"With its activities, resources, and opportunities for self-reflection, t
resource and fills a huge gap in the field of trauma. We are only be_
addressing compassion fatigue, secondary traumatic stress, and burnout is not supplemental but
central to creating trauma-informed agencies and systems. This workbook should be on the bookshelf
of anyone doing this work!"

> —**Lisa Conradi, PsyD**, president/founder of Conradi Consulting, LLC, and
> former director of clinical operations at the Chadwick Center, one of the
> largest trauma treatment centers in the U.S.

"This book features a wealth of information, including many neuro-based strategies to help the
helper heal from compassion fatigue, secondary traumatic stress, and burnout. A great companion
text for workshops geared towards assisting those who work with traumatized populations to reduce
inevitable work-related stress and improve their resilience."

> —**Vidette Todaro-Franceschi, PhD, RN, FT**, professor of nursing at the
> CUNY College of Staten Island and the Graduate Center at the City University
> New York and author of *Compassion Fatigue and Burnout in Nursing:*
> *Enhancing Professional Quality of Life*

"Compassionate care is the greatest gift that we can give to our community members who are facing
a challenge, but it can come at a cost. Dr. Steele has given us a gift with this publication. It dives
deeply into evidence-based solutions with excellent exercises and self-check assessment tools that
help us understand how best to stay healthy and resilient in this most worthy field of caregiving."

> —**Syd Gravel and Brad McKay**, retired Canadian police staff sergeants with
> distinction; currently senior police advisors with Badge of Life Canada and
> coauthors of *Walk the Talk – First Responder Peer Support: A Boots-on-the-*
> *Ground Peer and Trauma Support Systems Guide*

"This is an engaging journey in self-care for the clinician and caregiver."

> —**Jessica Hackenberg, PsyD**, psychotherapy coordinator for the VA's Northern
> Indiana Health Care System and assistant adjunct professor at
> University of Notre Dame

"In this work Dr. Steele invites us into a much deeper experience than understanding compassion
fatigue and secondary traumatic stress. He invites us into the practice of healing and walks us
through this process every step of the way. Every servant of traumatized people will benefit from
the 'sessions' in this book and the transformative experience waiting to be had."

> —**Jules Alvarado, MA, LPC**, international organizational wellness consultant,
> founder and senior clinical consultant with Alvarado Consulting and Treatment
> Group, and a foster parent the past 25 years

"This engaging, comprehensive, and cleverly designed workbook is a much-needed addition to the
self-care literature. Thoughtful narratives within sessions are accented with a range of useful tools
to nurture reflection, self-care, and personal development. This is a helpful resource with which to
check in with and look after ourselves and one another."

> —**Sarah Parry, PhD**, clinical psychologist and senior clinical lecturer at
> Manchester Metropolitan University in England

REDUCING COMPASSION FATIGUE, SECONDARY TRAUMATIC STRESS AND BURNOUT

Reducing Compassion Fatigue, Secondary Traumatic Stress and Burnout addresses the vital questions mental health providers have about self-care and its relationship to clinical practice.

Packed with activities, worksheets and interactive learning tools, the text provides neuro-based and trauma-sensitive recommendations for improving the ways clinicians care for themselves. Each "session" helps clinicians identify their personal self-care needs and arrive at an effective self-care plan that promotes resilience in the face of daily exposure to trauma-inducing situations and reduces the effects of compassion fatigue and burnout.

Integrating research with practical applications and best practices, *Reducing Compassion Fatigue, Secondary Traumatic Stress and Burnout* is an essential workbook for clinicians and organizations looking to enhance compassionate care.

William Steele, PsyD, MSW, is the founder of the National Institute for Trauma and Loss in Children (TLC), established in 1990 and a program of the Starr Global Learning Network since 2009. Dr. Steele has developed trauma-specific, evidence-based interventions programs and resources for practitioners currently being used in 55 countries.

REDUCING COMPASSION FATIGUE, SECONDARY TRAUMATIC STRESS AND BURNOUT

A Trauma-Sensitive Workbook

William Steele

Routledge
Taylor & Francis Group

NEW YORK AND LONDON

First published 2020
by Routledge
52 Vanderbilt Avenue, New York, NY 10017

and by Routledge
2 Park Square, Milton Park, Abingdon, Oxon, OX14 4RN

Routledge is an imprint of the Taylor & Francis Group, an informa business

Library of Congress Cataloging-in-Publication Data
Names: Steele, William, author.
Title: Reducing compassion fatigue, secondary traumatic stress, and
    burnout : a trauma-sensitive workbook / William Steele.
Description: New York, NY : Routledge, 2020. | Includes bibliographical
    references and index.
Identifiers: LCCN 2019036214 (print) | LCCN 2019036215 (ebook) |
    ISBN 9780367144081 (hardback) | ISBN 9780367144098 (paperback) |
    ISBN 9780429056734 (ebook)
Subjects: LCSH: Secondary traumatic stress. | Burn out (Psychology) |
    Job stress. | Human services personnel–Mental health. | Mental health
    personnel–Mental health.
Classification: LCC RC552.P67 S739 2020 (print) | LCC RC552.P67 (ebook) |
    DDC 616.85/21–dc23
LC record available at https://lccn.loc.gov/2019036214
LC ebook record available at https://lccn.loc.gov/2019036215

ISBN: 978-0-367-14408-1 (hbk)
ISBN: 978-0-367-14409-8 (pbk)
ISBN: 978-0-429-05673-4 (ebk)

Typeset in Interstate
by Apex CoVantage, LLC

Visit the eResources: www.routledge.com/9780367144098

To all the professionals, caregivers and responders faced with the daily challenges and sometimes overwhelming exposure to trauma victims and situations. The dedication, commitment and sacrifices you make to help survivors discover their strength and resilience, in the midst of great pain, echoes the spirit of your generosity and the compassion in your heart.

CONTENTS

x   *Contents*

ACKNOWLEDGMENTS

Over the past 30 years I have been privileged to work with, consult and train over 80,000 professionals, caregivers and responders. Their dedication to bringing best practices to survivors is unquestionable. Their expertise and wisdom are at work throughout this workbook. They have taught me so much and inspired this work and its focus on helping them remain resilient in the face of their daily exposure to trauma victims, situations and those individuals and/or situations presenting intense emotional challenges.

I especially want to express my gratitude to Misty Ramos, Executive Director of P.A.L.S. for Healing, who provided me with so many suggestions along the way. No book comes together without the help of editors so I also thank Anna Moore and her team at Routledge, and Apex CoVantage, for their expertise and guidance throughout the development and completion of this work.

AUTHOR BIOGRAPHY

Dr. Steele began his work in trauma in the early 1980s when he published the booklet *Preventing Teen Suicide*. This led to requests for training across the country. His experiences with nonfatal attempters and survivors of suicide was acknowledged in 1986 when the Michigan Chapter of the National Academy of Television Arts and Sciences awarded Dr. Steele's production of *Preventing Teen Suicide* a Michigan Emmy. In the mid-1980s he also began working with survivors of homicide and Parents of Murdered Children. He has assisted survivors and professionals following such tragic and traumatic incidents as the Gulf War, where he was one of the first Americans selected by the Kuwait government to assist with helping survivors and responders in the aftermath of that war. He assisted and trained survivors and professionals following such incidents as the bombing of the Murrah Federal Building in Oklahoma City, 9/11 in New York and Washington DC, Hurricanes Katrina and Rita, the 2009 murders of a high school coach in Iowa and a teacher in Texas, far too many suicides of school-aged children and teens, and the daily trauma children and adults experience that never receive national media attention.

Always a practitioner and passionate about bringing practitioners intervention strategies to help them and the survivors they are assisting, he founded the National Institute for Trauma and Loss in Children (TLC) in 1990. As its director for 23 years he created a legacy of trauma-specific, registered evidence-based intervention programs and resources now being used in 55 countries by many of the 60,000 professionals he trained while at TLC.

His more recent publications, *Trauma in Schools and Communities: Recovery Lessons from Survivors and Responders* and *Trauma Informed Practices with Children and Adolescents*, demonstrate his ability to translate theory into practical, timely trauma-sensitive strategies. Now retired from TLC, he continues to train and consult with schools and communities across the country to bring to others the wisdom given to him by the many survivors and responders of all ages he has met over the years who have struggled yet gone on to flourish.

INTRODUCTION

It's a Journey

This workbook invites you to go on a journey that begins by engaging you in several activities demonstrating that in no way are you alone in experiencing the unavoidable stress and unwanted reactions triggered and fueled by daily caring for and/or responding to trauma victims and/or trauma inducing situations.

Chapters are titled "Sessions" to reflect the interactive style of this workbook. The minute you begin the first session you realize that you are more a participant than a reader. This journey continues through seven sessions. Each session begins by asking you to answer a series of questions or complete several activities. This process identifies the various issues being covered and gives you an opportunity to evaluate your level of awareness and then compare your responses with the reported responses of your peers.

The term "journey" is used purposefully to reflect that arriving at an effective self-care plan to mitigate the negative effects of stress in our lives, inclusive of compassion fatigue (CF), secondary traumatic stress (STS) and burnout (BO), is dependent upon what you discover matters most in your personal efforts to remain resilient, compassionate and consistently effective while daily assisting, caring for and/or responding to trauma victims and those intensely emotional individuals and/or situations.

Self-care Is Personal

The following Reality statement, which is one of many posted throughout these sessions, reflects this need. Reality: *We all experience stress, but we experience it differently. This is why what works for me may not work for you. In fact, not knowing what that subjective experience of stress is like for you, what I might suggest you need to do to relieve yourself of that stress may be of no help whatsoever or make it worse rather than better.*

Therefore, before developing a self-care plan that best fits you, you need to identify those thoughts, mindsets, beliefs, attitudes and characteristics that are counter-productive to minimizing the effects of CF, secondary trauma and BO. For example, when I make a mistake or fail at something and tend to be self-critical and judgmental and get down on myself, I'm not engaging in self-compassion. We know that low levels of self-compassion are linked to high levels of CF and BO. On the other hand, if when faced with conflicts or challenges, I have a difficult time speaking up for myself, I'm not practicing self-efficacy, a characteristic of resilience, which we know supports compassion satisfaction and is essential for mitigating the effects of CF and BO and other sources of stress.

In this journey you'll be completing a series of assessments and activities and using various worksheets that allow you to determine your personal self-care needs, the actions that will help meet these needs and what will matter most to you in your efforts to remain resilient in the face of daily exposure to trauma.

The Experience Matters

Neuroscience and learning science have definitively demonstrated that the most effective learning process is one in which we are actively involved in activities that support what is being taught. For example, so often the literature simply lists the symptoms of CF/STS/BO. Passively reading these lists may bring new information to us that may or may not trigger a change. What becomes more beneficial is being asked to engage in an activity that asks you to describe in some detail how a symptom is expressed via behavior, thoughts and/or emotions. You're asked to engage in such an activity by developing a written narrative of eight statements each for CF/STS/BO. For example, the statement, *"There are days I don't return client's calls . . ."* would be considered BO if the rest of the statement read something like, *". . . because all they want to do is talk and I don't have the time."* This same statement could reflect secondary stress if the rest of the statement read something like, *". . . because hearing what happened to these clients just triggers to many unwanted reactions I have trouble controlling."* And, finally the same statement could be considered CF if the rest read, *". . . because I don't think any amount of caring will change anything."* This process not only helps you to evaluate your working awareness of how CF/STS/BO is experienced but will also make it much easier to recognize any one of these stressors in others and in yourselves.

Challenging the Work-Life Solution

During this journey, you're also asked to challenge several common statements made about what constitutes good self-care. For example, I'm sure most of you have read or have been told how important it is to have a work-life balance to counter the stress of daily exposure to trauma victims, materials and situations. However, if you are caring for others as your occupation and also raising a family, maintaining a work-life balance triggers an entirely different response than if you were single. Self-care must be personalized. Obviously, you are encouraged to strive for balanced self-care, however, spending time with family, friends, engaging in exercise and good nutrition alone, as valuable as they are for our well-being, may do little to offset the stress of the work you do. The reality is our thoughts, perceptions, beliefs, values, emotions and responses to everyday challenges, the ways we approach life, what we think, our mindsets, how we treat ourselves and the regulation of our emotions and behaviors must be in alignment with and supportive of the kind of self-care needed to mitigate the effects of CF/STS/BO.

Challenging Your Mindset

You'll learn, for example, about several interesting studies that illustrate how our mindsets not only influence our biology and the critical factors associated with good stress and bad stress but how they also influence our reactions to stressful situations inclusive of those associated with trauma victims, situations and materials. You'll then have the opportunity to evaluate your own mindsets and the negative impact they may be having on your ability to effectively manage and cope with the stress you face daily. The reality is that by altering our mindsets, we can alter our stress level without making major work-life changes.

It's Not Always a Choice

However, you'll also be introduced to another reality that dictates that we also need to respond to the physiology of stress by engaging in sensory-based processes versus cognitive processes. This reality is, *our reactions to stress at any given time are not a choice but a bio-neurological response often impossible to control cognitively*. Via the personal stories of two distinguished and well-respected leaders in the field of trauma, you'll discover how critical this is to recovering from and effectively managing the stress of what you do. You'll have the opportunity to engage in several sensory-based activities to experience firsthand how the simplest of movements can alter your reactions and why talk is often limited in its ability to regulate your reactions to the stress of what you do.

It's Not Entirely Your Responsibility

The literature often states that self-care is an ethical responsibility for all caregivers and responders. However, you'll discover through various examples that how well or how successfully you manage the stress of what you do, is not always a matter of the way you care for yourself; it is also categorically dependent upon how well the organization where you are working cares for you and your well-being. You'll discover the ways the corporate world is doing more for the wellness and well-being of its employees than some non-profit, human service organizations serving and responding to trauma victims or situations. This will help you better determine if the organization where you are working is engaging in those practices that help mitigate BO, STS and CF while supporting your overall well-being and enhancing your effectiveness with those you are caring for and/or responding to.

Self-reflection

There is another reality that is critical for determining what will matter most in your self-care efforts and sustaining your overall well-being, compassion satisfaction, effectiveness and success in all areas of your life; that process is self-reflection. Reality: *Failure to practice self-reflection is like being stuck on life's treadmill, always moving but going nowhere.* You have to be afforded the time to reflect on all the aspects and factors that either lead to or mitigate the effects of CF, STS and BO. This workbook affords you that opportunity in every one of its seven sessions.

In the final session you'll be asked to reflect on your assessment outcomes and complete several self-reflective questionnaires in order to arrive at your personalized, self-care priorities and action plans. This is where this journey ends and another begins; the one you decide to take to best manage the stress of what you do.

Your Way

Whatever actions you decide to take remember there is no one way or best way; your way is what you discover in this journey matters the most to you. Hopefully the experiences this workbook introduces you to become an agent of change, one that brings strengthened resilience against the stress of caring for and/or responding to those in trauma. If the discoveries in this journey keep you moving forward, please pass them on to your peers: alone we are at risk; together we are strong.

1 You Are Not Alone

Pre-session Questions and Activities

Before reading Session One, answer the following questions and complete the activities. Your answers can then be compared with those detailed in this session.

Pre/post-session questions and worksheets in the Appendix may be photocopied and/or downloaded from www.routledge.com/9780367144098

Answer all questions as best you can. If you seem to have no answer, give it your best effort as this will help reinforce what is learned throughout this session.

Questions

1. Define the major difference between CF, STS and BO using a one-sentence definition for each of these three types of stress.

   _____
   _____
   _____
   _____
   _____

2. What primary processes are altered by stress?

   _____
   _____

3. What is one of the reactions to STS and CF that make it difficult for professionals to share with their peers the stress they are experiencing?

   _____
   _____

4. Although the following two terms are used interchangeably and their differences debated, what one distinction do some make between vicarious trauma and STS?

   _____
   _____

5. What is the primary ethical responsibility stated in professional code of ethics of those who care for a trauma population, trauma victims and/or respond to potentially trauma inducing incidents?

   _____
   _____

6. Fill in what you believe is the percentage of STS or CF experienced by staff in the following areas.

   Child welfare_____, judges in criminal, family and juvenile court_____, social workers_____, hospice nurses_____, emergency department nurses_____, law enforcement officers_____, forensic investigators_____.

7. Approximately how much is spent in healthcare yearly as a result of BO?

   _____

   _____

Activities

1. List four stressors you experience as a result of the work you do. Following the fourth stressor add additional stressors you experience.

   _____, _____,
   _____, _____,
   _____, _____,
   _____, _____,
   _____, _____,
   _____, _____,
   _____, _____.

2. Circle any two of the stressors listed below that you have experienced.

   Intrusive (involuntary/unwanted) images, thoughts-sudden memories associated with cases . . . Distressing dreams about . . . Emotional/physical reactions triggered by reminders similar to those earlier case experiences, for example, when reviewing another case with similar details, walking into a similar environment, hearing case details similar to your experiences . . . Avoidance of thoughts, feelings, people, environments associated with trauma cases . . . Avoidance of conversations, activities or situations that carry reminders . . . Dreading seeing certain clients . . . Elevated arousal, such as being hyper-vigilant, jumpy, easily startled . . . Difficulty concentrating or focusing on details, gaps in memory, missing essential details . . . Trouble sleeping or staying asleep . . . Outbursts of anger or irritability . . . Becoming more impatient with clients . . . Feeling more detached, emotionally numb, flat . . . Thoughts of, "I've heard all this before," "Let's get this over with." . . . After a few minutes you stop listening to some clients . . . Distrusting your ability to any longer be helpful . . . Find it difficult to shut off work mode when home . . . Withdrawing from activities, friends you once enjoyed.

3. What does CF/STS/BO sound like or look like?

   Write out a minimum of six statements for each of these three stress types (CF/STS/BO) that reflect how one might feel, think and/or behave if experiencing each of these stress types.

   BO: For example, *My energy level sucks. It takes me forever to get things done now.*

   _____

   _____

   _____

   _____

CF: For example, *I'm getting mad with clients who think their situation is the worst. It's hard to feel for them the same way as I do about others who have it a lot harder.*

_____

_____

_____

_____

_____

STS: For example, *I am already thinking too much about my cases and some of the situations they've experienced even when I try not to.*

_____

_____

_____

_____

_____

Keep your answers with you as you read through this first session. Compare your responses with those you will find in the session. This process will help you compare what you know and what you might yet still need to know to best respond to the stress of the work you do.

Session One

You Are Not Alone: It's Not Your Fault

Imagine for a moment that you're at a workshop that is titled "Developing Resilience in the Midst of Daily Exposure to Trauma." The workshop flyer indicated that you would be learning about BO, STS, VT and CF: their prevalence, differences, how each impacts our performance, emotional, social and personal lives and all that can be done to remain resilient despite ongoing exposure to trauma populations and/or trauma inducing situations. After initial introductions, the presenter begins with a personal story.

Opening Statement: The Burning Pot

Allow me to give you a personal example of how stress can interfere with our thought processes, do damage and, in this example, end with a loss of $500 (rewritten from Steele, 2017):

Here I am a college educated professional, in my mid-thirties, single and living in a first-floor apartment with a door wall that led to an outdoor patio area. It was just several steps from the kitchen on the other side of a dining room table. One day the pot I was using to cook somehow caught fire. The flames rose over the edge and I had no fire extinguisher handy. I heard myself say, "'remain calm." My next thought was something like, "I got this." I'll just take the pot outside to the patio. I grabbed the pot and then walked over to the door wall but it was locked. Now visualize this. I sat that very hot, flaming pot on the linoleum covered floor to unlock the door wall. When I came back after putting the fire out, I saw what I had done. That's right. I saw the outline of the pot on the linoleum floor. It had melted the linoleum, which can't be patched. I thought I was thinking clearly under that minor stress. I could not believe what I had done. Besides losing my security deposit, I learned a valuable lesson.

Reality: *Stress alters the way we think and process information and subsequently how we behave. When that stress piles up, what we think and how we behave only gets worse, the stress only gets worse. Everyone caring for others is vulnerable to several types of stress.* (Answer to Pre-session One Question #2.)

This workshop is about

- increasing our awareness of different types and sources of stress, its various symptoms and the impact it has on our overall personal, emotional, cognitive and physical well-being and the quality of care we provide others,
- understanding that what we do leaves us vulnerable to personal and work-related stressors difficult to avoid,
- appreciating how prevalent these stressors are across helping professions; that they are not about our competence but our unavoidable reactions to continual exposure to the traumatic and demanding experiences of those we are attempting to help,
- developing neuro-based, trauma-sensitive, resilience focused, consistent self-care practices that minimize the impact of the kind of stress that is unavoidable when exposed to victims of trauma and those experiencing emotionally and challenging conditions* and/or to those responding to trauma specific situations, and
- remaining the best helper we can be despite what is the unavoidable, stressful challenges of caring for and protecting others.

Note: *Those experiencing emotionally challenging conditions could include a family member caring for an elderly parent, hospice nurses, EMTs, veterinarians and those working in animal welfare or teachers exposed to diverse student populations/traumatized students. One study conducted by the Humane Society of the United States (2003-2004) found in their sample of 1,000 animal control workers that over 56% self-reported extremely high risk for CF. Although research is just now beginning to examine CF/STS among teachers, we know that two out of three students struggle with stress dysregulation (SDR) creating a good deal of stress for educators (Transforming Education, 2015). There is another reality I want to present to you.

Reality: *Stress is not a bad thing. It can lead to professional growth, improved skills and greater resilience if, rather than ignoring it or minimizing it, we acknowledge it and manage it by engaging in neuro-based, trauma-sensitive, resilience-focused, consistent personal and professional self-care practices.*

Activity One: List, Look, Discover (Group/Individual)

Now imagine that the workshop room has 15 round tables and that there are 8 participants at each table; 120 participants are in attendance. Keep in mind that at your table there are a variety of different professionals working in various settings in different roles. At each table there is newsprint and markers, and a plain sheet of white paper for each participant. The presenter then prepares you for the following activity.

"Before we actually get to the content of this workshop, I'd like all of you to participate in two activities that will help lay the foundation for all we present today. Using the newsprint at your table you're asked to discuss and then list four stressors that really make what you do difficult at times. You're also instructed that after listing the fourth stressor you are to draw a line across the page underneath that sixth stressor and then continue to write down any other additional stressors that you face. You'll have several minutes to do this. When finished each group is to tape their newsprint up on the wall."

Processing the Activity

When all the lists are tapped on the wall, the presenter then says, "I want you to just look from where you're sitting at these lists and think about the conclusions you can arrive at about stress, even though you may not be able to read what's posted." Quickly what participants see is that everyone has drawn a line across the page after listing their fourth stressor and then more stressors are added. *The conclusions you have to draw about what you completed* and what is the usual outcome when this is done in a group are:

1. Everyone's dealing with stressors on the job.
2. Everyone's experiencing many more than four stressors.
3. Stress is not something that can be avoided when working with at-risk and/or traumatized populations.
4. You certainly are not alone with your exposure to stress; what others are experiencing you are experiencing.

Once participants arrive at these conclusions, sometimes with a little help from the presenter, the following reality statement is presented.

Reality: *You cannot expect to work with at-risk traumatized individuals or for an organization or program that services trauma victims or those experiencing emotionally challenging situations and not experience some form of stress. There are different forms. What is important at this point is acknowledging that stress comes with what we do.*

Following is a sampling of the more common stressors helpers identify. You'll likely find that what you wrote down is listed below. (*You can compare your Pre-session Activity #1 responses to those listed here.*)

*   nothing but high-risk clients, increase demand to do more in the same time, limited flexibility,
*   too much paper work/computer work, short lunch hours if any, increased isolation from other staff,
*   absence of peer review/support, insufficient training for dealing with clients,
*   little variation in client exposures/challenges, making life-changing decisions for clients,
*   responsible for client's lives, having to take over another worker's case, limited access to resources, thinking about client experiences even when I don't want to,
*   too many bad stories from clients, client deaths, safety issues, constantly in a "survival" mode,
*   physical threats, worry about law suits, high staff turnover,
*   expected to do more with less, too many deadlines, expected to respond to emails after regular work hours, and
*   limited availability to supervisors, opinions don't count for much, and only time we hear from management is when things go wrong.

As the presenter asks you to look at the list, he points out that many of these characteristics are associated with BO but also CF, which includes STS symptoms. He indicates the differences between these types of stress will be discussed shortly and that the primary purpose of this activity is to point out that caring for an at-risk and/or traumatized population is stressful and exposes us to various sources of stress.

Why Participants Rarely List CF/STS Symptoms: Old Mindsets

(*Answer to Pre-session One Question #3*) Rarely do participants list CF/STS symptoms. There is a reason for this. Experiencing symptoms of STS immediately triggers a fear response that in turn triggers old negative mindsets still reinforced by non-informed, and sometimes informed, supervisors and managers. One can be trauma-informed yet not engage interventions or responses that are not compassionate. For example, "It's part of the job. You're just going to have to forget about it or look for another job" is not a compassionate response. One old mindset says that if I let my supervisor know I am experiencing CF and/or trauma (STS) symptoms, they will question my psychological competence to do the job. This is a fear-driven mindset but one that still plays out in some environments. "You need some therapy" is not initially a compassionate response to this situation and indicative of an environment that is not itself compassionate.

Another old mindset is a self-induced, non-informed negative one that says, "What's wrong with me, I should be able to handle this." This mindset is often followed by efforts to repress the symptoms and thoughts associated with what has been traumatic. And then there is denial. This mindset says, "I've just had a couple difficult cases or situations I've had to deal with. It will pass. I don't need to worry about it."

Reality: *Experiencing CF/STS symptoms is very personal and often triggers mindsets that push us away from preventative and restorative self-care.*

These are some of the reasons why many do not list CF/STS reactions in this first activity and why participants are asked to complete a second activity.

Activity Two: Which Two Reactions (Group/Individual)

This second activity allows for

1. the normalization of CF/STS in environments servicing and/or responding to trauma victims,
2. a gradual, safe way to allow participants to accept and feel less fearful about CF/STS symptoms they may have had or are currently experiencing, and
3. the process of changing old, negative mindsets to ones that support self-care and resilience.

The second activity, *which you completed in the Pre-session One Activity #2*, asked you to circle any two stressors you have experienced. Possible stressors for attendees at the workshop include:

- intrusive (involuntary/unwanted) images, thoughts-sudden memories associated with cases,
- distressing dreams about emotional/physical reactions triggered by reminders similar to earlier case experiences, for example, when reviewing another case with similar details, walking into a similar environment, hearing case details similar to your experiences,
- avoidance of thoughts, feelings, people, environments associated with trauma cases,
- avoidance of conversations, activities or situations that carry reminders,
- dreading seeing certain clients,
- elevated arousal, such as being hyper-vigilant, jumpy, easily startled,
- difficulty concentrating, focusing on details, gaps in memory, missing essential details,
- trouble sleeping or staying asleep,
- outbursts of anger or irritability,
- becoming more impatient with clients,
- feeling more detached, emotionally numb, flat,
- thoughts of, "I've heard all this before," "Let's get this over with."

- stopping listening after a few minutes,
- distrusting your ability to any longer be helpful,
- finding it difficult to shut off work mode when home, and
- withdrawing from activities, friends you once enjoyed to the point of negatively impacting our personal relationships.

Participants are asked to look at this listing of symptoms and then use one of the 8.5-by-11-inch sheets of paper at their table to write down any two symptoms that they have experienced at any time while working with, attempting to help or assist individuals who have been exposed to trauma. When finished they're told to turn their paper face down, so they remain confidential, and that the presenter will come by to collect their responses. After "shuffling" the papers the presenter asks for help tapping these on the wall.

Now imagine yourself as a participant looking at 120 sheets of paper listing CF/STS symptoms. Seeing them tapped on the wall, you know you can draw the same conclusions made earlier.

1. STS/CF symptoms are not unusual,
2. STS/CF is not something that can be avoided when working with the traumatized population, and
3. that you certainly are not alone with your exposure to CF/STS; what others are experiencing, you are experiencing.

This process makes it much easier for participants to begin to accept that CF/STS comes with the work they do. At the same time, some will need to see more concrete data in the form of research, which will be reviewed shortly.

- From this point on, I will be talking with you as individuals participating in a series of seven sessions leading up to and including trauma-sensitive, neurologically based self-care practices to minimize the impact of the unavoidable stress you are repeatedly exposed to because of the work you do.
- Every session begins with pre-session questions and activities for you to complete and later use when developing a self-care plan that fits for you. As there is no one intervention that fits every traumatized individual, there is no one self-care plan that fits every professional. You need choices but choices that are based in neurologically and psychologically proven practices.
- At the conclusion of each session there are additional questions for you to answer that help identify and focus on what matters most to you from all that you learn in each session.

This process makes this a very personalized journey designed to minimize the stress of what you do while sustaining your resilience in the face of repeated exposure to trauma inducing situations, trauma victims and environments that may do little to support your resilience. Let's continue this first session.

Processing Activity Two

Given the outcome of above two activities, the conclusions I now make about you as a group is that there is very little difference between what you have identified as stressors and reactions from what your peers across the country have identified. Given your responses I know that the material presented will

- make sense to you,
- help you better determine the sources of your stress,

- encourage daily self-care specific to the effects of exposure to trauma, and
- allow you to walk away with practical strategies that will sustain your resilience and effectiveness in the face of the difficult situations and conditions you are exposed to on a regular basis.

Primary Differences

We are going to examine the differences between CF/STS and BO because knowing the specific sources of our stress can better help us determine what will be most helpful and useful in our efforts to take care of ourselves while remaining at our best when with clients or responding to trauma inducing situations. This is an ethical responsibility for us as well as for the organizations that services a traumatized population. Let's take a quick look at the primary differences between these stressors (see Tables 1.1 and 1.2) and then go into more detail.

This entire session is devoted to spending time examining these three stress related outcomes. It is critical to properly identify the causes or the source of our stressors. For example, it is important for us to be able to identify the reactions of BO as these relate to workplace or organizational practices that place us at-risk. Knowing this, our efforts can be directed at responding to those work place stressors and to evaluate the possible need to leave that environment all together. On the other hand, CF/STS represent our reactions to caring for others that can place us, and those we care for, at risk. If this is the source of our stress, there are a number of ways to respond differently to each to remain resilient and at our best as helpers. Let's discuss these differences in more detail and then look at the prevalence of these stressors across professions so you can again appreciate that they are unavoidable. (*Compare your answer to Pre-session One Question #1 with the following descriptions of PTSD, CF, STS, BO.*)

Table 1.1 Burnout Versus Compassion Fatigue

Burnout	Compassion Fatigue
Happens over time	Happens over time
Specific to work culture/practices	Specific to caring for others experiencing trauma or emotionally challenging conditions
Increased risk for compassion fatigue	May include burnout/secondary traumatic stress

Table 1.2 Secondary Traumatic Stress Versus Posttraumatic Stress Disorder

Secondary Traumatic Stress (STS)	Posttraumatic Stress Disorder (PTSD)
Triggered by direct/indirect exposure	Triggered by direct/indirect exposure
Does not meet full criteria for PTSD	Must meet full DSM-5 criteria inclusive of depersonalization or derealization*
May or may not co-exist with compassion fatigue and/or secondary trauma	May or may not co-exist with compassion fatigue and/or secondary trauma
Sudden onset or cumulative exposure-Brief intervention	Sudden onset or cumulative exposure-PTSD specific intervention

World Health Organization (WHO) (2016).
*Depersonalization refers to feeling detached from self, an outside observer of self; derealization refers to things not feeling real or feeling distorted.

Posttraumatic Stress Disorder (PTSD)

PTSD (posttraumatic stress disorder) is a response that some people develop after experiencing or witnessing a life-threatening event, like combat, a natural disaster, a car accident, or sexual assault. Symptoms are experienced for months, may come and go or be delayed for years after exposure to a traumatic event and most often required additional help to resolve.

Secondary Traumatic Stress

In a keynote address in 1982, Figley spoke of secondary victimization as a repercussion of caring for others in emotional pain (Adams, Boscarino, & Figley, 2006). In 1995 he referred to the phenomena as STS indicating its symptoms were similar to posttraumatic stress disorder but not meeting the full diagnostic criteria for PTSD. As we saw in the chart comparison, STS does now meet the DSM-5 Criterion A under PTSD.

PTSD Versus STS

PTSD has a full set of eight different symptom criteria that must be met in order for individuals to be assigned a diagnosis of PTSD. STS is a classification that indicates individuals are experiencing symptoms that are listed under the PTSD criteria but are not inclusive of all the symptom criteria needed to assign a PTSD diagnosis. STS may lead to PTSD if ignored and if trauma exposure continues so it is important to take STS seriously. Sometimes this can be self-managed for what it is; other times brief outside help may be the most beneficial intervention.

Note: STS is not a pathologic condition but responses/reactions considered not to be at all unusual among those caring for trauma populations and/or responding to potentially trauma inducing incidents.

STS is also sometimes referred to as vicarious trauma. The terms are used interchangeably, which is problematic. Let's explore this in more detail.

Vicarious Trauma

The term *vicarious trauma (VT)* was coined by Pearlman and Saakvitne (1995) around the same time STS was coined. They described VT as a profound shift in worldview, not generally experienced with STS and PTSD. This shift results in negative changes in beliefs and feelings about self and others. Today vicarious trauma, CF and secondary trauma are terms often used interchangeably. There is an ongoing debate as to whether there is a significance difference between them. (*Answer to Pre-session One Question #4.*) Some argue that unlike STS, VT involves issues related to counter-transference that compromises the clinician's effectiveness and places the client in harm's way.

Judith Herman's classic work *Trauma and Recovery* (1992) was the first to address the impact of repeated trauma on clients. She wrote, "while the victim of a single acute trauma may feel after the incident that she is not herself, the victim of chronic trauma may feel herself to be changed irrevocably or she may lose the sense that she has any self at all" (p. 86). It is this change that others defined as being the identifying factor experienced by those who repeatedly work with trauma victims that would classify them as experiencing vicarious trauma. This change develops as a result of the helper having difficulty with counter-transference issues.

Counter-transference can result in viewing self and the world differently in ways that now make it difficult for helpers to empathize; they overreact or inappropriately react (Fritscher, 2018). For example, I may become vicariously traumatized by the victims of sexual abuse and the stories they tell me to the point that it changes my view about sex, safety of my kids and leaves me unable to continue to assist victims because of the emotions and behaviors it triggers in me. On the other hand, those experiencing CF and/or STS may also experience a change in their "world view" that makes it difficult for them to continue to care effectively and/or interferes with the various aspects of their lives. What they experience is not necessarily vicarious trauma. The problem is that counter-transference issues can arise while helping any client including those who are not presenting trauma material (Figley, 1995). Therefore, it is argued that this does not make for differentiating between STS and VT. Clinicians or helpers who struggle with STS may or may not have counter-transference issues (Smith, Kleijn, Trjsburg, & Hutschemaekers, 2007).

It is interesting to note that the American Institute of Stress provides the following definition of CF: "(CF) also called "vicarious traumatization" or secondary traumatization (Figley, 1995). (It is) the emotional residue or strain of exposure to working with those suffering from the consequences of traumatic events." It differs from burnout, but can co-exist with burnout. Compassion fatigue can occur due to exposure to one case or can be due to a "cumulative" level of trauma exposure (American Institute of Stress (AIS), 2017). In other words, some define compassion fatigue as inclusive of vicarious trauma and secondary stress symptoms.

Francois Mathieu, Co-Executive Director of TEND, a wonderful resource for training and articles on CF, also wrote *The Compassion Fatigue Workbook* (2012). In a TEND® (2018) article titled "Defining Vicarious Trauma and Secondary Traumatic Stress: What Is Vicarious Trauma? What Is Secondary Traumatic Stress?" she wrote the following about the interchangeable use of terms: "At the end of the day, whether you call it STS or VT, what we are referring to is the impact of indirect (or direct) exposure to difficult, disturbing and/or traumatic images and stories of the suffering of others, humans and sometimes animals and the way that it might impact us as individuals and as professionals."

Given this debate and for purposes of easy reading we will simply refer to CF/STS as a range of responses that may or may not include counter-transference issues and the change in "world view" that has been associated with vicarious trauma. It may help to take a minute to look at the development of these competing terms.

CF

The term CF was first used in the context of a study of BO in nurses nearly two decades ago. At that time, Joinson (1992) coined the term to describe the "loss of the ability to nurture" that was noted in some nurses in emergency department settings. In 1995, Charles Figley, in his groundbreaking book *Compassion Fatigue: Coping With Secondary Traumatic Stress Disorder in Those Who Treat the Traumatized*, expanded the meaning of the term CF, and identified additional symptoms. He opted for the use of CF over STS, indicating that STS suggested a negative reference to a practitioner's competence compared to the term CF. He also argued that CF covered a wide range of professionals in various settings and roles such as those who care for animals/animal welfare. In comparison, STS is specific to those working with trauma victims and may be part of the CF experience for those working with trauma populations.

Empathy, Compassion

Just to be clear, empathy and compassion are related yet different. Empathy is being able to experience another's perspective and feel their emotions—"walk in their shoes." Compassion involves empathy but also involves the desire to help that individual with what may be challenging them.

Compassion involves more of a cognitive response-feeling for that person in a way that leaves us eager to do what we can to help (Well, 2017). Too much empathy (empathy strain) leaves us drained, overwhelmed and unable to help. CF is the decreasing ability to help due to being unable to distance ourselves from the emotions, the pain of others. How then does CF differ from STS/BO?

CF Versus STS/PTSD/BO

CF covers a wide range of helping professionals whereas STS/PTSD is specific to those who work with the traumatized population. CF and BO develop over time, whereas PTSD/STS can have a sudden onset and occur after one trauma exposure. CF/STS relates to those who care for others, whereas BO relates to work demands, the culture and its practices. Many use the term CF as being inclusive of STS, however STS is not always present in those experiencing CF.

BO

The American psychologist Herbert Freudenberger (1974) coined the term "BO" in the 1970s. He used the term to identify the consequences of severe stress in one's occupation. He indicated that BO leads to exhaustion, resulting from excessive work demands. He also indicated that professionals who look and act depressed are likely burned out. BO consists of three components: emotional exhaustion, depersonalization (cynicism) and feelings of ineffectiveness (diminished professional efficacy or lack of personal accomplishment) (Leiter, 2016). In the early years many of the characteristics now associated with CF were those described as BO in the research (Morse, Salyers, Rollins, DeVita, & Pfahler, 2012).

BO Versus CF/STS

BO can happen in any work environment. CF/STS relates to those caring in some way for others experiencing trauma or otherwise emotionally difficult situations such as cancer. BO becomes a risk factor for CF/STS. In many cases CF/STS is easier to change than BO, as BO requires major organizational changes in culture, policies and practices, which are further complicated by licensing boards, funding sources and leadership. BO may also require changing work places. Changing workplaces will not resolve CF if the new workplace is still serving traumatized, physically challenged individuals. CF/STS can be mitigated/resolved with brief intervention, education, cognitive reframing, sensory-based regulation practices and other self-care practices. BO requires significant organizational changes.

If you are a bit confused by these different classifications you are not alone. There is still a good deal of disagreement related to some of the differences presented. *What is not disputed are the symptoms that accompany these stressors.* This is why I will be focusing more on helping you become aware of and then identify your stressors via the symptoms you may be experiencing and then provide multiple self-care strategies for remaining resilient while doing the work you do.

Ethical Responsibility

Aside from all the terminology and the differences we've been discussing, we have a responsibility to pursue self-care strategies that help us minimize this stress. This responsibility is one of self-care.

Reality: *Rarely are we as professionals aware of the mandate that does dictate self-care responsibility, as self-care or the lack of, directly impacts the lives of those we are assigned to help and assist.*

(*Answer to Pre-session One Question #5.*) We have an ethical responsibility to those we serve to be informed about the stressors we face and to practice self-care that directs itself at minimizing the symptoms of these different stressors. It is an ethical responsibility that we implicitly agree to when obtaining a degree in the helping profession. Let me briefly show you what the different professions say about self-care in their code of ethics.

Social Workers

"Self-care is an ethical responsibility. The National Association of Social Workers (NASW) Code of Ethics states that 'a social worker's ethical behavior should result from their personal commitment to engage in ethical practice.' Ongoing self-care is the foundation of that 'commitment' to ethical practice" (Lipschutz, 2010).

American School Counselors Association

"Because of the multilayered demands of school counseling and the potentially devastating consequences of a school counselor's impairment, the ASCA Ethical Standards for School Counselors address self-care as an ethical mandate" (Williams, 2011).

American Counselors Association

The following is stated in section "C" of the ACA Code of Ethics: All counselors will "engage in self-care activities so they can work at their highest capacity" (American Counselors Association (ACA), 2016).

Psychologists

"When psychologists become aware of personal problems that may interfere with their performing work-related duties adequately, they take appropriate measures, such as obtaining professional consultation or assistance, and determine whether they should limit, suspend, or terminate their work-related duties" (Zur, 2016).

Mental Health Professionals

"Recognize that their effectiveness is dependent on their own mental and physical health. Should their involvement in any activity, or any mental, emotional, or physical health problem, compromise sound professional judgment and competency, they seek capable professional assistance to determine whether to limit, suspend, or terminate services to their clients" (Zur, 2016).

First Responders

"These principles declare that it is unethical not to attend to your self-care as a practitioner, because sufficient self-care prevents harming those we serve" (Green Cross Academy of Traumatology, 2010).

Nurses

The American Nurses Association Code of Ethics indicates: "The nurse owes the same duties to self as to others, including the responsibility to preserve integrity and safety, to maintain competence, and to continue personal and professional growth. Nurses should pay as much attention to taking care of themselves as they do their patients" (Purdue University, 2017).

Organizations

Organizations providing behavioral services to clients have the same ethical responsibility to you their employee. "Behavioral health program administrators should aim to strengthen their workforce; doing so requires creating environments that support the health and well-being, not only of persons with mental and substance use conditions, but of the workforce as well" (Hoge et al., 2007, p. 58).

The Asparagus Memory

Reality: *Now I could simply tell you here's what you need to do regarding your self-care, however, without giving you the information being presented, without engaging you in the activities we'll be going through and then processing the outcomes of these activities, the majority of you will never initiate the many self-care practices you'll have the option to select. Why is this?*

When as a child, I was first introduced to asparagus I gagged. I was told I couldn't leave the table till I ate it. I gagged again. When I then threw up on the table the asparagus was taken away. I've never eaten it since then. Let's say I convince you that asparagus is really good for you by informing you via research how it prevents certain diseases and enriches your health and longevity. You say, "Okay, I'll give it a try." On your first try the asparagus causes you to gag so you spit it out. You needed the research information to try but the physiological reaction convinces you that, no matter how good it's touted to be, your response is "I'm not eating it."

The information being presented here will build a strong case as to why it's important to engage in consistent self-care. However, to accept the practices that are presented you will need to experience some of the benefits as well as hear from your peers the benefits they have experienced. The activities will allow you to experience firsthand, without gagging, some of the self-care practices that will be recommended. You're given many options so you can select what is best for you. We'll also present plenty of documentation as to their benefits.

How Common Is CF/STS/BO?

That said let's look at the research and the prevalence of these various stressors across professions. As we do, I want you to again remember these are conditions that we simply cannot avoid because of the work we do and the situations and experiences we are exposed to via those we are attempting to help. (*Answer to Pre-session One Question #6.*)

Child Welfare

- University of California, Center for Human services studied 363 child welfare workers (Hatton Bowers, Brooks, & Borucki, 2014). The STS Scale, developed by Charles Figley and colleagues in 2004, was used to determine how many workers experienced 17 symptoms during the week previous to completing the scale. A half of these workers had scores indicative of experiencing posttraumatic stress disorder (PTSD) due to STS.
- In a previous study 34% of child welfare workers met criteria for PTSD due to STS (Salston & Figley, 2003). In addition, 75% of these workers reported having fair or poor health compared to peers not caring for trauma victims.

- In the previous listing of STS/CF symptoms, health symptoms were not listed, yet health issues, such as heart disease, diabetes, depression, do emerge as a result of prolong stress in those who do not engage in consistent self-care (Griffin, 2018; Schneiderman, Ironson, & Siegel, 2005).
- Additional studies show similar STS and health results among child welfare supervisors (Collins, 2018).

Judges, Attorneys, Court Workers

- Judges and court workers in criminal, family and juvenile court experience similar frequency of STS (Smith, 2017).
- In 2003, 105 judges working in criminal, family and juvenile court completed surveys on trauma while attending various judicial conferences. Based on the responses, 63% reported symptoms of work-related vicarious trauma (STS) (Jaffe, Crooks, Dunford-Jackson, & Town, 2003).
- In a study of 800 judges, 45% reported experiencing STS (Judicial Edge, 2018)
- Vrklevski and Franklin (2008) found that criminal lawyers scored significantly higher on measures of vicarious trauma and depression when compared to non-criminal lawyers.
- Symptoms of STS, such as sleep disturbances and nightmares, loss of appetite, hypervigilance and feelings of depression have also been identified among judges (Jaffe et al., 2003). These findings suggest that STS symptoms do occur among individuals serving in the legal arena.

Social Workers/Mental Health Workers

- When interviewed, 42% of social workers were found to be suffering from STS (Adams, Boscarino, & Figley, 2006).
- In another study, 70% exhibited at least one symptom of STS (Bride, 2007).
- One review of case managers working in mental health settings found that 1 in 5 had PTSD symptoms (Meldrum, King, & Spooner, 2018).
- Another study found that approximately one-third of individuals working in residential treatment experience symptoms of CF (Eastwood & Ecklund, 2008).
- 72% of mental health workers who provided clinical services to Katrina victims reported experiencing anxiety (Culver, McKinney, & Paradise, 2011).

Nursing/Medical/First Responders

- Abendroth and Flannery (2006) found moderate to high rates of CF in 79% of hospice nurses.
- Other studies indicate that 85% of emergency department nurses experience symptoms of STS (Gomez & Rutledge, 2009; Hoper, Craig, Janvrin, Wetsel, & Reimels, 2010).
- Years ago, Showalter (2010) demonstrated how commonplace CF is in the healthcare field although it remains underrecognized especially among nurses.
- Hoper et al. (2010) found that 85% of all nurses, regardless of role, experience CF.
- In another study, more than 25% of ambulance paramedics were identified as having severe ranges of post-traumatic symptoms (Beck, 2011).
- It is estimated that 30% of first responders develop behavioral health conditions including, but not limited to, depression and posttraumatic stress disorder (PTSD) (SAMHSA, 2018).
- According to the *Journal of Occupational Health*, approximately 20% of fire fighters and paramedics experience PTSD (DeMarco, 2018).

Law Enforcement

- Studies of PTSD and law enforcement can show anywhere from 5% to 50% presence depending upon what officers are exposed to, such as violent crime, and the frequency of that exposure. Some studies show that of the 900,000 police officers in the country, 19%, or 180,000, experience PTSD (Kirschman, 2017).
- Other studies suggest that 34% of law enforcement experience STS symptoms but do meet the criteria for PTSD (Kirschman, 2017).
- When it comes to forensic investigators, and those working on Internet crimes against children, 36% experienced moderate to high levels of secondary trauma (Perez, Jones, Englert, & Sachau, 2010).

(The following information and additional rates of stress across various police roles, such as investigating Internet crimes, can be found in Brady, 2012.)

- One study of 715 police officers found that 7%–19% of frontline police officers had PTSD. A 2006 study found that 20% of officers who responded to September 1, 2011, showed such severe difficulties they were referred for mental health (Maguen et al., 2009).
- In a random study of 100 officers in an urban setting 30% showed moderate to severe PTSD.
- Investigating child physical and sexual abuse cases is ranked as the third leading stressor behind being involved in a shooting and the shooting of an officer. The officers exposed to these three situations experience higher levels of PTSD/STS/CF than found in other law enforcement roles although this does not preclude experiencing moderate to severe STS/PTSD following exposure to other situations.

BO

- Of the 150,000 physicians who answered the 2018 Medscape annual physician survey, 42% reported being burned out (Medscape, 2018).
- In a 1999 study of more than 10,000 registered inpatient nurses, 43% had high degree of emotional exhaustion (Aiken, Clarke, Sloane, Sochalski, & Silber, 2002).
- Another study of 68,000 registered nurses in 2007 reported that 35%, 37% and 22% of hospital nurses, nursing home nurses and nurses working in other settings had high degree of emotional exhaustion. (The Maslach Burnout Inventory (MBI) is the gold standard for measuring BO. The above two studies used this inventory. A high level of exhaustion is equivalent to BO.)
- Studies estimate that anywhere between 21% and 61% of mental health practitioners experience signs of BO (APA, 2018).
- Nationally, child welfare worker turnover is estimated between 30% and 40% with an average tenure of fewer than two years, according to a U.S. General Accounting Office report (Stewart, 2016).
- A 2016 study by California State University, San Bernardino, found that social workers appear to be potentially more burned out and have less feelings of personal accomplishment than other human service workers (APA, 2018).

The research demonstrates that:

1. Stress is prevalent among those who care for a traumatized population and/or among those who are involved in potentially trauma inducing experiences, such as first responders.

2. Although stress levels are clinically significant across the roles examined, they tend to be at their highest among forensic investigators, those working on Internet crimes against children, first responders, and those who are continuously exposed to trauma clients and situations.
3. PTSD is associated with direct exposure whereas STS/CF is associated with indirect exposure as well as direct exposure.
4. Stress levels for the same individual can vary over time meaning that there are both external and internal risk factors involved.
5. BO is a risk factor for STS/PTSD/CF (Cieslak, Shoji, Melville, Luszczynska, & Benight, 2014).

The Cost of Stress

The psychological and physical problems of burned-out employees cost an estimated $125 billion to $190 billion a year in healthcare spending (Garton, 2017). Even greater are the costs of low productivity, high turnover, and the loss of the most effective personnel. In the helping profession there is also the cost to clients who are receiving inadequate and even harmful care from burned out helpers who miss critical signs that would otherwise help and/or protect clients psychologically and physically (HCPro, 2017).

These are some of the additional harmful health effects from excessive stress:

- damage to key brain structures and circuitry (McEwen & Morrison, 2013),
- reduced ability to cope with future stress and increased anxiety and chronic depression (Miller & Hen, 2015),
- the onset of post-traumatic stress disorder (Arnsten, Raskind, Taylor, & Connor, 2015),
- reduced immune system functioning (Dhabhar, 2014), and
- increased inflammation and depression (Slavich & Irwin, 2014).

Before ending this segment, I just want to define the difference between direct and indirect exposure, and then engage you in one additional activity that details the kinds of symptoms CF/STS/BO induces. (The following definitions are then presented describing exposure differences. They are presented with special attention given to the inclusion of criteria A4 under the DSM-5 PTSD diagnostic category. *It now indicates that those who care for others may qualify for the PTSD diagnosis.*)

Direct and Indirect Exposure

Direct Exposure

Firsthand experiencing of a trauma or witnessing a trauma happening to others

Indirect Exposure

Exposure to trauma situations via narratives/written material, case presentations or via the media

Note: Research is now showing that indirect exposure can trigger PTSD (May & Wisco, 2016). Actually, those of us who have spent years working with trauma victims knew this long ago but could not assign a PTSD diagnosis based on indirect exposure. This is why experienced leaders in the trauma field began to identify new classifications for stress symptoms. Recently, the DSM-5 did add a fourth PTSD exposure type under Criterion A 4 described as "repeated or extreme exposure to aversive details of a traumatic event, which applies to workers who encounter the consequences of traumatic events as part of their professional responsibilities" (Pai, Suris, & North, 2017).

Reality: *Given that STS/CF is not uncommon when working with or exposed to a traumatic population or traumatic situations, we must become familiar with these symptoms and, as an ethical responsibility, work diligently to minimize them by engaging in consistent, trauma-sensitive, neuro-based and resilience-focused self-care practices.*

In Session Two, we are going to spend time looking at and experiencing what we mean by neuro-based, trauma-sensitive self-care practices that science now confirms is critical to our being able to regulate our emotional, cognitive and behavioral responses to stress. What I want to do right now is engage you in a very brief, fun activity and then finish this segment with an activity that will descriptively detail the symptoms/warning signs for CF/STS and BO.

Activity: Back to Back (Group)

Note: This activity involves movement and becomes a great way to help us appreciate how the simplest forms of movement can reenergize us and improve focus and concentration as well as learning outcomes. In fact, research shows that simple movements have the ability to improve cognition, and mental performance in just seconds (Movement and Learning, 2014; Shoval, 2011, p. 462).

As an individual you can do this activity with your back to a mirror. Just follow the stretching instructions and while holding all three stretches turn and look at yourself in the mirror.

Participants in workshops I conduct generally are sitting more than they might at work; they are also attempting to process and absorb a lot of information. Their brains need re-energizing. I use this activity because it is fun and also helps alleviate the stress of learning and sitting. Any form of movement prior to engaging a task helps to improve focus (more on this later). It is also an activity I will refer to when talking about the physiology of trauma and its role in effective self-care. You have also been reading for some time and trying to assimilate the information you're reading about so your brain and body are also feeling a bit of stress. Read the following instructions and then do the series of stretches with your back to a mirror and then turn around following the last stretch holding all stretches.

First all participants are asked to pay attention to what their bodies and brain are feeling. The presenter asks them to pay attention as to whether they are feeling a bit stiff, tense, tired, experiencing a loss of energy, if their thoughts are wondering, if they are finding it a bit harder to focus or concentrate. They are then given the following instructions.

Participants are asked to pick a partner, stand up and get back to back. They are then instructed to reach to the sky extending their arms and hands as high as possible. They are told to hold this stretch while opening their eyes as wide as possible. It is suggested they feel the stretch in their forehead, from the top to the bottom of their eyes. Told to now hold these two stretches they are instructed to now open their mouths as wide as possible feeling the stretch in their jaws and even the neck muscles. Finally, they are told to keep hands and arms, mouth and eyes stretched out and wide opened as far as possible and then turn around and take a really good look at one another.

The room will be filled with laughter and everyone will feel energized. When they are asked to raise their hands if they feel a bit more energy and relaxed, most will raise their hands.

Note: If you have read the research related to sitting, you know that moving our muscles pumps fresh blood and oxygen through the brain and triggers the release of all sorts of brain- and mood-enhancing chemicals. When we are sedentary, everything slows, including brain function (Berkowitz &

Clark, 2014). If needed, *take a few minutes for yourself and get up and walk around for a minute before completing the final activity of this section, which will take 15–30 minutes.*

CF/STS/BO Warning Signs

There are many warning signs that tell us we are approaching or experiencing BO, CF or secondary trauma. These warning signs are comprised of thoughts, behaviors, emotions and physical conditions. When they are not recognized for what they are and mean, we simply do not respond in ways that support healthy self-care and resilience. The following statement describes a response that is certainly understandable given all the trauma material you are exposed to day after day. It goes like this,

> *"There are days I don't return client's calls."*

You tell yourself you'll call tomorrow when you have more energy. You may tell yourself this is tough work and you need a break every now and then, which is true. However, how many of you actually tell yourself that you may be experiencing the signs of secondary trauma or CF and need to further assess your behaviors, thoughts, emotions and physical conditions for additional STS/CF indicators? Most do not because we haven't been taught to associate thoughts and behaviors like this as strong predictors of CF/STS/BO.

In addition, given your busy days, the demands and all the distractions you face daily, you gloss over the signs, pay little attention to them, minimize, ignore or repress them so that stress becomes cumulative. As time goes on the quality of your work suffers, clients no longer get your best, placing some at-risk psychologically or physically, you experience more self-doubt about your skills, you find yourself with emotions and behaviors that are not at all like you, others are being affected by the changes in you and now recovering from all this stress will take longer.

Reality: *When we can recognize what is happening to us as a result of being exposed to a trauma population, traumatic situations and workplace culture, and practices that foster these stressors, we can take the necessary self-care measures needed to engage decisions and activities that are in our best interest personally and professionally, as well as comply with our ethical responsibility to those we care for-to care for ourselves.*

Let's try to identify the specific thoughts, behaviors, emotions, physical conditions associated with CF/STS/BO. We'll do this collectively via an activity I think you will find helpful.

Activity: What Does BO/STS/CF Sound Like or Look Like?

The purposes of this activity are to

1. help you evaluate your awareness and knowledge about the ways CF/STS is expressed via our thoughts, feelings and behaviors,
2. identify symptom differences between BO/STS/CF, and
3. to reframe necessary thought processes about the reactions to the stress we face.

Activity Instructions

If you did not complete Pre-session One Activity #3 listing statements that are associated with CF/STS/BO, do so now. For example, the earlier statement, "There are days I don't return client's calls" would be considered BO if the rest of the statement read something like, *"because all they want to do is talk and I don't have the time."* This same statement could be secondary stress if the rest of the statement read something like, *"because what happened to these clients just triggers to many unwanted reactions I have trouble controlling."* And, finally the same statement could be considered CF if the rest read, *"because I don't think any amount of caring will change anything."*

Note: You may have difficulty developing the narrative statements for CF/STS. Over the years, a great deal has been published about BO; its causes and symptoms are more familiar to most than those of CF/STS. However, enough material has been provided up to this point to frame several statements for each. One of the purposes of this activity is to help you evaluate your knowledge about the ways CF/STS expresses itself via our thoughts, feelings and behaviors. When you can do this, it is so much easier to more quickly recognize your stress reactions and their source or the cause, and in turn more appropriately intervene. So just do the best you can. It's a learning process that will make a difference.

Following Completion

To better recognize the signs, we have to be aware of how they are expressed in our thoughts, feelings and behaviors. Now that you have completed your descriptions, read the following stories for each stress reaction and compare what you wrote with the descriptors provided to see how aware you are of the ways stress is reflected in what we feel, think and do.

BO: Phil's Story: Two Years on the Job

I'm no longer happy when I come to work. Everyone is so overworked no one has time to talk to each other. Actually, there are more days that I don't really want to talk to anyone. I don't go to lunch with folks the way I used to. I feel like I'm in this alone. I'm tired and worn out by all the demands. I'm not sleeping well. My energy level sucks. It takes me a long time to come down after I get home from work. The paperwork never ends. The constant problems and situations my clients present have gotten overwhelming. I can't stand having to take over a colleague's client when I already have a full caseload. You do your job well and they just pile more on. It's just hard to care anymore with all the stress of this job. It's the same day after day. I'm numb most of the time, like there but not really there.

There's not a lot of recognition or support for that matter. Rarely does anyone ask how I'm doing anymore. We're always being told what to do but rarely why or asked for our opinion. I can't say that I feel like I matter that much. My supervisor can't be found half the time and when I do find her/him she/he always seems to be in a hurry or preoccupied. The meetings we have to attend suck most of the time. They keep going over the same stuff but nothing ever changes. If there is anything new they want to tell us about, it usually means more forms to fill out. I'm not answering my phone as much because I know it will mean more work or more complaints from someone. It's just getting harder for me to concentrate and get the work done and I'm more forgetful than usual. I seem to be getting more colds and my stomach is upset a lot. I'm just exhausted. I feel like I need a shot of something to just keep me going some days.

STS: Nancy's Story: Six Months After Starting Job

I think I'm being changed in not a good way by the kinds of clients I'm seeing day after day and hearing all the stuff that has happened to them. It's kind of depressing. Some days I just dread having to deal with some of my clients and I certainly don't want to hear my colleagues talk about their clients. There are days I don't return client's calls because I know they'll be calling about yet another crisis. Sometimes I just avoid them. I seem to be doing that with friends too. I'm not as happy as I used to be. I am already thinking too much about my cases and some of the situations they've experienced even when I try not to. I'll wake up in the middle of the night thinking about them. Even during the day I'll be busy doing something, and I start thinking about this one client's situation. It's like I can't shut it off. When I think about some of what I've been exposed to I get kind of jumpy, uneasy; that's not like me. It upsets me. My reactions are like they were when I was first exposed. Actually, I just feel more anxious about everything.

I keep wondering what the next horrific thing I'm going to have to deal with. It's like I'm constantly preparing myself or ready for something bad to happen. Some days I'm super alert, like nothing or no one around me is safe. Then there are days, when I just feel like giving up 'cause no way can I help my clients. It's hard to stay interested in something you know you just can't change. At home I'm getting so annoyed and angry at the slightest of things any more. It's not just at home. The other day I was in the grocery store and the cashier was taking her good old time talking to customers. She couldn't move any slower. I was just about ready to yell out something when she finally got to the person in front of me who only had two items. When she started checking me out, I didn't say one word to her. When she said have a nice day, I just ignored her. I was such a jerk. I notice that I seem to have memory gaps related to client material. I know there are days that I walk around like a zombie, just really detached. Physically, if it's not one problem it's another. I just have a lot of aches and pains. I kind of feel like I don't own my life anymore.

CF: Frank's Story, After 10 Years at Third Agency

I'm not getting a lot of satisfaction from the clients I have. Frankly it takes all my energy, so I can't say I really like what I'm doing anymore. I came out of school thinking I could really be helpful; I don't have that feeling anymore. It doesn't seem like anything I do is really helping my clients; I don't think anything really can. It seems like I hear the same stories over and over to the point that I stop listening after a while or jump ahead of where the client is at and silently finish their story in my head. I'm getting mad with clients who think their situation is the worst. It's hard to feel for them the same way as I do about others who have it a lot harder. I seem to be more tired and have little desire to the things I used to do. I know I've cut out a lot of my social activities; I just don't have the energy.

It doesn't take much to irritate me. My friend told me I've become really impatient. Some days I just can't think especially when I get a headache, which I'm getting more often. Drinking shuts it all down for a while until it's time to go back to work. I think I've used all my sick time. I'm just not as sharp as I was. On a couple of occasions, I forgot to get really critical information from clients. I'm not sure I want to do this work anymore. I'm not sure I can.

What's Next?

These narratives were not meant to be all-inclusive yet they do give us a good "sense" for the thoughts, emotions, physical reactions and behaviors that are associated with each stressor. This activity is also an introduction to the next session where we examine the subjective experiences of stress along with how our nervous system and the lower to mid-regions of the brain respond to stress. We'll explore these areas because *common sense tells us that when we are repeatedly exposed to trauma, via caring for or responding to others in trauma and doing so empathetically, we will eventually feel some of what they feel and what fuels their stress and the stress of our exposure to them and their experiences.*

We'll explore and engage you in an activity that demonstrates *why talk is initially limited in its ability to help find relief from the stress of repeated exposure in order to again emphasize that managing stress cannot be done well by simply trying to think our way out of it or by talking about it. In fact, we'll see that talk can make it worse for some.*

You'll be engaged in several activities that allow you to *experience what we mean by sensory-based practices and how beneficial and necessary they are for recovering from and managing the stress of exposure to trauma and for developing sustainable, trauma-sensitive, resilience-focused, effective self-care practices.*

All of this is a starting point, a foundation for committing to more effective and consistent self-care. However, as important as facts and research are for acknowledging the need for self-care, they are not as convincing as when we can also experience sensory and emotional changes associated with what is being taught and recommended. Both neuroscience and learning science demonstrate this, which you will have the opportunity in the next segment to experience firsthand for yourself. For this reason, learning how our bodies, our nervous system and our brain react to stress defines the kinds of activities that positively alter the negatively impactful stress of the work we do.

There is just one final activity for you to complete. Keep your answers as they will be used when working on your personalized self-care plan.

The Final Questions

There are a few final questions I'd like you to answer. These questions will be asked at the completion of every session. *Write down your responses so you can see them. It makes them more concrete and meaningful and easier to process. Hold onto to your answers because they will be used when preparing your personalized self-care plan.* For individual responders, it helps to narrow the focus or "focus down" to what matters most. This becomes a starting point for change. Your answers can also reinforce what you already know and need to continue doing on a regular basis, or if that has not been working, that you need to further explore the recommendations that are presented in this work.

Note: These are excellent questions to ask session attendees when working in a group, as they help everyone focus on what has been most personally meaningful. Sharing their responses with the group is also a wonderful way to acknowledge and reinforce a cross section of what has been learned. For a presenter it provides a quick assessment of what content the group values and what additional material might be helpful.

In a group setting what many will acknowledge about this session is that the research on prevalence was surprising. They'll express in several ways that they feel much better knowing what they have been experiencing is not uncommon and that this encourages them to look closer at their self-care practices. Some will ask how to tell the difference when some of the symptoms seem the same for the different stressors, which speaks to the need to complete appropriate CF/STS/BO scales and inventories reviewed later. Others have mentioned that organizations need to be held more accountable for their ethical responsibility to provide more self-care opportunities to staff. Still others will indicate that the activity What CF/BO/STS Sounds Like really helped them become more aware of their own thought processes, emotions and behaviors associated with the stress of what they do as well as better appreciate the stress driven behaviors and comments of some of their colleagues.

Post-Session One Questions

Write down your answers to the following questions. Keep these responses, as they will be used later when detailing self-care practices. This process will be completed at the ending of each session. The cumulative results will provide an outline of what you consider to be the most critical focal points in your self-care plan.

Questions

1. Of all that you have read and experienced up to this point, what surprises you the most?
   _____
   _____.

2. Of all that you have read and experienced up to this point, what one thought stands out the most for you?
   _____
   _____.

3. As you think about the one thought that stands out the most for you, how might it change the way you think about CF, secondary stress and BO?
   _____
   _____.

4. How has this changed what you feel you need to do about the unavoidable stress of what you do?
   _____
   _____.

References

Abendroth, M., & Flannery, J. (2006). Predicting the risk of compassion fatigue: A study of hospice nurses. *Journal of Hospice and Palliative Nursing, 8*(6), 346–356.

Adams, R. E., Boscarino, J. A., & Figley, C. R. (2006). Compassion fatigue and psychological distress among social workers: A validation study. *American Journal of Orthopsychiatry, 76*(1), 103–108.

Aiken, L. H., Clarke, S. P., Sloane, D. M., Sochalski, J., & Silber, J. H. (2002). Hospital nurse staging and patient mortality, nurse burnout, and job dissatisfaction. *JAMA,* 288, 1987–1993.

American Counselors Association (ACA). (2016). *American counseling association code of ethics.* Retrieved August 16, 2018, from https://counseling.northwestern.edu/blog/ACA-Code-of-Ethics/

American Institute of Stress (AIS). (2017). *Compassion fatigue.* Retrieved September 9, 2018, from www.stress.org/military/for-practitionersleaders/compassion-fatigue/

APA. (2018). *Research roundup: Burnout in mental health providers: Professional burnout in mental health practitioners and strategies for managing and preventing burnout.* Retrieved August 9, 2018, from www.apapracticecentral.org

Arnsten, A. F., Raskind, M. A., Taylor, F. B., & Connor, D. F. (2015). The effects of stress exposure on prefrontal cortex: Translating basic research into successful treatments for post-traumatic stress disorder. *Neurobiology of Stress, 1,* 89–99.

Beck, C. (2011). Secondary traumatic stress in nurses: A systematic review. *Archives of Psychiatric Nursing, 25*(1), 1–10.

Berkowitz, B., & Clark, P. (2014). *The health hazards of sitting*. Retrieved August 28, 2018, from www. washingtonpost.com/apps/g/page/national/ . . . health-hazards-of-sitting/750/

Brady, P. Q. (2012, May 1). *Crimes against caring: Compassion fatigue, burnout and self-care practices among professionals working with crimes against children*. Boise State University Scholar Works, Criminal Justice Graduate Project and Thesis.

Bride, B. E. (2007). Prevalence of secondary traumatic stress among social workers. *Social Work, 52*(1), 63–70.

Cieslak, R., Shoji, K., Melville, E., Luszczynska, A., & Benight, C. C. (2014). A meta-analysis of the relationship between job burnout and secondary traumatic stress among workers with indirect exposure to trauma. *American Psychological Association, 11*(1), 75–86.

Collins, J. (2018). *Addressing secondary traumatic stress*. Retrieved August 9, 2018, from www.cwla.org/ addressing-secondary-traumatic-stress/

Culver, L., McKinney, B., & Paradise, L. (2011). Mental health professionals' experiences of vicarious traumatization in Post-Hurricane Katrina New Orleans. *Journal of Loss and Trauma, 16*(1), 33–42.

DeMarco, H. (2018). *The other victims: First responders to violent disasters often suffer alone*. Retrieved August 4, 2018, from https://khn.org/ . . . /the-other-victims-first-responders-to-horrific-disasters-often-suffer-i. . .

Dhabhar, F. S. (2014). Effects of stress on immune function: The good, the bad, and the beautiful. *Immunologic Research, 58*(2–3), 193–210.

Eastwood, C. D., & Ecklund, K. (2008). Compassion fatigue risk and self-care practices among residential treatment center childcare workers. *Residential Treatment for Children & Youth, 25*(2), 103–122.

Figley, C. (1995). *Compassion fatigue: Coping with secondary traumatic stress disorder in those who treat the traumatized*. New York: Brunner/Mazel.

Freudenberger, H. J. (1974). Staff burnout. *Journal of Social Issues, 30*, 159–165.

Fritscher, L. (2018). *Counter-transference in therapy*. Retrieved January 20, 2019, from https://www.verywellmind. com

Garton, E. (2017). *Employee burnout is a problem with the company, not the person*. Retrieved August 16, 2018, from https://hbr.org/ . . . /employee-burnout-is-a-problem-with-the-company-not-the-person

Gomez, D., & Rutledge, D. N. (2009). Prevalence of secondary traumatic stress among emergency nurses. *Journal of Emergency Nursing, 35*(3), 199–204.

Green Cross Academy of Traumatology. (2010). *Ethics of self -care*. Retrieved August 16, 2018, from www.ncbi. nlm.nih.gov/books/NBK207194/box/part2_ch2.box30/?report . . .

Griffin, M. R. (2018). *10 health problems related to stress you can fix*. Retrieved July 29, 2018, from www.webmd. com/balance/stress . . . /10-fixable-stress-related-health-problems

Hatton Bowers, H., Brooks, S., & Borucki, J. (2014). *Associations between health, workplace support, and secondary traumatic stress among public child welfare workers: A practice brief*. Northern California Training Academy, University of California Davis, Davis, CA.

HCPro, Nurse Leader Insider. (2017). *The dangers of compassion fatigue*. Retrieved August 17, 2018, from www. hcpro.com/NRS-330485-868/The-dangers-of-compassion-fatigue.html

Herman, J. (1992). *Trauma and recovery*. New York: Basic Books, p. 6.

Hoge, M. A., Morris, J. A., Daniels, A. S., Stuart, G. W., Huey, L. Y., & Adams, N. (2007). *An action plan for behavioral health workforce development: A framework for discussion*. Rockville, MD: Substance Abuse and Mental Health Services Administration, p. 58.

Hoper, C. L., Craig, J., Janvrin, D. R., Wetsel, M. A., & Reimels, E. (2010). *Compassion satisfaction, burnout, and compassion fatigue among emergency nurses compared with nurses in other selected inpatient specialties*. Retrieved August 1, 2018, from www.ncbi.nlm.nih.gov/pubmed/20837210

The Humane Society of the United States (HSUS). (2003-2004). *Compassion satisfaction/fatigue self-test: Animal care: Compassion fatigue: Coping with secondary traumatic stress disorder*. Washington, DC: Humane Society of the United States.

Jaffe, P. G., Crooks, C. V., Dunford-Jackson, B. L., & Town, M. (2003). *Vicarious trauma in judges: The personal challenge of dispensing justice*. Retrieved September 4, 2018, from https://onlinelibrary.wiley.com/doi/ abs/10.1111/j.1755-6988.2003.tb00083.x

Joinson, C. (1992). Coping with compassion fatigue. *Nursing, 22*, 116–120.

Judicial Edge. (2017). *Nearly half of all judges have suffered from this condition*. Retrieved August 4, 2018, from www.judges.org/nearly-half-judges-suffered-condition/

Kirschman, E. (2017). *Cops and PTSD: Why you should care, what you can do*. Retrieved July 30, 2018, from www.psychologytoday.com/us/blog/cop-doc/201706/cops-and-ptsd-0

Leiter, M. (2016, December). Latent burnout profiles: A new approach to understanding the burnout experience. *Burnout Research, 3*(4), 89–100.

Lipschutz, R. (2010). *Ethics corner: Self care – an ethical responsibility*. Retrieved August 17, 2018, from naswil.org/news/chapter-news/ . . . /ethics-corner-self-care-an-ethical-responsibility/

Maguen, S., Metzler, T. J., McCaslin, S., Inslicht, S. S., Henn-Haase, C., Neylan, T. C., & Marmar, C. R. (2009, October). Routine Work Environment Stress and PTSD Symptoms in Police Officers. *The Journal Nervous Mental Disorders, 197*(10), 754–760.

Mathieu, F. (2012). *The compassion fatigue workbook: Creative tools for transforming compassion fatigue and vicarious traumatization*. New York: Routledge.

May, C. L., & Wisco, B. E. (2016, March). Defining trauma: How level of exposure and proximity affect risk for posttraumatic stress disorder. *Psychological Trauma, 8*(2), 233–240.

McEwen, B. S., & Morrison, J. H. (2013). The brain on stress: Vulnerability and plasticity of the prefrontal cortex over the life course. *Neuron, 79*(1), 16–29.

Medscape National Physician Burnout & Depression Report. (2018). Retrieved August 10, 2018, from www.medscape.com/slideshow/2018-lifestyle-burnout-depression-6009235

Meldrum, L., King, R., & Spooner, D. (2018/2002). Secondary traumatic stress in case managers working in community mental health services. In C. R. Figley (Ed.), *Treating compassion fatigue* (pp. 85–106). New York: Routledge.

Miller, B. R., & Hen, R. (2015). The current state of the neurogenic theory of depression and anxiety. *Current Opinion in Neurobiology, 30*, 51–58.

Morse, G., Salyers, M. P., Rollins, A. L., DeVita, M. M., & Pfahler, C. (2012, September). Burnout in mental health services: A review of the problem and its remediation. *Administration Policy Mental Health, 39*(5), 341–352.

Movement and Learning. (2014). *What the researchers say*. Retrieved December 18, 2014, from http://movementandlearning.wordpress.com/about/

Pai, P., Suris, A. M., & North, C. S. (2017 March). Posttraumatic stress disorder in the *DSM-5*: Controversy, change, and conceptual considerations. *Behavioral Sciences, 7*(1), 7.

Pearlman, L. A., & Saakvitne, K. W. (1995). Treating therapists with vicarious traumatization and secondary traumatic stress disorders. In C. R. Figley (Ed.), *Compassion fatigue: Coping with secondary traumatic stress disorder in those who treat the traumatized* (pp. 150–177). New York: Brunner/Mazel.

Perez, L. M., Jones, J., Englert, D. R., & Sachau, D. (2010). Secondary traumatic stress and burnout among law enforcement investigators exposed to disturbing media images. *Journal of Police and Criminal Psychology, 25*(2), 113–124.

Purdue University. (2017). *Importance of self-care for nurses*. Retrieved August 16, 2018, from https://nursingonline.pnw.edu/articles/self-care-for-nurses.aspx

SAMHSA. (2018). *First responders: Behavioral health concerns, emergency response, and trauma*. Retrieved August 4, 2018, from www.samhsa.gov/ . . . /supplementalresearchbulletin-firstresponders-may2018.pdf

Salston, M., & Figley, C. R. (2003). Secondary traumatic stress effects of working with survivors of criminal victimization. *Journal of Traumatic Stress, 16*, 167–174.

Schneiderman, N., Ironson, G., & Siegel, S. (2005). *Stress and health: Psychological, behavioral, and biological determinants*. Retrieved July 20, 2018, from www.ncbi.nlm.nih.gov/pmc/articles/PMC2568977/

Shoval, E. (2011). Using mindful movement in cooperative learning while learning about angles. *Instructional Science, 39*(4), 453–466.

Showalter, S. E. (2010). *Compassion fatigue:* What is it? Why does it matter? Recognizing the symptoms, acknowledging the impact, developing the tools to prevent compassion fatigue and strengthen the professional already suffering from the effects. *American Journal of Hospice & Palliative Medicine, 27*(4), 239–242.

Slavich, G. M., & Irwin, M. R. (2014). From stress to inflammation and major depressive disorder: A social signal transduction theory of depression. *Psychological Bulletin, 140*(3), 774.

Smith, J. M., Kleijn, W. C., Trjsburg, R., & Hutschemaekers, G. (2007). How therapists cope with clients' traumatic experiences. *Torture, 17*(3), 203–215.

Smith, W. (2017). *Secondary or vicarious trauma among judges and court personnel.* Retrieved August 17, 2018, from www.ncsc.org/ . . . /2017/Secondary-or-Vicarious-Trauma-Among-Judges-and-C. . .

Steele, W. (2017). *Optimizing learning outcomes: Proven brain-centric, trauma-sensitive practices.* New York: Routledge, Taylor and Francis Company.

Stewart, C. (2016). *High staff turnover, burnout puts child welfare system in crisis: Up to a quarter of Ohio's child welfare caseworkers leave the job each year.* Retrieved June 23, 2018, from www.daytondailynews.com/. . . / high-staff-turnover-burnout-puts-child-welfare-s. . .

TEND®. (2018). *Defining vicarious trauma and secondary traumatic stress: What is vicarious trauma? What is secondary traumatic stress?* Retrieved from www.tendacademy.ca/ . . . /defining-vicarious-trauma-and-secondary-traumatic-st. . .

Transforming Education. (2015). *Let's talk about self-management: Marshmallows, stop signs, squeezy balls and teaching.* Retrieved August 5, 2018, from www.youtube.com/watch?v=Oq9POEdptZ8.

Vrklevski, P. L., & Franklin, J. (2008). *Vicarious trauma: The impact on solicitors of exposure to traumatic material.* Retrieved July 15, 2018, from journals.sagepub.com/doi/pdf/10.1177/1534765607309961

Well, T. (2017). *Compassion is better than empathy.* Retrieved May 12, 2019, from https://www.psychologytoday.com/us/blog/the-clarity/201703/compassion-is-better-empathy

Williams, R. (2011). *The importance of self-care.* Retrieved August 16, 2018, from www.schoolcounselor.org/magazine/blogs/ . . . 2011/the-importance-of-self-care

World Health Organization (WHO). (2016). *International statistical classification of diseases and related health problems.* 10th ed. (ICD-10). Geneva, Switzerland: WHO.

Zur, O. (2016). *Ethical principles of psychologists and code of conduct (APA).* Retrieved August 16, 2018, from www.zurinstitute.com/ethicsofburnout.html

2 Stress From a Different Perspective
Part One—It's a Reaction and It's Subjective

Pre-session Questions and Activities

Answer all questions as best you can. If you seem to have no answer, give it your best effort as this will help reinforce what is learned throughout this session.

Questions

1. What is the one word that best captures or describes the experience of grief?
   _____

2. What is the one word that best captures or describes the experience of trauma?
   _____

3. Briefly describe what is meant by our subjective experience.
   _____
   _____

4. When the limbic area of our brain is activated what other process does it limit access to?
   _____
   _____

5. What two feelings best describe the experience of terror?
   _____, _____.

6. Is the following statement true or false, "our bodies can and do overreact to stressors that are not life threatening"? Yes ____ No ____

7. True or false? "Our reactions to stress at any given time may not be a choice but a bio-neurological response often impossible to control cognitively."

   Yes ____ No ____

8. Dr. Peter Levine has stressed for years that trauma is (two words) is as much a (two words) _____ as it is a (two words) _____ _____.

9. Does talking about (trauma) what happened make it better?
   _____

10. As best you can briefly describe what is meant by neuromodulation.
    _____

11. List 10 questions you might ask someone about the stress they are experiencing to better define how they are subjectively experiencing that stress.

1. _____?
2. _____?
3. _____?
4. _____?
5. _____?
6. _____?
7. _____?
8. _____?
9. _____?
10. _____?

Session Two

Stress From a Different Perspective: Part One

It's a Reaction—It's Subjective

Opening Statement

Two sessions are needed to examine stress from a different perspective. The purpose of this session is to

1. talk about two different aspects of stress, the first being the subjective experience of stress and the second being the physiological response, and
2. how these become an integral part of effective self-care. The session following this one is devoted to mindsets associated with stress, our reactions to it and our efforts to remain resilient in the face of the unavoidable and ongoing stress of what we do.

Years ago, when I stopped thinking about trauma as a set of formal diagnostic criteria and became more interested in what the subjective experience was like for trauma survivors, it changed the way I went about helping.

Reality: *Identifying the subjective experiences of the stress we experience because of what we do, will help identify what will matter in our efforts to alleviate and/or manage that stress.*

Think about this. When we look at trauma victims, we see symptoms. Unfortunately, trauma symptoms can be misleading and mistaken for depression, attention deficit problems, oppositional defiant disorder (ODD), conduct disorder, reactive attachment and other disorders. Basically, symptoms are outward indicators that something is not right. We really don't know what an individual is struggling with internally until we discover, by being very curious, what they now think and believe about

- themselves following their experience,
- the present and future,
- the environments they must navigate their way through,
- the people in those environments, and
- the feelings and sensations they now experience as a result of what they were exposed to, what happened to them.

In other words, our subjective experience refers to how an experience changes the way we view ourselves, others and the immediate world around us.

Fear, constant worry, hurt, anger, sometimes revenge, thoughts of what's wrong with me, guilt and shame are just a few of those subjective experiences. Survivors reinforced that my being curious enough to explore with them what their lives were now like, allowed them to feel no longer alone, that I was with them in their world. The interventions they helped me develop to work through and positively change their subjective experiences went through rigorous research and became evidence-based interventions now being used in 55 countries (Steele, 2015; Steele & Kuban, 2013; Steele & Malchiodi, 2012).

Helping trauma victims identify their subjective experiences helps to determine what will matter most in their efforts to survive and our efforts to help them. This also holds true in our efforts to best manage the stress of what we do.

In the first part of this session we'll draw several parallels between the subjective experiences of trauma and those of CF and secondary trauma.

Reality: *This approach matters greatly because it can help us to more easily identify and appreciate those strategies that not only support, but also sustain our efforts to remain resilient while doing this difficult work.*

Secondly, I believe it is also critical to understand the physiology of stress as that physiology dictates how we find relief from and/or best manage the stress we are exposed to in ways that talk alone cannot accomplish. In the second part of this session we'll discuss trauma physiology. Neuroscience confirms the fact that stress is not primarily a cognitive experience but a physiological one and as such is often best reduced and/or managed using non-cognitive processes, or what I refer to as sensory-based activities. Sensory-based activities are those activities that do not involve traditional talk approaches.

Reality: *These activities will help you to appreciate why certain non-cognitive approaches to self-care are recommended and how quickly they can change how we are reacting to the stress we're exposed to daily.*

Keep in mind that we will not be talking about BO in this segment as BO relates specifically to work conditions. Yes, those work conditions can very definitely impact our physiology and thinking in ways that hurt us and, at times, other people; however, we'll cover those responses and conditions when we look at organizational stress. Let's begin by examining the subjective experiences of trauma and compare those with CF and secondary trauma.

Trauma as a Subjective Experience

Activity: Describe Trauma (Group/Individual)

Before going any further, I would like you to write down your answers to the following two questions, a third question will follow in just a minute.

1. What is the one word that best describes the experience of grief?
2. What is the one word that best describes the experience of trauma?

Let me now ask you: What one word did you write down that best describes the experience of grief? In past workshops like this, your peers generally present several descriptors. However, the one word most commonly presented by them is "sadness." When we say people are grieving, we usually say they are feeling sad.

Now what one word did you write down to best describe the experience of trauma? Again, past participants present a variety of descriptors. Actually, when I've presented these two questions to thousands of your peers in the past, the response to which word best describes grief is offered without hesitation, "sad" being the most immediate and frequent response. However, there is more hesitation and multiple words used to describe trauma: fear, pain, scarred, overwhelmed and lost are just a few. After 20 years of working with both victims of grief and trauma, I found the one word that best describes the experience of trauma is "terror" (Steele, 2003). My sense is that fewer of you wrote this word down than those who wrote "sad" to describe grief. This said, let's now try to describe the experience of "terror" in order to arrive at a working definition of trauma that clearly dictates the focus of interventions. You may be surprised to discover how its subjective experience, although not as intense, is similar to those of CF and secondary stress. Please take a minute to write down your answer to this question.

3.   What two feelings best capture the experience of "terror"?

Before I present the answer to this question, I want to spend a bit more time on why it is so important to examine our subjective experiences to stress regardless of the source of that stress.

Compared to grief our understanding of trauma is still in its infancy, yet there is much we do know thanks to neuroscience and its research into how our brains and nervous systems respond to stress. We do know that the subjective world of trauma victims is changed by their experience *as is ours as a result of attempting to help victims*. We know *this subjective world is an implicit one that acts and reacts to the sensations triggered by what we now see, hear and sense to be a potential threat* (Rothchild, 2017); *a world where we are poised to act, not because of what we think, but because of what we sense* (Kolk, 2015; Steele & Malchiodi, 2012).

Now did you ever try to calm a trauma victim by saying, "Everything will be okay." Trying to help change what a victim is experiencing using talk initially does not help much. Changing their experience dictates the need to first know how they are currently experiencing their world to then determine the kinds of experiences that will help change their subjective views and beliefs into ones that support their strength and resilience.

To better manage our own stress, we also need to direct our efforts not at the symptoms but how it has changed the way we are now experiencing ourselves, the work we are doing.

For example, you tell me you are really stressed out. What I want to know is what that subjective experience is like for you. Some of the questions I might ask are,

- What's the worst part of that stress for you?
- What upsets you the most about that worst part?
- When do you feel it the most?
- Where do feel it the most in your body?
- Who or what intensifies it?
- Who or what helps to reduce it?
- What does that stress make you feel like doing?
- How does it change what you think about yourself, the work you are doing?
- If that stress could talk, what would it say to you?
- If it could listen, what would you say to it?
- Does anyone else know about your stress?
- When they found out, what did they say to you?
- What worries you the most about your stress?

- In comparison with other worries you may have, would you put this worry in the top one third of your biggest worries, the middle third or lower third?

I could go on but even with these few questions I am going to have a far better idea as to

- its intensity,
- how it may be changing the way you view yourself, your sense of competence, the work you are doing,
- how it is impacting you at a physical level and an emotional level,
- what triggers its intensity and who or what helps to soothe it,
- how it's altering your ability to manage in that environment or under the conditions associated with that stress, and
- how others may or may not be helping.

In other words, this information is going to make it easier to introduce you to new experiences to better change and manage your unique responses. Let's look at a few examples.

Examples

Q. *When do you feel it (stress) the most?* If you tell me you begin feeling it when you are getting ready to go to work, I know there are going to be a number of workplace issues that may or may not be resolvable. Obviously more questions regarding the workplace culture and conditions need to be pursued. On the other hand, you tell me the stress hits you in the afternoon, I would want to know what you do on your lunch hour, if you take lunch, what you do mid-afternoon to regulate your responses to the stress of the earlier part of the day. Your stress response may be situational or a failure to take morning stress breaks. There could be a number of possibilities that are resolvable.

Q. *How does it change what you think about yourself, the work you are doing?* If your response to this is that you want to be helpful but are not feeling competent enough to help the clients assigned to you, then additional training and/or further education is where you might want to direct your efforts. Helping you with competency, skill building is also a responsibility of the workplace. If your supervisor is not providing the support needed or the workplace provides little incentive to further your education, the focus would be on looking for a workplace that does.

Q. *Have you told anyone about the stress you are experiencing?* If you have not, that is a problem in itself. If you reply "yes" I would ask the next question.

Q. *When they found out, what did they say to you?* If you tell me they said you needed to suck it up or find another job, you are not the problem. They're right about finding another job, another workplace that is more supportive; they are not right that you need to just suck it up.

Q. *What is your biggest worry?* If your biggest worry is that you are finding it more difficult to manage your emotional reactions to victim's stories/situations and you tell me that, in comparison with other worries, this is in the middle third of all your worries, I would suggest that we need to further assess the possible cause. I would wonder if this is the result of having no client diversity. If this were the case, I would want to check to see if there are other BO factors taking place in your work environment that are contributing to your exhaustion. I might wonder if you're not getting sufficient supervision to address transference issues. I might wonder about your own past history and whether the work is triggering unresolved issues. I would also want to evaluate your self-care practices, how frequently you engage in self-care, how balanced your efforts are and what you do to regulate your reactions at the time your emotional responses are triggered. Any one of the answers to these questions then makes it easier to determine the next step, the action needed.

Over Intervening

Why are these questions so important? When I was assisting schools across the country with how best to respond to traumatic situations, I cautioned them to give students a choice as to what they felt would help them the most because not all students exposed to the same situation have the same response. This holds true for you as well. You can be exposed to the same stressors as your peers yet have very different reactions. If I tell you to meditate 15 minutes a day, which is a standard prescription related to reducing stress, it may do little for you because it fails to address what is driving that stress, for example, wondering whether you are competent enough to help victims.

Reality: *To restate, my personal experiences to the same experience you experienced may involve some similar responses yet also be quite different.*

One question I suggested to school crisis team members that helps quickly identify student's subjective experience is, "Since this happened, what worries you the most?" I can't tell you how many times I've heard some students, for example, express great sadness after a non-violent loss or fear after a violent incident. On the other hand, there were those students exposed to the same incident whose major concern was wondering if the high school football game scheduled for that Friday night was still going to be played.

Reality: *We all experience stress, but we experience it differently. This is why what works for me may not work for you. In fact, not knowing what that subjective experience is like for you, what I might suggest you need to do to relieve yourself of that stress may be of no help whatsoever or make it worse rather than better.*

We'll return to this in greater detail when walking through the development of a personalized self-care plan that fits your experience versus a "one cure fits all" approach. So, let's see what descriptors you used to describe the experience of 'terror."

Terror Is Feeling...

Once again when I've conducted trainings with your peers across the country and asked them what two feelings best described the term *terror*, they often identify symptoms, such as being unable to forget, having intrusive memories and recollections or unable to relax, to mention a few. These reactions are associated with PTSD/STS yet fail to capture the overall experience that fuels these reactions. What survivors have described to me over and over again is that their terror caused them to *feel unsafe and powerless to do anything about their situation.* (Feeling unsafe can include feeling physically unsafe and emotionally unsafe.)

If this is the subjective experience of terror, then our interventions need to be redirected at restoring that sense of safety and empowerment by introducing victims to new experiences, which help to renew that sense of safety and power. When we can identify our own specific subjective experiences to stress, it is so much easier to know what will matter the most to help us with that stress.

The Subjective Experience, STS and CF

Let's draw a parallel between the subjective experience of trauma and that of secondary stress and CF. Keep in mind that both CF and STS are stress responses and both can induce the following reactions. These reactions may not be as intense as those associated with the terror of trauma yet are part of what we experience when experiencing CF and/or secondary trauma.

- We experience a state of ongoing readiness (hyper-vigilance) for the next trauma or intense stress-inducing situation we might face.
- Our view of who and what is safe in our home and/or work environment changes.
- We feel a loss of power over our physiological and/or emotional responses when triggered by reminders of that stressful experience.
- As we experience feelings not felt before or not felt with such intensity, we come to feel unsafe with our emotions.
- We worry that our feelings will "leak" out, that others will discover that we are not managing as well as we say we are doing and question our competency.
- We do not feel as emotionally safe among our colleagues.
- We fear how they may think of us if they discover the stress we are experiencing.
- We pull back from them, avoid them when we can, isolate ourselves more often.
- We do our best to avoid clients who intensify that stress.
- If we can't avoid them, we stop listening, try to redirect their focus or not return their calls in a timely manner.
- We start wondering if we will be able to continue to do what we do.
- We feel powerless to change anything.
- We're not driven by reason and logic any longer but by what we sense will make for even more stress.
- Reason and logic take a back seat to rationalizations. These rationalizations are stress driven reactions and often create more problems for us, for example, how we interact with clients, the quality of our work, our performance.
- We no longer do what is logical and reasonable but what we now sense we need to do to protect ourselves, to hold onto what sense of power we may have left.

It's a Mid-brain Response

There are other reactions that are driven by our fears and sense of powerlessness; however, what is so important to appreciate is that often we are not aware of the changes that are taking place in us. We may have some vague sense that we are under stress but not the level of intensity, the ways it is affecting our work, our performance, our colleagues, our clients or those we are trying to help. This is understandable. It is what repeated exposure to stressful clients, situations and conditions do to our brain, our physiology.

It's Not Denial

Remember the burning pot story. I felt totally calm and in control. I said to myself, "I can handle this." I did not handle it well. My cognitive processes were interrupted or taken over by my mid-brain and nervous system reaction to what was experienced as stressful. People often use the term "denial" to refer to those whose performance at work, interactions and reactions reveal their stress but are "denied" by that person. In reality, this is not always denial but a survival response to what is being experienced in that region of the brain where reason, logic, language doesn't exist, where everything is driven by fear, where we see and experience things differently than those around us.

It's Not a Cognitive Experience

For the last 30 years I've said that trauma is not primarily a cognitive experience but a sensory experience, one that is first experienced in the lower, mid-regions of the brain. The neuroscience of stress documents this, and as such supports those sensory-based interventions that change what is being experienced in the lower, mid-regions of our brain. If, in fact, stress is not primarily a cognitive experience, reason tells us talk and other cognitive processes will be initially limited in its efforts to remove that stress. What then is often much more helpful initially? To answer this, we need to spend time looking at how our brain responds to stress/trauma/trauma material/trauma incidents. This will set the foundation to how we can best alter the effects of stress and CF.

The Physiology of Stress

Zebras Don't Get Ulcers

Stress physiology is a disciplined science, meaning it examines how variables like emotions, our beliefs, our position and the ways others respond to us trigger and sustain the stress response and what that sustained stress response does to our body and mind. Acclaimed professor of biology and neurology at Stanford University, Robert Sapolsky has spent years researching and studying the effects of stress on the processes of our brains and bodies. His book *Why Zebras Don't Get Ulcers: The Acclaimed Guide to Stress, Stress-Related Diseases and Coping* (Sapolsky, 2004) is a must read for anyone seriously wanting to prevent the damaging mental and physical side effects of sustained stress.

Zebras don't get ulcers because their stress response is only triggered for brief periods of danger. When they face a physical threat, their bodies gear up for fight or flight. When the physical threat is over, their stress response is shut down. As humans, our body, like that of the zebra, is extremely adaptable in responding to short-term physical emergencies. When it's over we are over with it. However, when we worry for months about various things like work conditions, clients, paying the bills, relationships and family, or even anticipate something going wrong, our stress response remains on alert.

Reality: *When we are exposed regularly to trauma victims, conditions and materials, and/or we worry for months about various things like work conditions, we have the same stress response that we have to a physical crisis but it never gets shut down because other worries and exposure to trauma clients, situations or material continues.*

In other words, we become more vulnerable to CF, secondary stress and BO. The fact is, unless we learn, like the zebra, how to shut our stress down when not facing real danger yet are exposed regularly to stressful conditions, we become vulnerable to CF/STS/BO. Let's then take a closer look at how our brains and bodies function under stress to discover how we can better manage that stress.

Activity: Our Brains Under Stress (Group/Individual)

How does our brain function under stress, regardless of the source of that stress? Let me begin with more of a non-technical description adapted from Daniel Siegel's "Hand Model of the Brain" (Siegel, 2012) that I describe in "Optimizing Learning Outcomes" (Steele, 2017, p. 12):

> I want you to make a fist but put your thumb inside your hand. Now as you look at your fist also look at your forearm. Your forearm represents your reptilian brain, the first part of our brain that developed. The reptilian brain had three primary functions when it faced a possible

or real threat; flight, flight or freeze; the very same reactions we have when facing stress that is overwhelming or consistent. Now open your hand and wiggle your thumb. Your thumb represents the next part of our brain to develop: the limbic region, the mid-brain also referred to as the emotional brain. There is no language, there is no reason; there is no logic in this part of the brain.

Via the amygdala, hypothalamus this part of our brain simply responds to what it senses needs to happen in order to survive.

Now close your fist once again. Your fingers represent the last part of brain to develop; the cortex region and your fingertips represent the frontal cortex. The cortex and the frontal cortex are those regions of the brain where language, reason and logic do exist and where the functions needed to learn as well as help regulate our primal survival responses take place. Now open your fist once again and wiggle your thumb.

As you wiggle your thumb think of the daily stressors you experience and the fact that this part of our brain remains very active. When our mid-brain remains stressed from constantly responding to the stress of the environment we work in and exposure to the traumatic experiences of the people we are attempting to help, our performance begins to suffer along with our mental and physical health. Living in stress is like a foundation built on a growing sinkhole; sooner or later that foundation will collapse. This is not new information. Interestingly the Yerkes-Dodson Law of 1908 (Wikipedia, 2013) concluded that,

Reality: *The quality of our performance on any task, whether physical or mental, is related to our level of stress (emotional arousal). If we are feeling either very low or very high levels of emotion arousal, then our performance is likely to be impaired.*

Activity: Video

At this point I would show a video segment related to stress and our brain. I suggest that you Google "YouTube Got Stress?" and watch this brief three-minute video that does a good job of giving us a sensory understanding of how ongoing stress affects us (https://www.youtube.com/watch?v=Ogb7KYLtVLY).

In earlier years we didn't have neuroscience to support theories on stress. Today the research is quite abundant. Stress triggers predominant processes in the limbic/subcortical and right hemisphere of brain (Perry & Szalavitz, 2006), limiting access to the cortex (upper brain) and left hemisphere (Levine & Kline, 2008). This minimizes our ability to reason, to think things through, to focus and process information. *Cognitive processes take second place to stress.* Because stress is primarily a physiological response, our systems need actions other than cognitive processes to regulate that stress.

Heart Rate and Trauma Stress: Children of Waco

Bruce Perry (Supin, 2016, pp. 7-8) gives us a wonderful example of how this works when he describes his experience with the 21 children rescued from the Waco, Texas, Branch Davidian cult standoff. When he arrived, the children were in the custody of the FBI and Child Protective Services. Perry was greeted by a Texas ranger who wanted no one doing therapy on these children. He offered the ranger a deal. He told him if he took the pulse of one of the girls who was sleeping soundly and if it was under 100 he would leave. The normal resting rate for a girl her age is around 80. Her pulse was

160. He and his team stayed for months. When stressed, our heart rate is elevated. We may show no outward signs yet *the body knows*.

Over time what they observed is that the Waco children had about three hours of therapeutic intervention a day, not one minute of it was formal therapy. What they witnessed is that children would seek small doses of support throughout the day, an adult or activity that would make them laugh, another who gave good hugs. Their heart rates began to go down with these small doses of physiological regulators, which became buffers from further symptoms.

Reality: *"A stressful situation, whether something environmental, such as a looming work deadline, or psychological, such as worry about losing a job, can trigger a cascade of stress hormones that produce well-orchestrated physiological changes"* (Harvard Health Publishing, 2018).

By nature, trauma is terrifying and as such leaves us vulnerable to a myriad of reactions. We understand this. We don't argue about his. On the other hand, we tend to respond a bit differently to everyday stress; we minimize it, ignore it and have a hard time accepting that is presents serious challenges to our nervous system and the functions of our brain.

Reality: *Our bodies can and do overreact to stressors that are not life-threating, such as work pressures.*

I want to present an even more technical description of how our brains and nervous systems respond to stress because I do think it helps us to appreciate the delicate balancing act our body is engaging every minute, as well as what it needs most when dealing with ongoing stress.

The Alarm Goes Off, the Command Center Takes Over

Adapted from Harvard Health Publishing (2018)

Our eyes, ears and body are the first to capture what is stressful. The amygdala, our fear center that supports emotional processing, is also often referred to as the "smoke detector." It sends a warning signal to the hypothalamus, referred to as the "command center" that then triggers our nervous system (Autonomic Nervous System-ANS), which readies the body to fight or flee.

The Autonomic Nervous System: Gas Pedal/Brake

Think of the nervous system as having a gas pedal (the sympathetic nervous system) that pumps up our body for action, and the parasympathetic system (the brake pedal), which hopefully slows or calms everything down. When the alarm goes off, our command center (the hypothalamus) initiates a second response referred to as the HPA axis: the hypothalamus, the pituitary gland and the adrenal glands. The HPA produces several hormones-corticotropin (CRH) that go to the pituitary gland, which then releases adrenocorticotropic (ACTH) and this then travels to the adrenal glands and releases the "stress hormone" cortisol, which is a steroid.

Reality: *When our stress level remains constant/chronic, the release of cortisol continues and becomes the primary cause of memory and concentration problems, anxiety, depression, weight gain and numerous health issues including life-threatening ones like heart disease* (WebMD, 2018).

What's Really Interesting

The gas pedal accelerates our readiness, gives us the fuel we need to avoid, run from or fight off the stressors. This happens so fast we are not aware of all the processes taking place; it's so fast our visual, auditory center hasn't had time to fully process what has happened. In other words,

Reality: *Under stress our body acts first, our cognitive processes after*, and

Reality: *Even low-level stress is like a car idling on high for a long period.*

Sooner or later, if not turned off, it runs out of gas. Being a weekend warrior doesn't change much nor does drinking or medicating as a regular *go-to* stress reliever help. If we do not engage in consistent self-care practices that help regulate our motor (nervous system/brain), we too will run out of gas and also incur damage along the way in the form of BO/CF/STS/PTSD and numerous physical conditions. The documented physical outcomes of prolonged stress left unattended include but are not limited to respiratory conditions; elevated levels of stress hormones and of blood pressure; increased risk for hypertension, heart attack or stroke, diabetes; a burned-out immune system; anxiety; depression and overall wear and tear on the body leading to additional health problems (Mayo Clinic Staff, 2018).

What Today's Trauma Specialists Say

Today's leaders in the field like Babette Rothchild (*The Body Remembers*, 2017); Bessel van der Kolk; Peter Levine, founder of Somatic Experiencing (*In an Unspoken Voice*, 2011) and Stephen Porges (*Clinical Applications of the Polyvagal Theory*, 2018), among others, have substantially documented that our bodies need as much attention as our psyche when under stress.

Reality: *Our reactions to stress at any given time are not a choice but a bio-neurological response often impossible to control cognitively*.

Dr. Porges is a distinguished behavioral neuroscientist and professor of psychiatry who developed the Polyvagal theory. He has done so much to help us understand how the vagus nerve helps us with regulation. The vagus nerve has a number of branches, which connects with our brain, lungs, stomach and guts; thus, it's called the polyvagal theory. Basically, via abundant research he discovered that our behavior is tied to our physiology. In other words, we can only behave in a way that our physiology allows us.

The MRI Experience

Being a scientist and psychologist, Dr. Porges was interested in his own brain so he made an appointment for an MRI. As he is being moved into the tubular scanner, he senses a bit of anxiety and says, "Stop. I need a glass of water." After he finishes his water and when they move him further into the scanner, his body starts responding with a panic attack. As much as he tried, he couldn't reason it away. He had to get out and get out of there fast to some place safe. He had no idea his body would respond the way it did. When it did, he needed to act, to do something different with his body to reduce that stress. What he learned from this is that:

Reality: *Our physiology can profoundly change the way we respond. It can also profoundly change the negative effects of stress. It's very difficult to think away the effects of stress because our physiology is in need of a different experience*.

If interested in hearing him tell his story you can Google "YouTube The Polyvagal Theory: Looking At Trauma From A New Perspective" (https://www.youtube.com/watch?v=MKkDAOW2yd4).

Actually, Dr. Porges' experience is to some degree similar to experiences of law enforcement, firefighters, other first responders and military. They are trained through repetition to enter into the dangerous situations they encounter at a cognitive level, being very observant and making decisions based on the knowledge they have as to what procedures are the safest to initiate given what they observe. However, as happened to Dr. Porges, these responders will at some point be exposed to situations that immediately trigger emotional, mid-brain responses that then shut down those cognitive processes and the stress/survival response takes over. The other aspect of this work that leaves them vulnerable to stress is that they remain hyper-alert, their systems are constantly ready for the next danger. In some ways the gas pedal is on the floor so their systems simply run of gas at some point leaving them vulnerable to the stress of the work they do in the form of PTSD and other physical and mental difficulties. They too need the kind of self-care that helps to regulate that hyper alert response. It's similar to the story Dr. Perry told about the children of Waco.

Vital First Step to Relieving Stress: Calm the Fear Center

Dr. Peter Levine is the founder of The Somatic Experiencing method, which is a body-oriented approach to the healing of trauma and other stress disorders. It has been his life's work, resulting from his multidisciplinary study of stress physiology, psychology, ethology, biology, neuroscience, indigenous healing practices, and medical biophysics, together with over 45 years of successful clinical application.

Dr. Levine has stressed for years that "trauma is a physiological phenomenon, rather than a purely psychological one," and as such he wrote, "psychologists, psychiatrists and other helping professionals need to understand the core mechanisms of how to stabilize the body's reactions to traumatic stress on the physical level in order to help children and teens (and adults) regulate their sensations and emotions" (Steele & Malchiodi, 2012, p. 5-6). When we fail to regularly regulate these stress responses and when exposure to stress is consistent and/or repetitive, we remain in an activated arousal/survivor response that predisposes us to CF/STS and BO.

You might be interested in hearing Dr. Levine's personal reactions about the sudden trauma he experienced when he was struck head on by a car while walking across the street. You'll hear how he was unable to process the questions the paramedics were asking him and how dangerously high his blood pressure was until one gesture from a pediatrician who happened to be there, was experienced at a sensory level and helped regulate his nervous system and slow down his heart rate so he could begin to process things at a cognitive level.

View his story by Googling "YouTube Dr. Peter Levine on working through a personal traumatic experience" (https://www.youtube.com/watch?v=9hP2KJ3UgDI).

What does this experience tell us? It tells us that the first level of stress reduction ought to be at a physiological/sensory level and only thereafter, if needed, an integrated physiological-cognitive one some refer to as *bottom-up* and *top-down* approaches. More on this shortly, but first let's look a bit more at the limitations of talk.

Activity: Talk Is Limited (Group)

This is a fun activity that helps participants experience how hard it can be to try to find the words to describe the effect of a traumatic experience. It will bring a lot of laughter and reenergize the group. It takes about 15 minutes. All participants will need a plain sheet of paper and a pen or pencil.

- Inform participants that they are to pick a partner and then rearrange their chairs so they are back to back. Next tell them that the first task will be for one of the partners to draw a picture of whatever they want and, that while the one partner is doing this, the other is to sit quietly and not look at what their partner is doing. Ask them to choose the one who will do the first drawing and then give the initial drawers a minute or two to draw whatever they like.
- Next, instruct the drawers to stop for a minute while you present the next task. Instruct them to do the following. The person who did the first drawing is to attempt to provide their partner with information so they can attempt to replicate this initial drawing. This means recreating the original drawing, its objects, their same size and location on the paper. *However, the partner giving the instruction cannot name any of the objects in their drawing.* For example, they cannot say

draw a picture of the sun and put it in the upper right-hand corner nor can they say put a circle in the upper right-hand corner, as a circle is an object. Furthermore, they cannot watch what their partner is now drawing nor can the one drawing ask any questions or look at the original drawing. Then instruct the group to not share their drawings with one another until you instruct the entire group to do so.

- Give the group a couple minutes to replicate the first drawing. Once the drawing has started, take the opportunity to walk around the room to see how they are doing as well as determine when to tell the group to stop and then instruct them to show their drawings to one another.

The room will be filled with laughter and lots of talk. Having done this activity over 100 times, the outcome is always the same.

The Outcome: I will ask for a show of hands as to how many actually replicated their partners drawing: the same object, size, placement on the paper, etc. Rarely do more than one-third of the group raise their hands. There will be many who have drawn a completely different object. If time permits, I will ask participants what made this difficult for some while others were in "sync." If time does not allow for this, I will make the following observations.

- When I took away your ability to name the objects in the original drawing, I was limiting your language, your ability to find ways to describe your drawing to your partner. This is what happens in trauma; our cognitive processes, our access to language, significantly diminishes. This makes it difficult for others to know what that experience was like for you and for you to connect to others via language.
- Those of you trying to replicate the original drawing were not able to ask questions for more detail, clarification and guidance. Also, how you interpreted what your partner was describing to you will be greatly influenced by your personal experiences. For example, if both of you are boaters and your partner tells you to think about what you love doing during the summer, the chances are with a little more description you'll draw a boat similar to what your partner first drew. Some of you did do just that; the majority did not.
- Now obviously if you could have seen what your partner drew, you would have been able to connect, be in tune with your partner. This seems simple enough but is very profound. If we cannot see what trauma victims now see when they look at themselves and the world around them, as a result of what happened to them, how can we connect with them and appreciate what will matter most to them in their efforts to survive. This means that many trauma victims need to be provided alternative ways to express themselves, to communicate to us what their world is now like. Drawing, art, music poetry, journals, drama, dance are just a few of the ways this can be accomplished.

This activity can actually be used with a variety of groups to demonstrate important aspects of effective communication. For our purposes, it reinforces what we have to say next about traditional talk approaches with trauma victims and the physiology of trauma that dictates, initially a different approach to coping with trauma, inclusive of self-care for us as helpers and responders.

Talking About It Makes It Worse

In many cases initially talking about what happened only makes it worse (Barron, 2015). Researchers at the University at Buffalo and University of California, Irvine obtained data from a random sample of 2,000 Americans after the September 11, 2001, terrorist attacks. "What they discovered surprised the participants who chose not to discuss their feelings right after the attacks often fared better over the subsequent two years than those who did" (Kingsbury, 2008). Dr. Spencer Eth (van der Kolk, 2015, p. 231) found a similar response in 2002 from 225 who escaped from the Twin Towers. When asked what was the most helpful, they replied, "acupuncture, massage, yoga and EMDR in that order." Eth's survey suggests, along with others, that the most helpful interventions are those focused on relieving the physiological symptoms of their trauma.

If you think about this, the more we talk about what happened to us, the more we remain in the past, in that trauma experience, rather than in the present. Now for some that is the best intervention; for others repressing the experience by not talking about what happened results in array of symptoms that eventually interfere with various areas of their lives. At some point, they will need to tell their story but in a way that keeps them in the present. We'll get to that process in a minute.

"When interviewed following 9/11, many educators also told me what was most helpful to them was the use of the many of the health clubs who opened their doors to educators so they could use the pools, the hot tubs and receive massages" (Steele & Kuban, 2013, p. 24). How does this support what we know about the physiology of stress?

Over the years, I have met with many survivors who were directly exposed to a variety of traumatic incidents such as the Gulf War, the bombing of the Federal building in Oklahoma, 9/11 with survivors from both New York and Washington DC, hurricanes Katrina and Rita and far too many traumas involving school shootings and other forms of violence. These survivors had very high levels of exposure to the visuals, the sounds, the smells, the terror and the chaos experienced in such situations. After the first few days, they also reported that talking only intensified the primary reactions they first experienced at those tragic incidents. I remember one clinician I met saying that a few months after the 9/11 attack, area restaurants did an informal survey and found that the consumption of mashed potatoes had tripled. What are mashed potatoes? That's right, comfort food.

Over and over I heard that it was comfort foods like mashed potatoes and sensory experiences like exercise that was getting survivors from one day to the next.

Reality: *Our bodies, our physiology is the first to respond to trauma and, as such, needs to be attended to or, said differently, needs to be regulated.*

Reality: *When we are stressed, regardless of the source, we need to do something to soothe, calm our overly active physiological reactions to that stress.*

The Wall Street Journal Says So

I do not have a formal source to cite regarding the consumption of mashed potatoes after 9/11 but there is no doubt that when we are stressed, we seek comfort of some kind. Some of you may be too young to remember this but many of us do, as we saw our savings almost wiped out. On September 29, 2009, eight years after 9/11, the Dow Jones registered its largest point drop ever and the Standard & Poor's 500 had its biggest percentage drop since 1987. Personally, all I could think about was having to work years to recoup what little we had saved for retirement. It was a significant loss that put our future in question. It was a very stressful time. We were powerless; there was nothing we could do immediately or in the short run to recoup that loss.

What Stock Soared?

What is so interesting about this is that basically all stocks plummeted except for one. Any guesses as to which company's profits skyrocketed during that time? In the September 30th issue of *The Wall Street Journal* (2008, c6) the following day they ran a brief story on the rise of Campbell's stock despite the plunge. It was titled, "We Want Comfort When Stressed." This was the explanation given by the Campbell's Soup spokesperson on their secret for success. Good old fashion chicken noodle or tomato soup does bring comfort. So here is yet another example of how our bodies are impacted by stress and as such need calming.

Write It–Change It

Journaling has always been a non-talk healing process. We now have research to show that writing about a trauma experience(s) is as effective, likely more than traditional talk therapy or Cognitive Processing Therapy (CPT). Bray (2018) reports that research demonstrates that Written Exposure Therapy (WET) was just as effective as CPT, took half the time and far fewer dropped out of this five-session treatment than those in the CPT group: 126 male and female military and non-military victims of trauma participated.

Reality: *Often many find it difficult to talk about their trauma experiences just as we find it difficult to talk about our CF/STS reactions to the work we do. Using sensory-based activities or communicating without words is often far more helpful and powerful than talk;* **this holds true for self-care practices as well.**

In Bessel van der Kolk's book *The Body Keeps the Score* (2015), which everyone working with trauma victims should be required to read, in Chapter 14, he talks about the limits of language and the fact that at some point it is necessary to use the body as a bridge to facilitate the use of language. When we begin to talk about a traumatic experience, the visual memories, physical sensations and emotions of that experience are activated and can easily choke efforts to find the words to describe those memories. The body needs to be used to establish what he calls "islands of safety." He helps clients identify different postures or movements that are safe and grounds them, keeps them in the present while experiencing a sense of control or power over their reactions to those traumatic memories.

An example of this use of the body is that of a child who becomes anxious when going to school. "A child's body might become tense and breathe shallow when talking about school and just the opposite when talking about home. In this situation, asking children to experiment with breathing (shallow and abdominal) or with different body postures or actions when talking about 'school' (a stressful sensory memory), until they feel sensations similar to those associated with 'home' (a calming experience), teaches them that they can empower themselves to regulate their reactions to stressful events" (Steele & Malchiodi, 2012, p. 77).

Reality: *When we are exposed to chronic stress, we need to engage our bodies in the very same "grounding" processes in ways that help to regulate our nervous system responses to ongoing stress.*

Activity: Move to Change (Group/Individual)

I use this activity frequently in trainings to demonstrate how a simple change in posture can change our feelings and thoughts. Try this yourself. It takes no more than three minutes. Participants are given the following instructions.

- First, I want you to get comfortable. We're all going to take three deep breaths and let the air out very slowly. . . . Alright take that first deep breath, hold it for a few seconds, alright now exhale very slowly. Okay, let's do this two more times.
- Now, I want you to take a minute to focus on some stressful experience you are having. . . . Take a minute to pay attention to where in your body or what part of your body responds the most as

you think about this stress or stressor. . . . Do you feel a particular emotion? Where do you feel it? What one thought really stands out for you about this stress or stressor?

- Now I want you all to stand up with your feet shoulder width apart and your arms folded over your chest. Hold this position for a minute while thinking about that stressor . . . pause. *How does this position change the way you feel about this stressor? Is that feeling more intense than when you were sitting down or less intense? When you took this pose what thought jumped into your mind about this situation? Hold onto this for a minute.*

- Now I simply want you to place your hands behind your back and lower your head-chin to chest if you will. . . . Hold this pose for a minute . . . pause. *Now how does this position change the way you feel about this stressor? Is that feeling more intense than when you were sitting down or less intense? In this pose what thought jumped into your mind about this situation? Is it different from the previous thought? Hold onto this for a minute.*

- Now I want you to sit down and clasp your hands behind your neck and just lean back a little in your chair and hold that pose for a minute while you think about that stressor. . . . *Now how does this position change the way you feel about this stressor? Is that feeling more intense than when you were sitting down or less intense? In this pose what thought jumped into your mind about this situation? Is it different from the previous thought? Hold onto this for a minute.*

- Now one more posture change. I want you to lean forward and place your elbows on the table and rest your head in the palm of your hands and hold this pose for a minute while thinking about that stressor . . . pause. *Now how does this position change the way you feel about this stressor? Is that feeling more intense than when you were sitting down or less intense? In this pose what thought jumped into your mind about this situation? Is it different from the previous thought? Hold onto this for a minute.*

- Okay let's all take in a deep breath . . . hold for a few seconds . . . then exhale slowly.

Once the activity is completed, I will ask for a show of hands as to how many experienced a change in the way they felt and thought about that stressor when they took a different pose? The majority of participants will raise their hands; a few may not.

Summary of Activity

I only had you hold those postures for a few seconds and yet you began to experience shifts in your emotions and thoughts associated with your stressor. This is how we can use our bodies to begin to regulate our reactions to challenging situations. Now a few of you did not hold up your hands and that is fine. The fact is none of these postures may have been what your body needed to experience a change. Perhaps you needed to move around, go for a walk or perhaps music would have altered your feelings and thoughts. It's different for each of us. What works for you to get the desired response may not work for me. There are plenty of options we'll look at later; below are just two.

Reality: *When our bodies are stressed, we need to engage them in an activity that helps regulate the unwanted physiological responses to stress.*

Group Activity: Movement to Energize Our Brain

Before summarizing this session and asking you to complete two brief activities, I'd like to show you this 13-minute TED Talk video from a neuroscientist and what she discovered about the effects of movement on our brains and our moods. As she nears the end of the video, she asks her audience to stand and do several activities. At this point stand up and follow her instruction. Keep in mind that she mentions 30 minutes of movement as beneficial, neuroscience show that 1-3 minutes is also beneficial in regulating stress, disrupting the stress cycle, reenergizing us and increasing our focus. These will be identified in the self-care session.

To access the TED Talk, Google "The Brain-changing Benefits of Exercise/Wendy Suzuki."
Session Summary

1. We've established that stress is first a physiological response and, as such, efforts to alleviate and/or manage that stress need to be initially directed at resetting that response at a physiological level via the use of the body as a resource. The session on self-care presents a number of such activities, which take very, very little time and can be done at work.
2. We've also established that stress is a subjective experience and, as such, triggers various sensations, feeling and thoughts that make our response unique from others exposed to the same stress. Identifying our subjective experiences also helps us to better identify what will matter most in our efforts to remain resilient in the face of that stress.

Activity: Your Subjective Experience

At this point I want you to take a minute to answer the following questions about your subjective experience to the stress you experience. It can be related to any source of stress you are experiencing. Allow your responses to be as spontaneous as possible. When finished there will be two more brief questions to answer.

What's the worst part of the stress you are experiencing?

_____

What upsets you the most about that worst part?

_____

When do you feel it the most?

_____

Where do feel it the most in your body?

_____

Who or what intensifies it?

_____

Who or what helps to reduce it?

_____

What does that stress make you feel like doing?

_____

How does it change what you think about yourself, the work you are doing?

_____

If that stress could talk, what would it say to you?

_____

If it could listen, what would you say to it?

_____

Does anyone else know about your stress?

_____

When they found out, what did they say to you?

_____

What do you wish they would have said to you?

_____

What worries you the most about your stress?

_____

In comparison with other worries you may have, would you put this worry in the top third of your biggest worries, the middle third or lower third?

_____

Final Task

As you look at your answers, circle the ones that stand out the most for you or matters the most to you. Write your answers down here.

_____

_____

Question One: How might you change the way you now think about this particular stressor?

_____

_____

Question Two: What might you try differently to regulate that stress response the next time you experience it?

_____

_____

Question Three: In these past two sessions we discussed the stress of trauma but also that our reactions to all forms of stress are as much physiological as they are psychological. As you think about it now, how would you rate your overall stress level - not just related to the work you do but also to the stress you face in your personal life/home life? Check the percent that best reflects your current stress level. (*This information is for your eyes only so be as honest as possible as this, and other information, will help you develop a personalized self-care plan that is most effective for you. You'll be using your answer when we evaluate stress levels and sources prior to developing your self-care plan.*)

10%-20%____, 20%-30%____, 30%-40%____, 40%-60%____, 60%-70%____, 70%-100%____.

Post-Session Questions

Write down your answers to the following questions. Keep these responses, as they will be used later when detailing self-care practices.

Questions

1. Of all that you have read and experienced up to this point, what surprises you the most?

    _____

    _____

2. Of all that you have read and experienced up to this point, what one thought stands out the most for you?

    _____

    _____

3. As you think about the one thought that stands out the most for you, how might it change the way you think about CF, secondary stress and BO?

    _____

    _____

4. How has this changed what you feel you need to do about the unavoidable stress of what you do?

    _____

    _____

References

Barron, C. (2015). *When not talking about past trauma is wise*. Retrieved August 31, 2018, from www.psychology today.com/ . . . /201501/when-not-talking-about-past-trauma-is- . . .

Bray, B. (2018). Putting PTSD treatment on a faster track. *Counseling Today*, August 27, 2018 (*A Publication of the American Counseling Association*). Retrieved September 14, 2018, from https://ct.counseling.org/2018/08/putting-ptsd-treatment-on-a-faster-track/

Harvard Health Publishing. (2018). *Understanding the stress response*. Retrieved September 2, 2018, from www.health.harvard.edu/staying-healthy/understanding-the-stress-response

Kingsbury, K. (2008). *Talking out trauma: Not always a help*. Retrieved August 31, 2018, from content.time.com/time/health/article/0,8599,1812204,00.html

Levine, P. (2011). *In an unspoken voice: How the body releases trauma and restores goodness*. Berkeley, CA: North Atlantic Books.

Levine, P., & Kline, M. (2008). *Trauma proofing your kids*. Berkeley, CA: North Atlantic.

Mayo Clinic Staff. (2018). *Chronic stress puts your health at risk*. Retrieved September 2, 2018, from www.mayoclinic.org/healthy-lifestyle/stress-management/in . . . /stress/art-20046037

Perry, B., & Szalavitz, M. (2006). *The boy who was raised as a dog: And other stories from a child psychiatrist's notebook--what traumatized children can teach us about loss, love, and healing*. New York: Basic Books.

Porges, S., & Dana, D. (2018). *Clinical applications of the polyvagal theory: The emergence of polyvagal-informed therapies*. New York: WW Norton & Company.

Rothchild, B. (2017). *The body remembers volume 2: Revolutionizing trauma treatment*. New York: WW Norton & Company.

Sapolsky, R. M. (2004). *Why zebras don't get ulcers*. New York: Henry Holt & Company.

Siegel, D. (2012). *Hand model of the brain*. Retrieved January 26, 2016, from www.youtube.com/watch?v= gm9CIJ74Oxw

Steele, W. (2003). Helping traumatized children. In. S. L. A. Strausner & N. K. Philips (Eds.), *Understanding mass violence: A social work perspective* (pp. 41-56). New York: Allyn and Bacon.

Steele, W. (2013). *Optimizing learning outcomes: Proven brain-centric, trauma-sensitive practices*. New York: Routledge.

Steele, W. (2015). Play therapy for children experiencing grief and traumatic loss. In D. Crenshaw & A. Stewart (Eds.), *Play therapy: A comprehensive guide to theory and practice* (pp. 304-320). New York: Guilford Press.

Steele, W., & Kuban, C. (2013). *Working with grieving and traumatized children and adolescents*. Hoboken, NJ: Wiley.

Steele, W., & Malchiodi, C. (2012). *Trauma-informed practices with children and adolescents*. New York: Routledge.

Supin, J. (2016, November). The long shadow: Bruce Perry on the lingering effects of childhood trauma. *The Sun*, 7-8.

van der Kolk, B. (2015). *The body keeps the score: Brain, mind and body in the healing of trauma*. New York: Penguin Books.

The Wall Street Journal. (2008, September 30). We want comfort when stressed: Campbell's Soup Spokesperson on Campbell's secret to success. *Wall Street Journal*, C6.

WebMD. (2018). *What is cortisol?* Retrieved September 3, 2018, from www.webmd.com/a-to-z-guides/what-is-cortisol

Wikipedia. (2013). *Yerkes-Dodson law*. Retrieved August 8, 2018, from https://en.wikipedia.org/wiki/Yerkes-Dodson_law

3 Stress From a Different Perspective
Part Two—New Mindsets Equal New Results

Pre-Session Activities

Answer all questions as best you can. If you seem to have no answer, give it your best effort as this will help reinforce what is learned throughout this session.

Activity One: Match the Mindsets

Review the following mindsets in Category A established in the first two sessions. Following your review, select the appropriate mindset for each of the statements regarding CF/STS/BO listed in this section. (Answers included in this session following the initial comments about mindsets.)

Category A: Mindsets Established During the First Two Sessions

A.   The stress I feel is not because there is something wrong with me but because of what I am exposed to while caring for or responding to trauma victims and/or situations.

B.   I need to attend to even the smallest amount of stress in order to consistently perform at my best.

C.   No matter how we approach trauma victims or situations, we are all vulnerable to CF/STS.

D.   Stress is a response to the conditions we are exposed to, not the result of how smart we are or how well we do our job.

E.   Although not pathological, many of the reactions of CF/STS are unavoidable and dictate the need to respond to them before the cumulative effect makes resolving that stress more difficult and involved.

F.   Stressful physiological reactions dictate the need for physiological, sensory-based interventions.

G.   Even if I do not have direct exposure to trauma victims or situations, being a supervisor or manager of staff who do, increases my risk of experiencing secondary trauma.

H.   Even though we are exposed to the same stress our colleagues are exposed to, our subjective reactions are unique to how we experience those stressors. Therefore, what works for them may not work for me.

I.   We can't possibly know what will be best for those repeatedly exposed to stressful situations without knowing how they are experiencing themselves, those around them.

J.   It's okay to not want to talk about trauma details we experience. However, I still need to engage in some activity that will help my body find relief from the physiological sensations and emotions that stress has induced because the body remembers.

K.   If the majority of my stress is the result of a stress inducing work culture and practices, I should think about finding a different work environment.

L.   Self-care is an ethical responsibility I assume when I agree to care for and/or respond to trauma victims or situations.

Category B: New Mindsets

Match each of these new set of mindsets with the appropriate mindset (MS) listed in Category A. Identify the mindset you select using its corresponding letter.

1. CF and secondary stress can actually be easier to resolve than BO, which is precipitated by organizational culture and practices often slow to change. MS____
2. Our subjective experience refers to how we now view/think about ourselves, the people around us, the environment where we work in, the work we do, our present and future as a result of what we have been exposed to. MS____
3. Even though law enforcement, fire fighters, military are trained to enter potentially dangerous situations at a cognitive level, to shut down their emotional reactions yet remain hyper alert, their systems are also vulnerable to the stress of the work they do. MS_____
4. Indirect exposure – what we read, what we hear discussed about trauma situations – can induce secondary trauma. MS_____
5. CF, STS, stress in general is common, not at all unusual among those caring for trauma victims, those who are emotionally challenging and/or responding to trauma situations. It is unavoidable. MS_____
6. No matter the source, stress alters our cognitive processes and our performance. MS_____
7   It is our subjective experience that best helps to define the focus of what will matter most in our efforts to best manage the ongoing stress of what we do. MS_____
8. Talking about the details of the trauma we are exposed to can be more harmful than not talking about those details. MS_____
9. Stress, trauma is not a choice; it's a reaction, a physiological reaction. MS_____
10. CF, STS is not pathological. MS____
11. I should not fear that by telling others about the stress I experience, that they may question my competence. MS____
12. When I take on the role of caring for or responding to trauma victims and situations, I agree to a code of conduct. MS____

Activity Two: Develop a Mindset

A mindset is a core belief that influences how we interact with the various environments we navigate daily, with the people in those environments and the conditions we face in in those environments.

Following is a scenario that is rarely talked about nor addressed in training. It presents a situation that will create a good deal of stress. As best you can, write down a mindset that would help support you through this difficult time.

Scenario: Caring for or responding to trauma victims, we expect that some will be non-compliant, resist suggested changes, become angry, show little resolve, ask that we do everything for them, that we perform miracles, "yes-but" everything we suggest, create roadblocks to their own healing despite all our efforts, not accept our help, drop out of treatment. *We never expect them to die, take their own lives or be killed, or to be physically or sexually abused while in our care.* When a client suddenly dies or is severely harmed while in our care, our personal and professional lives are shaken. When this happens, it is quite easy to develop cognitive reactions that end up wounding ourselves.

We second-guess our competency (*If only . . . I'm not smart enough to be . . .*). We feel somehow responsible (*I should have known . . .*). We will wonder what is wrong with us (*Why didn't I . . . ?* or *I shouldn't be having all these reactions*). Our anxiety is intensified wondering what staff may be thinking about us (*She must not have. . . . She ignored. . . . She misread the signs. . . . She didn't listen . . .*). It's intensified even more as we may fear any number of adverse reactions from the family, what an investigation will reveal, the negative press it may bring to us and the agency and whether we will lose our job (*People always want to blame someone so there is a strong reality of losing the job*).

My mindset would be,

_____

_____

_____

_____

_____

Questions

1. As best you can describe what you believe defines effective effort.

   _____

   _____

2. As best you can list what you would consider to be four characteristics of effective effort, which are also characteristics of resilience. _____ , _____ ,

   _____ , _____ .

3. How might you respond to the person who says, "My manager did not greet me today; he is probably disappointed with my work."

   _____

   _____

4. How might you respond to the person who says, "I don't want to tell my supervisor about my last visit because it went so badly"?

   _____

   _____

Session Three

Stress From a Different Perspective: Part Two

New Mindsets Equal New Results

The purposes of this session are to

1. reinforce the mindsets established in the first two sessions as these begin to dictate how we approach self-care as a way to protect against and minimize the stress reactions of CF and secondary stress due to the work we do,
2. identify the characteristics of mindsets that support *effective effort* especially given our vulnerability every time we attempt to assist and/or respond to trauma victims and situations, and
3. define the difference between a mindset and the process of reframing, both of which are important to sustaining our resilience and effectiveness.

Opening Statement

Learning how to change how you respond to stress via specific neuro-based, trauma-sensitive practices is a whole lot easier when you have the kind of mindsets that supports that change and when you can experience the value of those suggested changes for yourself. We know our brains are wonderfully adaptive and open to change. In reality, self-care is about changing how our brain and nervous system reacts to minimize the impact of the stress we experience when responding to trauma victims and/or situations. The good news is that we now know that our brains are quite adaptable. We can "hack" into our brain and change the way it responds. In fact, one of the greatest discoveries in the past several hundred years is that of neuroplasticity. Neuroplasticity is the "brain's ability to reorganize itself by forming new neural connections throughout life" (MedicineNet, 2018).

Note: For a brief two-minute video demonstrating neuroplasticity, Google "Neuroplasticity YouTube" and click on the Sentis Brain Series (https://www.youtube.com/watch?v=ELpfYCZa87g).

The way we reorganize our brain or modify our brains response is "through activity or experiences, which also includes mental activity and our thoughts" (Cleary, 2015). We partially covered "our thoughts" in session one by identifying several different ways to think about CF, secondary stress and BO. In session two we partially covered the kind of activities that allow us to experience a modified response to stress. Many more activities will be presented. As Cleary and others have indicated, our thoughts, our beliefs frame how our brains respond to what we experience. For this reason, we are going to use this entire session to focus on the power of a mindset.

Mindset

A mindset is a core belief that influences how we interact with the various environments we navigate daily, with the people in those environments and the conditions we face in in those environments.

Milkshakes and Mindsets

Science has demonstrated repeatedly that our mindset influences outcomes in all areas of life. For example, participants in one study were given two milkshakes. Each shake was described differently. Each produced a different outcome. The first milkshake was called the *Sensi Shake*. Participants were told that it contained only 140 calories, zero fat and only 20 grams of sugar. When they returned two weeks later, they were given the *Indulgent Shake*. They were told it had 620 calories, 30 grams of fat and 56 grams of sugar. On both occasions they were hooked up to an IV to measure ghrelin levels. Ghrelin is referred to as the hunger hormone. When ghrelin levels increase significantly, they signal the body that is time to stop eating: our hunger has been satisfied. After drinking the *Sensi Shake* ghrelin levels increased only slightly. After drinking the *Indulgent Shake* ghrelin levels increased three times more to a level satisfying hunger. However, each shake had the same *Sensi Shake* ingredients demonstrating that our mindset influences our biological responses (Crum & Corbin, 2011). This is very convincing research; our mindset matters. To change results, change your mindsets.

Whether the stress you are experiencing is recent, built up over time or has become chronic, neuroplasticity allows us to change how we feel physically, emotionally and cognitively and it can change the way we behave, interact and respond. It is interesting to note that as far back as 2011, the Director of the National Institute of Mental Health (NIMH) has encouraged "the 21st century discipline of clinical neuroscience" to include brain plasticity-based strategies in providing clinical care (White, 2011).

Reality: *Just as a mindset can alter biological outcomes, it can alter how we react to stress in ways that positively change our stress reactions and support effective and sustained performance and overall well-being.*

Growth Mindset

Carol Dweck, researcher, Stanford University professor and author of *Mindset: The New Psychology of Success*, among other works, has documented that there are "growth mindsets" that demonstrate how intelligence, learning capacity and performance are all changeable. In essence a growth mindset says, "we can change"; and a fixed mindset says, "we are limited." Dweck completed a very interesting study (Regan & Meehan, 2018) about praising effort versus intelligence that I would like to share with you to support the difference a mindset can make on performance.

Note: For a five-minute graphic video illustration of this study, Google "Growth Praise Mindset— How Words Impact Our Development YouTube" (https://trainugly.com/portfolio/peerfeedback/).

The Study

In Dweck's study, 400 fifth graders were given an easy IQ test. Following the test, half the group was praised for their intelligence ("You are really smart"), the rest of their group for their effort ("You really worked hard at this"). Both groups were then given the opportunity to take a harder test or take a test similar to the first one where they would well. Amazingly, 60% of those praised for their intelligence to the easier test while 92% of those praised for their effort took the more difficult test. What this demonstrated is that those praised for their intelligence heard, "Oh you value me because I am really smart so I will not do anything to change that." The kids praised for their effort on the other hand heard, "You won't criticize me for making a mistake but let me learn from it and continue to work hard."

In the next step all students were given an impossible test. What they discovered is that those praised for their effort actually worked harder and longer on this test than those praised for their intelligence; they were easily frustrated and gave up early. In the final part of this study, all students were given a test similar to the first test. Once again, an amazing result: Those praised for their intelligence did 20% worse, while those praised for effort raised their average score by 30%. One simple mindset can influence profound change.

How Well Did You Do?

Let's see how well you matched the listed mindsets with the statements provided.

1. CF and secondary stress can actually be easier to resolve than BO, which is precipitated by organizational culture and practices often slow to change. **MS−K** *If the majority of my stress is the result of a stress inducing work culture and practices, I should think about finding a different work environment.*
2. Our subjective experience refers to how we now view/think about ourselves, the people around us, the environment where we work in, the work we do, our present and future as a result of what we have been exposed to. **MS−H**. *Even though we are exposed to the same stress our colleagues are exposed to, our subjective reactions are unique to how we experience those stressors. Therefore, what works for them may not work for me.*
3. Even though law enforcement, fire fighters, military are trained to enter potentially dangerous situations at a cognitive level, to shut down their emotional reactions, yet remain hyper alert,

their systems are also vulnerable to the stress of the work they do. **MS-C.** *No matter how we approach trauma victims or situations, we are all vulnerable to CF/STS.*

4.   Indirect exposure - what we read, what we hear discussed about trauma situations can induce secondary trauma. **MS-G.** *Even if I do not have direct exposure to trauma victims or situations, as a supervisor or manager of staff who do, increases my risk of experiencing secondary trauma.*

5.   CF, STS, stress in general is common, not at all unusual among those caring for trauma victims, those who are emotionally challenging and/or responding to trauma situations. It is unavoidable. **MS-A.** *The stress I feel is not because there is something wrong with me but because of what I am exposed to while caring for or responding to trauma victims and/or situations.*

6.   No matter the source, stress alters our cognitive processes and our performance. **MS-B.** *I need to attend to even the smallest amount of stress in order to consistently perform at my best.*

7.   It is our subjective experience that best helps to define the focus of what will matter most in our efforts to best manage the ongoing stress of what we do. **MS-I.** *We can't possibly know what will be best for those repeatedly exposed to stressful situations without knowing how they are experiencing themselves, those around them.*

8.   Talking about the details of the trauma we are exposed to can be more harmful than not talking about those details. **MS-J.** *It's okay to not want to talk about trauma details we experience. However, I still need to engage in some activity that will help my body find relief from the physiological sensations and emotions that stress has induced because the body remembers.***

9.   Stress, trauma is not a choice; it's a reaction, a physiological reaction. **MS-F.** *Stressful physiological reactions dictate the need for physiological, sensory-based interventions.*

10.   CF, STS is not pathological. **MS-E.** *Although not pathological, many of the reactions of CF/STS are unavoidable and dictate the need to respond to them before the cumulative effect makes resolving that stress more difficult and involved.*

11.   I should not fear that by telling others about the stress I experience, that they may question my competence. **MS-D.** *Stress is a response to the conditions we are exposed to not the result of how smart we are or how well we do our job.*

12.   When I take on the role of caring for or responding to trauma victims and situations I agree to a code of conduct. **MS-L.** *Self-care is an ethical responsibility I assume when I agree to care for and/or respond to trauma victims or situations.*

**Repeat, Repeat, Repeat.

The brief video about neuroplasticity you watched at the beginning of this session made two points: our brains are malleable, adaptable and changeable; however, it takes repetition of activities, experiences and thoughts for new patterned responses to become automatic. I want you to remember this when we look at self-care plans and practices because it does take some effort for even the briefest of actions or simplest of thoughts to rewire our responses to stress.

Reality: *Through repetition, the brain lays down neural connections. Eventually whatever is repeated becomes so efficient that it will run automatically without our awareness* (Cleary, 2015).

For this reason, let's review the mindsets we've established at this point one more time.

- No matter how we approach trauma victims or situations, we are all vulnerable to CF/STS.
- Even if I do not have direct exposure to trauma victims or situations, being a supervisor or manager of staff who do, increases my risk of experiencing secondary trauma.

- The stress I feel is not because there is something wrong with me but because of what I am exposed to while caring for or responding to trauma victims and/or situations.
- Stress is a response to the conditions we are exposed to not the result of how smart we are or how well we do our job.
- Although not pathological, many of the reactions of CF/STS are unavoidable and dictate the need to respond differently.
- I need to attend to even the smallest amount of stress in order to consistently perform at my best.
- Unwanted physiological reactions dictate the need for physiological, sensory-based interventions.
- Even though we are exposed to the same stress our colleagues are exposed to, our subjective reactions are unique to how we experience those stressors. Therefore, what works for them may not work for me.
- We can't possibly know what will be best for those repeatedly exposed to stressful without knowing how they are experiencing themselves, those around them.
- It's okay to not want to talk about it. However, I still need to engage in some activity that will help my body find relief from the physiological sensations and emotions that stress has induced because our body, our non-thinking brain remembers.
- If the majority of my stress is the result of a stress inducing work culture and practices, I should think about finding a different work environment.
- Self-care is an ethical responsibility I assume when I agree to care for and/or respond to trauma victims or situations.

New Mindsets

New mindsets will continue to be presented to provide cognitive support for ongoing recommendations in the areas of organizational practices, culture, engagement and supervision practices that help minimize the stress of what we do, for strengthening our resilience and growth despite ongoing exposure to trauma victims and situations, for self-assessments and self-care planning. The newest mindsets just established in this session are:

- it is never too late to change how our brain reacts to stress,
- to rewire our reactions, we must repeat the *actions and thoughts* supportive of the desired change, and
- it takes effective effort.

It's Not Always Easy to Do

When it comes to changing through repetition, we need to acknowledge that because of the work we do, it is not always easy to repeat the practices that we have determined will help us best manage our stress. The very nature of caring for or responding to trauma victims and situations also means being exposed to frequent crises precipitated by victims and clients as well as workplace demands like paper work that make routinely engaging self-care practices difficult.

Reality: *Routinely engaging in self-care practices takes effort.*

Let's face it; there are days that simply exhaust us. If we have families, they also demand our time when we get home. If we are on call or expected to respond to emails after hours, it's very difficult to relax while our nervous system is on alert. However, we can stabilize that stress response or regulate so it remains manageable and minimally impactful.

Brief Breaking Periods

The previous reality statements can be used to reinforce the need to engage in very brief stress reduction, stress regulation activities throughout the workday.

Reality: *The reality is that because of the work we do our sympathetic nervous system (the gas pedal) is already accelerated and preparing for the unexpected, for crisis and exposure to trauma before we actually get to our workplace parking lot. It then builds during the workday unless we have control of the brake pedal.*

The good news is that neuroscience also shows us that it only takes 3-5 minutes to initiate our parasympathetic nervous system response or put the brakes on our stress response (Kalish, 2018; Ward, 2018; Donvito, 2016). If at least once every two hours or better yet every hour, we take 3-5 minutes to engage in the kinds of self-regulation practices we'll identify when talking about self-care, we can prevent the cumulative effects of stress. If we wait till the end of day it simply takes longer to come down and as the day goes on, we become less efficient and effective. Brief does mean brief. For example,

Reality: *Simply changing our posture for 2 minutes reduces the stress hormone cortisol by 20%* (Cuddy, Wilmuth, & Carney, 2012).

Effective Effort

It does take effective effort to reach the point where we do these neuro-based, *brief breaking periods* routinely. However, not all effort is effective. As an avid golfer, I know practice is essential to success. I've also learned over the years that hitting a bucket of balls at the golf range is not effective practice. Effective practice is focusing on a goal, then trying different approaches until we find which routine, what type of swing, what club works best to achieve the results we want and then we go back and continue to practice those moves until they become a natural body, automatic response when standing over the ball on the golf course where it counts. So, what constitutes effective effort?

Pre-session Question #3

How did you define effective effort in Pre-session Question #3? The most common response from your peers is that effective effort means to keep trying. The problem with this response is that trying means different things to different people. For some, trying means simply getting answers from others, copying what others have done or trying once and then giving up when what was tried didn't work. However, if your response includes the elements in the definition below, you understand effective effort.

The Director of Professional Learning and Curriculum Design for Mindset Works provides the following descriptive definition of effective effort.

> Effective Effort is purposeful and targeted. When I am really trying effectively, I am doing a LOT! I pause and quietly think. I problem-solve. I research. I tinker. I figure out what isn't working and change my strategy. I furrow my brow, and I don't stop until I figure it out.
>
> (Diehl, 2017)

What Diehl is describing here are *four characteristics of resilience*, which are essential in our efforts to minimize the negative influence stress can hace on all aspects and areas of our lives.

Resilience Characteristics

Pre-session Question #4

What characteristics of resilience did you identify in the pre-session question? Generally your peers identify a host of characteristics many of which are associated with resilience. The common responses are the ability to bounce back, never giving up, staying positive, seeking help when needed and some mention not being afraid to take risks. What I do not often hear described as characteristics is curiosity, persistence and the courage to continue when vulnerable. So let me walk you through the definition of effective effort just presented and pull out for you four resilient characteristics.

Curiosity

The first characteristic of resilence described by Diehl is curiosity: *I quietly think, I research, I tinker, I figure out what isn't working*. This is exactly what I am asking you to do related to thinking differently about stress, about approaching stress differently, trying a variety of activities, cognitive processes and mindsets. It will be a bit of an adventure but that makes us resilient.

Persistence

The second characteristic also found in resilient individuals is persistence: *I furrow my brow, and I don't stop until I figure it out*. Never giving up could reflect a fixed mindset, which is not the same as persistence. Persistence is the key to succeeding at changing.

Some will mistake persistence for stubbornness. Stubbornness is rigid, an unwillingness to change one's attitude or position. *Persistence is keeping focused on what we desire even when we need to change how we're trying to make it happen*. The experiences in these sessions will help you "figure out" what works best for you to sustain your best effort in the midst of daily exposure to trauma victims and incidents.

Risk Taking

The third characteristic of resilience is risk taking: *I figure out what isn't working and change my strategy*. Getting out of our comfort zone is never easy and does induce some stress. However:

Reality: *"Outside of our comfort zone is where the magic happens."* (Anonymous)

Another way to think about risk is that every time we try something new, we discover something new about ourselves, what fits, what works, what doesn't work. No one self-care plan fits everyone. The numerous activities in this workbook may briefly take you out of your comfort zone while allowing you at the same time to discover what works for you.

Courage

The fourth characteristic is the courage to continue while vulnerable: *I don't stop until I figure it out*. In many ways, vulnerability defines what we feel when we care for or respond to those in trauma. We can't predict the outcome, we may influence it a bit, but we can't control it. We find ourselves in situations where we have no answers, where we ourselves feel overwhelmed at times and yet we continue to respond and care the best we can.

In her #1 *New York Times* bestseller *Dare to Lead: Brave Work, Tough Conversations, Whole Hearts* (Brown, 2018), Brené Brown teaches us what it means to "dare greatly, rise strong, and brave the wilderness." Based on seven years of new research conducted with leaders, change makers and culture shifters, she tells us how important empathy, connection and the courage to continue is to becoming our best. We don't avoid difficult conversations and situations; we lean into vulnerability when it's necessary to do good work. In her book (Brown, 2018, p. xviii), she writes, "The courage to be vulnerable is not about winning or losing; it's about the courage to show up when you can't predict or control the outcome."

Note: All leadership staff and those pursuing a leadership role in organizations and programs that serve trauma victims ought to be required to read and implement the four skill sets that make up successful leadership as defined by Dr. Brown, a Doctor of Social Work at the University of Houston who holds numerous awards for her work on vulnerability, shame, empathy and courage and how these make for great leaders.

To listen to her TED Talk on vulnerability, simple Google "The Power of Vulnerability TED Talk" (https://www.ted.com/talks/brene_brown_on_vulnerability?language=en).

I just ask that you keep these characteristics of resilience/effective effort in mind as you're asked to engage actions and develop or take on mindsets that are new for you in your efforts to prevent reactions of CF, secondary trauma and BO or, if needed, to recover from them.

Reality: A resilient mindset is critical during the worst of times, which anyone caring for or responding to trauma victims will at some point experience.

Allow me to spend a minute talking about a response to trauma exposure that is seldom discussed, yet is a universal reaction for many survivors, as well as those working with survivors. I would imagine that many of you reading this work have experienced these reactions and have done so in silence.

Self-induced Secondary Wounding

Self-induced wounding is often a silent process following exposure to a traumatic incident where a survivor begins to second-guess their responses, feel guilt and shame for what they did or did not do and question their competency and moral character. It's silent because survivors understandably keep these thoughts to themselves. I've met with hundreds of survivors over the years following the suicide death of students, violent death or suicide of colleagues, the sudden death of clients, the abuse of children while in the care of protective services and while in the midst of a disaster. Some refer to these reactions as survivor guilt; it is much more than guilt as our entire psyche is attacked. It is part of the STS response. Unless someone normalizes these responses that individual's mindset about themselves, others and the world is going to create a very deep and open wound that will not heal easily.

Secondary wounding is self-induced

- when comparing our actions and reactions to the behaviors and reactions of other survivors,
- by real or perceived expectations others have of us or we have of ourselves, and
- when we compare our behaviors and reactions to norms in our society or work culture that are associated with being an "okay person" versus "not okay person."

First responders as well as those caring for, servicing or treating traumatized individuals are vulnerable to this wounding when things suddenly go bad with those they are trying to protect and assist. We're vulnerable to

- second-guessing our competency—*If only . . . I'm not smart enough to be . . .*
- feeling somehow responsible—*I should have known . . .*

- increased anxiety wondering what staff may be thinking about us–*She must not have. . . . She ignored. . . . She misread the signs. . . . She didn't listen. . . . No one is talking to me about it. . . . They must think I'm incompetent.*

- distrusting our view of self–*I ignored what they said. I'm so stupid. I'm a professional. I shouldn't be having all these reactions. If only. . . . I'm not smart enough to be a good childcare worker/therapist. I should have. . . . It's my fault. He was my best friend. I should have known he was thinking about killing himself. It's my fault.*

- attacking our own psyche–*Had I not been so scared, maybe I could've helped the others. I'm such a coward. What's wrong me? I should be able to control these reactions. They tell me I'll be better if I talk about what happened, but I don't want to. It's too hard. What's wrong with me? What's happening to me?*

These new mindsets/beliefs are intensified even more as we fear any number of adverse reactions from family, peers–*Everyone thought I was a really good (therapist, child care worker, hospice nurse, officer, etc.), now they'll never trust me again.*

We'll fear what an investigation might reveal; the negative press it may bring to ourselves and the agency and whether we will lose our job. People always want to blame someone, so there is a strong reality of losing the job.

Note: Hospice workers and others who anticipate the death of those they are helping can also experience challenging reactions like the ones just described. Just a few of the factors that can contribute to such mindsets are: disagreement about the goals of care, conflict with other care team members, difficulty controlling client's pain/symptoms, treatment errors, effects of treatment, not being there when their patient/client dies, client family dynamics that complicate care choices and preferences, becoming over involved with client.

Allow me to now address the tough scenario I asked you to develop a mindset for in our Pre-session Activity Two. I use this scenario because it does happen, yet few speak about it and, in my experience, frequently do not respond appropriately when it does happen. Even the literature is sparse. Let's review this scenario.

Scenario: Caring for or responding to trauma victims, we expect that some will be non-compliant, resist suggested changes, become angry, show little resolve, ask that we do everything for them, that we perform miracles, "yes-but" everything we suggest, create roadblocks to their own healing despite all our efforts, not accept our help, drop out of treatment. *We never expect them to die, take their own lives, be killed, or be physically or sexually abused while in our care.* When a client suddenly dies or is severely harmed while in our care our personal and professional lives are shaken. When this happens, it is quite easy to develop the kind of self-induced wounding mindsets I just described. We will need a growth mindset to counter these.

Compare the mindset you arrived at in the Pre-session Activity Two Task with the following mindset.

Mindset: One situation, incident or experience does not define what I can become unless, in the midst of my vulnerability, I fail to take the time and continued actions (effective effort) that are needed to learn from my experience until I arrive at a new beginning that works for me.

Points for Discussion

The effective effort mindset is in my own words; although they work for me, they may not work for you. The words you use must fit for you and reflect the characteristics of effective effort, which are also characteristics of resilience: curiosity (figuring out what does/did not work); risk-taking (changing what I'm doing); persistence (until I find what works); courage (to continue my effort when vulnerable/being self-compassionate).

Inherent in this mindset is that we understand the importance of courageously moving forward, not hiding, when feeling our most vulnerable, when we do not have immediate answers, when there is doubt and anxiety, when there are feelings we may not have experienced in the past. It takes personal courage to learn from and recover from such situations.

Reality: *In the process of moving forward, having connections with those we trust, processing what happened with a supportive supervisor and, if needed, seeking trauma-sensitive crisis intervention or brief therapy from an outside source might all be part of moving forward courageously.*

I also believe it is critical to use the Internet to read what others have experienced and learned from difficult experiences similar to our own. Their experiences can help normalize some of what we may be experiencing, provide strategies for moving forward and alleviate some of our anxiety.

Reality: *Our mindset points us in a desired direction. The effort, the action we take gets us there.*

Resetting Mindsets

It's time to check and reset our mindset when exposed to interactions with others, their behaviors or comments, and/or situations that overwhelm us, anger us, make us anxious and uneasy, that make it difficult to do our job, that challenge our skills or competency, that lead to negative thinking or excessive worry. I believe this goes a bit deeper than simply changing a negative thought into a positive one.

How did you respond to Pre-session Questions 3 and 4?

Following are some of the responses I've heard from your peers to Pre-session Statement #4 that read, "I don't want to tell my supervisor about my last visit because it went so badly."

They are overreacting. They are making assumptions about their manager. I would tell them they should be more positive. Sounds like they might be afraid of their supervisor's reactions. Maybe the problem is the supervisor or manager. This person doesn't seem to have much confidence in their work.

Collectively they've identified several possibilities for the negative reactions toward the manager and supervisor. Indirectly they are suggesting a need to further explore the source of these expressed mindsets. Why is this important?

The Experience Matters

As far back as 1930, Alfred Adler (1930) coined the term "private logic" referring to how our experiences shape our thoughts and our thoughts shape our behaviors. For example, if you tell me you are a really good friend and then you hurt me, I'm going to take a step back. That hurtful experience immediately changes what I think about you and I will act accordingly. I will keep my distance, trusting will be difficult, when with you I will be sensitive or on alert and ready to be hurt again. I will need a number of different kinds of experiences with you to be able to trust again. Our experiences shape our thoughts and our behaviors. This has been proven repeatedly. The trauma-specific, evidence-based interventions I developed years ago provided victims the opportunity to return to what happened to them but to experience it differently through a variety of experiences that changed for the better how they now viewed themselves, the people around them, their future.

I tell you this because *I find the concept that to change how we are reacting we need to change or positively reframe what we are thinking to be an over simplification.* Yes, there are times when someone gives us a different way to think about what is happening that makes sense and encourages a different reaction or response from us. This then would be our initial way of helping.

Consider the examples provided by The Resilience Alliance Training Manual (NYC, 2011, p. 49) of reframing into positive thoughts the two negative thoughts presented in Pre-session Questions 3 and 4.

"My manager did not greet me today. He is probably disappointed with my work."

Reframing this in a positive way would change this negative thought to "I'm jumping to conclusions. So far my manager has been pleased with my work—he may just be having a bad day."

The second statement was, "I don't want to tell my supervisor about my last visit because it went so badly."

A positive reframing would be, "Even though it didn't go well, my supervisor can help me think through how to make it better next time."

If this change in thinking works for these individuals, that is wonderful. We always want to respond to a problematic thought process or behavior with the least intrusive approach. Again, this may be all that is needed. However, if their reactions surface again, more work is needed to explore the possible subjective mindset these individuals have about their performance and/or their supervisor/manager. This raises the question of how we go about this.

Reality: *There are times when our reactions are tied to a past experience that shaped a mindset that now drives our reactions and behavior, both of which can only be changed by changing our experience.*

How to

With any negative thought, it is important to first isolate the elements of that negative thought. In the above two cases there are two elements, the supervisor/manager and the performance of the worker. Once these are isolated, it is then important to try to identify how that individual is subjectively experiencing each element through self-reflection or by curiously exploring what their core mindset or belief is about each. Let's do this now.

About the Work/Performance

Both initial thoughts reflect that these individuals believe they may not be performing well. What is at the core of this belief? The reflective questions I might ask to get at the subjective ways they are experiencing how well or not well they are doing are:

- What do you believe you are doing well?
- Has anyone told you that you are not doing well?
- What did they tell you; how specific were their comments?
- How does what you are not doing well differ from what you are doing well (different clients, different subject matter, different tasks, different skills, etc.)?
- What suggestions were offered by those commenting on your performance?
- Have you tried these?
- What do you believe kept them from helping?
- Is this confined to a particular issue or type of client/situation that is more difficult for you than another?
- What is the worst part of those situations or interactions with others or specific clients that make it difficult for you?

- Does this situation or type of client remind you of similar experiences or people that were difficult in the past?
- Do you want to improve your skills, or does this have you questioning whether you want to continue to do this work?
- Who or what do you think would help you overcome this difficulty?
- Given access to these resources do you believe you can be more effective?
- What would be the easiest first step that you could take to help change what you are now experiencing?
- What would you consider to be an acceptable outcome? In what time frame do you believe this can be accomplished?

Reflective questions about issues with your supervisor/manager (S/M):

- Do you feel that your S/M treats you fairly?
- Have you found that they have been as helpful as you would like?
- In what way have they not been helpful?
- Have you felt comfortable talking about areas of weakness with your S/M?
- When you tell them of your concerns, a difficulty you are having has their response been helpful or one that tells you he/she is not going to be helpful with your difficulties such as, "This is the nature of what we do; either get used to it or think about changing careers"?
- Does your S/M remind you of similar experiences you've had in the past with people like your S/M?
- Do you feel emotionally safe with your S/M, that what you say or express is safe?
- What has your supervisor/manager said to you or done in the past that causes you to be uneasy with this relationship?
- What have others said about your S/M that might cause you to be uncomfortable with them?
- If you were supervising yourself what might you say about your performance and reports?
- If you could, would you look for another supervisor/manager?
- Do you need to think about getting the support you are looking for from outside supervision or from peers?
- If you believe your S/M is not likely to change, what can you now do to continue to improve while avoiding conflict with your S/M?
- What resources would be helpful in this endeavor?
- What would you consider to be an acceptable outcome?
- In what time frame do you believe this can be accomplished?

Reflective questioning is really about taking the time to be curious rather than analytical.

Reality: *Curiosity is the cornerstone of empathy* (Siegel, 2007; Smith, 2012) *and also a wonderful way to create a positive connection with others* (Hughes, 2009). *Curiosity is a way to say "You Matter" to create a sense of engagement, which is one of the leading factors associated with staff satisfaction, retention and resilience* (Gallup, 2018).

The reflective questions are designed to curiously examine the underlying mindsets of individuals because our underlying mindsets influence how we respond to the many aspects of the work we do. Going through this process will definitely point out whether there are earlier experiences with performance and/or individuals that are triggering these negative responses. Responses will most definitely also help to isolate not only the problem area but provide a sense of what kinds of experiences these individuals may find helpful. As these are identified, they are easily supported using the characteristics of effective effort. (We also review in Session Five the STS core competencies of a trauma-informed supervisor.)

Summary

Preventing, minimizing the stress of what we do, the reactions associated with CF, STS and BO is best accomplished by working from the "bottom up" as described in Session Two and, as described in this session, from the "top down." We want the management of stress, CF/STS/BO to be a neurologically integrative process or as some say a *balanced use of both our thinking and emotional brain*. From the "bottom up" we regularly need to engage in those activities that regulate our nervous system, our emotional, mid-brain responses to stressors, while establishing growth mindsets to help us from the "top down" *pause and quietly think, reflect, problem-solve, research, tinker, figure out what isn't working and change our strategy, furrow our brow, and don't stop until we figure it out.*

The other aspect of managing our stress is related to how the organization we are working for is or is not supporting their ethical responsibility to assist us with self-care management. Their management practices can intensify the stress of what we do, increase BO, cause rapid turnover or support a toxic environment that presents us with numerous challenges some of which we can overcome, others that will not likely change. In the next two sessions we'll discuss a number of organizational factors that can contribute to our well-being or our stress.

Post-session Questions

Write down your answers to the following questions. Keep these responses, as they will be used later when detailing self-care practices.

Questions

1. Of all that you have read and experienced up to this point, what surprises you the most?

   _____

   _____

2. Of all that you have read and experienced up to this point, what one thought stands out the most for you?

   _____

   _____

3. As you think about the one thought that stands out the most for you, how might it change the way you think about CF, secondary stress and BO?

   _____

   _____

4. How has this changed what you feel you need to do about the unavoidable stress of what you do?

   _____

   _____

References

Adler, A. (1930). *The problem child*. New York: P. G. Putnam's Sons.

Brown, B. (2018). *Dare to lead: Brave work. Tough conversations. Whole hearts*. New York. Random House.

Cleary, I. (2015). *What is neuroplasticity?* Retrieved September 17, 2018, from iancleary.com/neuroplasticity/

Crum, A. J., & Corbin, W. R. (2011). Mind over milkshakes: Mindsets, not just nutrients, determine ghrelin response. *Health Psychology, 30*, 424–429.

Cuddy, A. J. C., Wilmuth, C. A., & Carney, D. R. (2012, September). The benefit of power posing before a high-stakes social evaluation. *Harvard Business School Working Paper, No. 13–027*.

Diehl, E. (2017). Growth mindsets for learning: Effective effort. In W. Steele (Ed.), *Optimizing learning outcomes: Proven brain-centric, trauma sensitive practices* (p. 122). New York: Routledge.

Donvito, T. (2016). *15 5-second strategies for shutting down stress ASAP*. Retrieved December 2, 2018, from www.rd.com/health/wellness/quick-stress-relief/

Gallup. (2018). *Gallup Q12 employee engagement survey*. Retrieved August 15, 2018, from https://q12.gallup.com/public/en-us/Features

Hughes, R. (2009). Attachment focused treatment for children. In M. Kerman (Ed.), *Clinical pearls of wisdom* (pp. 169–181). New York: W. W. Norton.

Kalish, A. (2018). *12 ways to reduce your stress in 5 minutes or less*. Retrieved December 2, 2018, from www.themuse.com/advice/12-ways-to-reduce-your-stress-in-5-minutes-or-less

MedicineNet. (2018). *What is neuroplasticity?* Retrieved October 4, 2018, from www.medicinenet.com/script/main/art.asp?articlekey=40362

NYC. (2011). *The resilience alliance training manual*, p. 49. Retrieved October 3, 2018, from www.nccwe.org/.../2011.../Resilience_Alliance_Training_Manual_-_September_2011...

Regan, T., & Meehan, T. (2018). *Growth mindset feedback and praise*. Retrieved October 6, 2018, from https://trainugly.com/portfolio/peerfeedback/

Siegel, D. (2007). *The mindful brain: Reflections and attunement in the cultivation of well-being*. New York: W.W. Norton.

Smith, J. (2012). *Theories of counseling and psychotherapy: An integrative approach*. Los Angeles: Sage.

Ward, M. (2018). *Need a break? Try these 6 research-backed ways to de-stress in 5 minutes*. Retrieved December 2, 2018, from www.today.com/health/how-deal-stress-daily-basis-t126882

White, C. (2011). Brain circuitry model for mental illness will transform management, NIH mental health director says. *BMJ, 343*, d5581. doi:10.1136/bmj.d5581

4 Tough Conversations, Well-being, Engagement

Pre-session Questions

Answer all questions as best you can. If you seem to have no answer, give it your best effort as this will help reinforce what is learned throughout this session.

1. What does the following information suggest? In 1995, Charles Figley brought our attention to the secondary stress or the cost of caring. The National Child Traumatic Stress Network (NCTSN) supported by the Substance Abuse and Mental Health Services Administration (SAMSHA) was founded in 2000. It became the primary source for information in all areas of trauma and called for organizations serving trauma populations to become trauma informed. The National Center for Trauma-informed Care (NCTIC) was established in 2005 to inform practitioners of promising and evidence-based trauma treatments. Its primary focus was on the treatment of trauma victims not the stress of caring. It wasn't until the spring of 2012 that the Center for Advanced Studies in Child Welfare held a very comprehensive conference focused on Secondary Trauma and the Child Welfare Workforce. It wasn't until six years later, in 2018, that one major statewide child welfare organization, serving thousands of traumatized children and families, initiated its first workforce assessment of secondary trauma and BO among its staff.

    _____

    _____

2. What does the following suggest? In 2007 Prudential Financial initiated its first employee Health Risk Assessment Questionnaire that covered five dimensions associated with staff well-being. They used that outcome to develop additional services to help their employees reduce high levels of stress and depression.

    _____

    _____

3. Have you read the stories of those businesses, programs and organizations who have received the American Psychological Association Awards for Center of Excellence and Psychologically Healthy Workplaces? Yes___ No ___

4. Have you read the #1 2018 *New York Times* bestseller by Dr. Brené Brown, *Dare to Lead: Brave Work, Tough Conversations, Whole Hearts* (New York: Random House)? Yes___ No___

5. Have you read the 2006 *New York Times* bestseller *12 Elements of Great Managing*, by Rodd Wagner and James K. Harter (New York: Gallup Press)? Yes___ No___

6. Have you read Markus Cunningham and Curt Coffman's 2000 book *First, Break All the Rules: What the World's Greatest Managers Do Differently* (New York: Simon and Shuster, also available through Gallup Press)? Yes___ No___

7.   Have you read the *New York Times* bestseller by Rath and Harter, *Wellbeing: The Five Essential Elements* (New York: Gallup Press, 2010)? Yes ___ No ___

8.   Define the difference between wellness and well-being.

Wellness is
_____
_____

Well-being is
_____
_____

9.   List what you consider to be 5 areas of well-being.
_____ , _____ , _____ , _____ , _____ .

10. What do well-being and wellness have to do with stress?
_____
_____

11. What would you consider to be a few of the shared reactions to the stress of everyday life: financial, health, relational, social and spiritual (having purpose in life) that also are experienced with CF/STS/BO?

_____ , _____ ,
_____ , _____ ,
_____ , _____ ,
_____ , _____ .

12. What one element or factor has repeatedly been shown to improve employee attendance, performance, the quality of service provided, worker satisfaction and retention?
_____

Session Four

Tough Conversations, Well-being, Engagement

Opening Statement

Social worker and psychologist, Dr. Brené Brown has spent 27 years studying what gives meaning to our lives. Working with transformational leaders across the globe and studying over 400,000 pieces of data she has identified what constitutes daring leadership. Her newest of four *New York Times* bestsellers, *Dare to Lead: Brave Work, Tough Conversations, Whole Hearts*, tells us that leadership is not about "power, status or titles but about taking responsibility for recognizing the potential in people and ideas and having the courage to develop that potential" (Brown, 2018, p. 4).

This is where "tough conversations" about organizational responses and responsibilities regarding employees caring for and responding to trauma situations and victims of trauma needs to be initiated. What we need to also keep in mind is that any form of work-related stress is best approached at an organizational, as well as an individual level. In their meta-analysis of 90 studies on stress management interventions published between 1990 and 2005, LaMontagne, Keegel, Louie, Ostry, and Landsbergis (2007) revealed that in relation to interventions targeting organizations only, and interventions targeting individuals only, interventions targeting both organizations and individuals (i.e., the systems approach) had the most favorable positive effects on both the organizations and the individuals.

In This Session

The purposes of this session are to

1. focus on organizational well-being and engagement as primary factors in the reduction and management of worker stress inclusive of STS,
2. examine how these factors improve performance, the quality of service provided, retention and engagement. In our next session we focus on several issues regarding the mandate of providing trauma-informed care within a trauma-informed culture followed by individual intervention process between supervisors and supervisees related to the prevention of and recovery from STS.

Note: For simplicity, the terms "organizations" and "TSOs" refers to any program, agency, institution and setting in which its employees provide services to those who present with emotionally challenging conditions or situations, those who have been traumatized and/or those who have been exposed to trauma inducing incidents and/or conditions. TSOs are inclusive of those who identify their organizations as trauma-informed, as well as those, who do not refer to themselves as formally trauma-informed, yet are serving and/or responding to emotionally challenging individuals and/or situations. The term "trauma populations" refers to emotionally challenging clients who may or may not have trauma histories yet cause compassion strain and stress for those assisting them. Let's begin by reviewing a few historical facts related to organizational care for its employees.

Organizational Mindset

Historically little has been written about leadership of non-profit organizations compared to corporate leadership. As a result, non-profit leaders have looked to businesses and their leadership models. Consider the following

Reality: *A mindset that accepts that employee well-being is a responsibility of leadership and a benefit for all involved, inclusive of organizational well-being, and has been and is far more prevalent in business than in the world of those serving trauma populations.*

Historically, the mindset of those organizations serving traumatized populations has been that professionals in the helping field are somehow immune to stress and as professionals should be able to manage whatever stress they might experience. Thanks to the work of leaders in the field of trauma and organizations, such as the National Child Traumatic Stress Network (NCTSN), the National Center for Trauma-Informed Care (NCTIC), Green Cross and the Child Welfare League of America (CWLA), we now understand that stress of employees/responders working with a trauma population is not a sign of weakness but an unavoidable response to repeated trauma exposure.

The call to assist and support staff in the area of secondary stress is now being acted upon by many organizations. It has, as we will see, taken many years, too many to get to where we are today.

However, I want you to consider that this recent focus on STS, although much needed and long over-due, is unfortunately a narrow if not fixed mindset that fails to address the larger, growth-oriented mindset and understanding of what constitutes well-being related to employee stress; a view that businesses have understood and focused on for years.

As a result of efforts by businesses to provide on-site assistance to their employee's well-being in several "life domains" they are experiencing cultures that are less stressed, far more engaging, enhancing overall performance, staff satisfaction, higher retention rates and organizational well-being. For these reasons we need to have a "tough conversation" and ask the following questions,

- Is focusing on the prevention and alleviation of STS a growth mindset or a fixed mindset?
- Are leaders of TSOs really demonstrating that they understand that stress, whatever its sources, negatively impacts quality of care, consistency of performance and performance outcomes, worker engagement, organizational culture, workplace satisfaction, professional growth within the organization and retention rates?
- Are leaders, especially policy makers, even funding sources, demonstrating that they understand the responsibility they have to help support the potential of employees, as a way to sustain the quality of care provided clients and consumers by the organizations they govern, license and/or fund?
- What is the difference between well-being and wellness programs, and what do these have to do with CF/STS/BO?
- What one element or factor has repeatedly been shown to improve employee attendance, performance, quality of service provided, worker satisfaction and retention and are TSOs doing what they can to support and/or improve in this area?

Before going any further let me also point out that CF is distinct from STS yet also inclusive of STS and BO. However, much of the literature focuses on an organizations responsibility to assist staff with the alleviation or prevention of STS often without mentioning its relationship with CF and BO. My use of the term STS therefore will be inclusive of these two components and the stress associated with each of these, as all three are frequently present in TSOs along with an absence of attention to other critical employee well-being factors.

Leadership Role

Dare to Lead is a book about acknowledging the responsibility today's leaders have toward those they are leading. It's about the courage it takes to lead in an ever-changing world and, within our focus, a very stressful one. It's about *daring to actively care for and be connected to* the people leaders are leading. As the author, Dr. Brené Brown writes, "care and connection are irreducible requirements for wholehearted, productive relationships between leaders and team (staff) members" (Brown, 2018, p. 12).

Ultimately, it's about a visible leadership growing a culture that actively supports the well-being of its employees. Given what we know about the "cost of caring" the stress of repeated exposure to trauma clients, conditions and situations within TSOs, leadership's efforts related to developing a culture of employee well-being is essential to the resilience of employees and the organization. Bloom (2006) and Bloom and Sreedhar (2008) brought our attention to how organizations serving trauma populations can easily become a traumatized organization and as such become change resistant, avoidant, controlling and dissociated from their employees-primary survival responses of freeze, fight and flight.

Fortunately, thanks to the founding of the National Child Traumatic Stress Network (NCTSN) in 2000, we have become far more trauma-informed as organizations and leaders of TSOs. Obviously, those we respond to are also receiving much better care for their trauma related conditions and symptoms. However, attention on the well-being of those providing services and assistance to the traumatized has only recently become a focus. As I said earlier this is long overdue and greatly needed but is, in my opinion and that of many others, too fixed on STS symptoms.

In this session we are going to examine:

- How the focus on STS is a narrow, if not a fixed mindset regarding the ethical responsibility organizations have to assist its staff with the stress they experience.
- How the corporate world has been successfully addressing employee stress long before many TSOs and programs serving trauma population.
- Organizational responses to the stress of those who are assisting trauma populations,
- What goes into developing a culture of well-being where employees can flourish, where their potential can develop, where their best care is consistently given to the traumatized population they serve, and
- What you want to consider before taking a position in an organization whose primary clients are those victimized by trauma and/or emotionally challenging situations and conditions.

Note: Dr. Brown's TED Talk on the Power of Vulnerability is in the top five viewed TED Talks with over 30 million views. You can view it by Googling "TED Talks The Power of Vulnerability July 9, 2017" (https://www.ted.com/talks/brene_brown_on_vulnerability?language=en).

After viewing her talk, I think you'll understand what I mean when I tell you that it's very difficult to put the topic of organizational care of staff into a "neatly tied together package" as there are many variables. However, the hope in looking at the issues and having this discussion is that organizations will adjust their mindset as needed to address the well-being of staff that includes but goes beyond a focus on STS. As we will see, this goes beyond offering tuition reimbursement, health insurance and 401ks.

Organizational Response to STS

The website of NCTSN (2018) states the following about organizational response to secondary stress, "Individual and supervisory awareness of the effects of this indirect trauma exposure is a basic part of protecting the health of the worker and ensuring that children consistently receive the best possible care from those who are committed to helping them."

I think we need to be more specific and state that protecting the health of the worker goes beyond a focus on secondary stress. If the primary motivation for protecting the worker from this stress is to ensure "that children (all clients) consistently receive the best possible care from those who are committed to helping them" then TSOs are compelled and responsible for developing a much broader growth mindset as to what constitutes stress and the "health of the worker."

I certainly do not want to sound unappreciative or righteous about the hard work and countless hours so many have devoted to bringing attention to the need for organizations to acknowledge the secondary stress of its workers and how this relates to the care they provide. Over 30 years of spending countless hours with survivors of homicide, suicide, those exposed to school shootings, violent and accidental death, catastrophic fires, hurricanes, bombing of the Federal Building in Oklahoma, 9/11 and far too many other incidents, I am friends with secondary stress. I know how important it is for organizations to acknowledge it as an unavoidable work hazard and assist workers in managing it. However, as critical as this is, organizations must do more. We need to look at stress from a larger lens than one focusing specifically on preventing and/or resolving STS because,

Reality: Stress is stress. Regardless of its source, stress affects our bodies, our emotions, cognitive processes and performance even when sources such as CF/STS and BO are not significant stress sources. We might resolve STS, for example, but if other sources of stress exist, our emotions, cognitive process and performance (the care of clients) will be impacted.

Let's start this discussion by briefly discussing the answers you provided for the first two questions/scenarios in the pre-session questions and activities.

Answers to Pre-session Question #1

The first case scenario showed a dated timeline from 1995 to 2018 during which CF, BO and secondary trauma has been discussed, researched and acted upon by some. What your peers most frequently mention is the amount of time it seems to have taken for organizations to actively address STS with those who do the day-to-day work with victims of trauma. As Bloom (2006) and others (Sharp, 2013) have made clear, especially regarding organizations serving the traumatized,

Reality: *Organizational change can be a complex process especially in the non-profit sector because of overseeing funding sources, compliance management groups, licensing agencies, leadership styles and old mindsets of those in the role of policy making and organizational leadership. However, the argument can be made that the mindset of leadership related to staff well-being has not been a priority equal to that of the care provided clients.*

Let me provide some additional information regarding this first scenario. This first pre-session scenario mentioned the founding of the National Child Traumatic Stress Network (NCTSN) in 2000. In 2008, NCTSN published "Child Traumatic Stress: What Every Policymaker Should Know: A Guide from the National Child Traumatic Stress Network" (Gerrity & Folcarelli, 2008). This very comprehensive 58-page document was written to educate policymakers about the scope and impact of childhood trauma, to effective solutions that can be implemented with the support of informed public policy, and to provide information about additional resources. *Unfortunately, it did not mention secondary stress issues facing staff providing this service and that policy addressing the unavoidable stress of caring for a trauma population is an equally essential component for effective care of the traumatized.*

The earliest dated publication I could find providing information about STS by NCTSN was 2011 with the publication of "Secondary Traumatic Stress: A Fact Sheet for Child Serving Professionals" (NCTSN Resources, 2011). Many of the NCTSN web pages are not dated so there may have been an earlier publication; however, the Internet search did not cite earlier publications.

In 2012 NCTSN did identify seven practices that programs, agencies and service providers of a service system with a trauma-informed perspective must provide: number 7 states "maintain an environment of care for staff that addresses, minimizes, and treats secondary traumatic stress, and that increases staff resilience" (NCTSN, 2012). Also, in the spring of 2012, the Center for Advanced Studies in Child Welfare held a very comprehensive conference focused on Secondary Trauma and the Child Welfare Workforce. Actually, numerous conferences about STS were conducted that year. NCTSN also published several new resources on STS and provided a number of webinars on the issue. Wilson, Pence, and Conradi (2013) of the Chadwick Center, one of the largest hospital based child advocacy and trauma treatment centers in the nation, far advanced in its trauma approach to care, indicated in 2013 that "*Actively working to increase staff resilience to secondary traumatic stress (STS) involves seeking ways to reduce the risk of STS among all personnel - from the receptionists, to transcriptionists, to the frontline professionals and their supervisors.*" As stated, this focus on STS is very important and, in this statement, focuses on all personnel, which is wonderful. What I wish it would have also addressed is assisting all personnel with STS *and other life-work stressors* that negatively impact employee well-being to reflect more of a growth-oriented mindset.

Every year since 1995, when Dr. Figley brought attention to CF and secondary stress, an abundance of articles and research studies have been conducted and published about the two. However, it wasn't until approximately 17 years later, in 2011–2012, when many started to take action to encourage organizations to attend to STS among its staff. Now, here we are in 2018 and some major organizations are just now beginning to focus on the secondary stress impact on their staff and how they might help them with that stress. This is good news and we must continue to encourage TSOs to engage in this focus, yet with a more expansive growth mindset regarding staff well-being and reduction of varied sources of workplace stress. Let's explore this responsibility further.

Fixed or Growth Mindset?

The good news is that the old mindsets that staff are responsible for their own self-care and that professionals ought to be able to manage their own stress have significantly shifted to STS as unavoidable and that organizations do have, as cited in Session One (Hoge et al., 2007, p. 58), a responsibility, an ethical responsibility to assist staff in the prevention of or recovery from STS. However, once again, I propose that this mindset is fixed on fixing STS rather than a much more expansive growth-focused mindset of what contributes to the resilience, sustainability of quality care, performance, potential, work satisfaction and retention of those who are repeatedly exposed to a trauma population, even when STS is being prevented and/or managed. Let's examine this by way of the brief Prudential case presented in the second pre-session scenario.

Answer to Pre-session Question #2

Note: Before answering this question, let me tell you that a few have criticized me for using a corporate example as opposed to a non-profit one. I often hear that business/corporations have far more financial resources than TSOs and that change in organizational settings is a complicated process compared to the flexibility of leadership in the corporate world. My responses are

1. It's not really about resources as much as it is about mindset. When the well-being of staff is elevated, health care costs go down as does the cost incurred by the high level of turnover often experienced in TSOs. For example, if the wellness/well-being efforts provided staff reduced turnover by 10 employees, the organization would save approximately $540,000 in cost to recruit and retrain new employees; this is more than enough to initiate a broader onsite range of well-being programs. According to the Texas Senate Finance Committee it cost $54,000 to retrain a new social service worker (Governing, 2016).

    Furthermore, "once turnover persists, it creates conditions that lead to a seemingly never-ending cycle: experienced caseworkers don't have time to mentor new ones, caseloads increase, backlogs develop, tempers flare, pressures rise and burnout shows no signs of fading" (Governing, 2016). In other words, the culture becomes a stressful one, not an engaging one, a resilient one, one that encourages staff to not only remain but also do their best work. So, if STS among staff is reduced by a focused effort on educating and assisting staff with STS but BO/turnover rates remain high, has anything really changed? Under these conditions can we really expect client care to be at its best or employee performance and engagement in the organization to be at best? The answer is "no."

2. Is it complicated? No, change in this area is really not complicated. The reality is and the point about to be made is that the corporate world has been developing broad programs in the area of employee wellness and well-being longer than most non-profit, mental health, human service agencies. The outcomes of their efforts teach us a great deal about this approach TSOs can

take to better assist staff in multiple areas of stress. Essentially, as we'll see, they discovered and have demonstrated that employee well-being means organizational well-being. This has to be a leadership mindset at the highest levels that is also endorsed and acted upon by administrators, managers and supervisors and employees.

3.   Is it hard work? Yes, it takes *effective effort* as well as a leadership mindset of a kind that Dr. Brown described; one that embraces the importance of leadership *connecting and caring* for its employee's potential and well-being in order to create a culture of *productive relationships*.

I don't want to get ahead of myself so let's look at the Prudential story.

The Prudential Story: A Growth Mindset

In 2007, Prudential understood that there were multiple areas in employees' lives that lead to stress and that the stress of their employees really mattered when it came to retention, engagement in the organization, performance outcomes and a culture of well-being. Concerned about the levels of stress and depression among their employees, they administered, for the first time in 2007, their Health Risk Assessment Questionnaire. This was approximately five years before organizations and professional associations across the country began making very visible efforts via conferences, etc. to bring attention to secondary stress in TSOs.

What was unique about Prudential's questionnaire is that it evaluated five life domains – financial, physical, emotional, social and spiritual.

I left the non-profit world in 2014 after 45 years of working in organizations assisting trauma victims. I was never asked to complete a Health Risk Assessment or any other assessment that involved the five areas of life that Prudential evaluated. If we needed help, we were directed to the organization's Employee Assistance Program (EAP), which was our responsibility to follow up with. Other than health insurance, some educational reimbursement and 401Ks, that many could not contribute to because their salaries went to mortgages and basic care for families, well-being *on site programs* for staff were all but non-existent. I want you to compare what your organization provides with what Prudential offers. This is important because it presents a growth mindset for what I consider to be a responsibility of TSOs that again goes beyond a focus on STS. We'll also see in a bit that it is also smart and rewarding for all involved.

The APA Center of Excellence Award

Every year the American Psychological Association honors one organization with its Center of Excellence Award (APA, 2018) and several others with its Psychologically Healthy Workplace Award. The Center of Excellence Award highlights the effective application of psychology in the workplace – whether addressing mental health, applying good behavioral science to safety practices, using learning theory to strengthen training efforts, or employing a host of other ways that psychology can promote well-being and performance. The Psychologically Healthy Workplace highlights employee involvement; health and safety; employee growth and development; work-life balance and employee recognition. Additional factors that are considered include employee attitudes and opinions, the role of communication in the organization and the benefits realized in terms of employee health, well-being and organizational performance.

In 2017 Prudential Financial received the Center of Excellence Award from the APA for its effort to make the mental health and wellness of its staff manageable. I cite their story because their efforts were directed at reducing high levels of stress and depression among their employees, which is what is frequently experienced in TSOs funded to serve trauma populations. In addition, Prudential did something out of the ordinary; they evaluated five domains of living that can induce stress and impact overall performance, work attendance and retention.

(The following description is adapted from APA Center for Excellence Awards description, 2018.) As I indicated a few minutes ago, Prudential's Health and Wellness team introduced Prudential's first annual employee Health Risk Assessment Questionnaire in 2007. It evaluated the financial, physical, emotional, social and spiritual lives of employees for stress related issues. More than three-quarters of Prudential 20,000 employees took the assessment in its first year. The outcome revealed "stress and depression were indeed significant risk factors for its employees. The following year, during the nation's economic downturn, the data also revealed that more than a third of employees were experiencing stress related to finances. From this point on employee well-being became a major focus."

As a result of Prudential's assessment outcome, leaders worked to better meet the well-being needs of its employees. Let's look at some of these efforts. (The following is adapted from Prudential's Comprehensive Approach to Supporting Health, 2018.)

Among some of the services available, often on site at no cost to Prudential employees and their families, are personal budget coaching, internal counseling, assessments and training, as well as life coaching, adult care coaching and financial management. Prudential's health and wellness team is innovative in the topics they choose for programs as well as the formats. The team often works closely with Prudential's corporate communications department to take advantage of the company's intranet, town hall meetings, online newspaper, as well as links to internal videos, called "PRUTubes." These videos have featured employees talking about their personal challenges such as a senior executive discussing his alcohol addiction and his division president describing how the condition resulted in performance counseling and referral to their behavioral health services that resulted in that employee's eventual advancement in the company. Three employees shared their experiences with domestic violence and how they sought help. Some 1,000 employees participated in the event, either in person or via live video stream, and many others watched the video later.

The director of their behavioral health services described her own experiences with depression, noting the irony of someone responsible for the behavioral health needs of 20,000 people seeking care for herself. She indicated that treatment had helped her live a richer life and she encouraged others to seek treatment if needed. All agree that these efforts to address the well-being of staff help "build a culture where no health challenge is unmentionable." The benefit of their growth-oriented mindset regarding stress has been enormous for the employees and the company, as each year factors for stress and depression have steadily declined while engagement, retention and performance have improved.

I encourage leaders to visit the Prudential site for a fuller description of what they do for employee wellness and well-being. Simply Google "Workplace Mental Health-Prudential Financial, Inc" (https://www.workplacementalhealth.org/Case-Studies/Prudential-Financial-Inc).

Note: By the way, 10 years after Prudential initiated the Health Assessment Questionnaire, the latest study released by PwC found that a quarter of U.S. workers said financial worries caused them health problems; 40% said finances distracted them at work and 15% said these problems made them miss work, according to the study, which surveyed 1,600 working U.S. adults aged 21 to 75 (Pinsker, 2018). That is why companies are providing a more robust menu of voluntary financial wellness benefits, sometimes with cash incentives or discounts, to help employees manage their money.

"They are starting to see that a 401(k) is not enough. Employees say: I have present-day needs I have to take care of before I can take care of retirement," said Chris Whitlow, chief executive officer of Edukate, a workplace financial wellness provider (Pinsker, 2018).

Organizational Well-being

Has your organization made a demonstrated effort to not only provide ongoing support for STS but also your well-being?

Before you answer this, let's spend a bit more time on why a well-being mindset is so essential and far more inclusive of the stress employees experience beyond STS. If your employer supports your efforts to resolve and/or help prevent the effects of secondary stress, which is what these sessions are about, that is wonderful. However, if you are also struggling with financial and/or social well-being issues, the stress of that struggle will still negatively impact how you perform your workplace responsibilities (Kohll, 2017) even after finding relief from or managing STS. As I stated in the introduction of this session,

Reality: *Stress is stress. Regardless of its source, stress affects our bodies, our emotions, cognitive processes and performance even when sources such as CF/STS are not significant sources of stress. We need to keep in mind that helpers bring their own personal life stress into the work place and these also influence performance, engagement and the care of others and, in fact, present additional risk for or vulnerability to CF/STS/BO.*

It is interesting to note that in the same year Prudential conducted its Health Risk Assessment and began attending to more than employee health needs, Hoge et al. (2007, p. 58) wrote, "Behavioral health program administrators should aim to strengthen their workforce; doing so requires creating environments that support the health (wellness) and well-being, not only of persons with mental and substance use conditions, but of the workforce as well." That was in 2007 and many organizations are just now getting on board, while the broader well-being/wellness concept addressing stress across five domains was initiated years ago by the business/corporate world. Needless to say, many TSOs are just now addressing STS and behind in accepting and adopting a well-being responsibility and approach.

Goodwill

There are always exceptions. One prime example is that of the Goodwill Industries of North Central Wisconsin. Their philosophy, as stated in the 2013 CARF Connection Blog is quite clear. "Goodwill NCW supports its *people-first value* through a *commitment to care for team members as whole persons who have complex lives*. The organization's leaders recognize that *any challenges that team members are facing in their personal lives do not disappear when they come to work*. In fact, the weight of those challenges can hinder team members from bringing their best to the tasks at hand. The organization has responded by nurturing a culture of holistic wellness in the workplace."

I encourage you to read how they use wellness coaches and chaplains on site to help employees with emotional, spiritual, psychological, physical or financial stress to strengthen the resilience and well-being of its 1,400 employees and their organizations performance. That effort started in 2007, the same year Prudential began its efforts to improve the well-being of its staff. Does your TSO provide on-site assistance with these five areas of life? It is interesting to note that although Goodwill Industries is a non-profit organization, it has always had a business focus.

Reality: *Businesses and corporations have a richly active history of focusing on, assessing and engaging in programs and practices supporting the wellness and well-being of its employees.*

Defining Well-being

In 2010 the *New York Times* bestseller *Wellbeing: The Five Essential Elements* (Rath & Harter, 2010) defined the concept of well-being in the work place to include physical, community, career, financial and social well-being, which is similar to the Prudential effort. (At the time, social well-being was inclusive of emotional/psychological, spiritual well-being.) Yes, concern about profit margins as well as growth and the sustainability of their success in what has now become a global marketplace is a strong motivator but not the only one. Many have already realized that organizational growth, success and sustainability are, in fact, dependent upon the wellness and well-being of their employees.

Reality: *Quite simply stated, stressed employees, regardless of the source of that stress, are not high performers; they are not engaged in the overall goals and values of the organization or maintaining a positive work place culture and their stress becomes the stress of their peers.*

You might find it interesting that The World Health Organization (WHO) defines health as a state of complete physical, mental and social well-being and not merely the absence of disease or infirmity. WHO provides us with the ICD or International Classification of Diseases, which also includes PTSD and BO (WHO, ICD-10, 2018). It should be mentioned that it does not include CF nor does the APA's DSM-5. This will be addressed a bit later, as CF is real and hopefully will, at some point, be included as a diagnostic category.

A Tangible Connection

"There is growing awareness and appreciation among people managers that these three words (health, wellness, well-being) have a tangible connection to employee productivity, engagement, absenteeism, workplace safety and performance" (Bevacqua, 2018). Let's take a closer look at how some define wellness and well-being.

Wellness and Well-being: What Is the Difference and Does It Matter?

How did you answer Pre-session Questions 8 and 9? Many of your peers have an intuitive sense as to the primary difference between wellness and well-being. They know that wellness reflects issues around physical health while well-being addresses a number of areas in our lives. When asked to identify the five areas of well-being, most identify mental health and emotional health and many mention work–life balance. Few mention financial, spiritual and social well-being, yet these are the categories most frequently cited in the definitions of well-being.

The Difference

Wellness and well-being are two terms still used interchangeably but there is a difference. In organizational settings, wellness is generally focused on programs related to employee's health, the prevention of illness, treatment and recovery. It's about how well our bodies are functioning and from this perspective includes stress management efforts, such as exercise, nutrition and sleep. Well-being programs, on the other hand, focus on mental health, emotional health, social, spiritual and financial well-being; some definitions also include career fulfillment (Faulkner, 2017; Kohl, 2017).

Note: From this point on we'll add career fulfillment as a sixth well-being category. Although employers want their employees to become skillful at what they do, career fulfillment is a broader issue. Career fulfillment speaks to advancement opportunities but also opportunities to assume different roles within the profession, for example, trainer, certified specialists, educational writer, marketing specialist, etc. This effort also is associated with less BO. Okay, back to well-being.

Reality: *"Well-being is becoming a core responsibility of good corporate citizenship and a critical performance strategy to drive employee engagement, organizational energy, and productivity. No longer an optional or narrowly focused element of the rewards menu, well-being is now front and center as a business imperative for leading high-performance companies"* (Agarwai, Bersin, Lahri, Schwartz, & Volini, 2018).

Obviously, the recommendation is that TSOs approach the stress of its staff with such a growth-oriented mindset and responsibility.

Spirituality in the Workplace: A Necessary Well-being Component

Because someone always asks, let me define what is meant by spiritual wellness in the workplace. Spiritual wellness in the workplace is not about religion but about "defining meaning and purpose in life; self-awareness; and connectedness with self, others, and a larger reality" (KU, 2018). It's about aligning what we do and how we interact with others around us with our values and beliefs. Spiritual wellness is about "individuals and organizations seeing work as an opportunity to grow and contribute to society and its community in a meaningful way. It is about care, compassion and support of others, about integrity and people being true to themselves and others. It means individuals and organizations are attempting to live their values more fully in the work they do" (Srivastava, 2018).

Reality: *Spiritual intelligence is the key to personal fulfillment and good work performance and can lead to a more satisfying and productive work place. It is a component of self-care as it supports finding meaning and purpose in our lives, which in turn allows us to more easily adapt to stressful situations.*

In the session on assessments, the *Spiritual Intelligence Self-Report Inventory* is reviewed. It's really about evaluating our cognitive processes and behaviors in the face of stress and how these responses reflect possible barriers to self-fulfillment. The following question is not on this scale but reflects a 'spiritual' conflict that can be experienced in the process of trying to do our job. It's an important question that gets at whether we feel we are being true to our self at work.

"Am I having to do things that go against my better judgment (what I value, what I believe)?"

If the answer to this is "yes," then this conflict is a source of stress, not conducive to work place engagement, professional growth nor our well-being. This "spiritual" well-being question helps reveal if we are in a culture that is counter-productive to our performing at our best and a roadblock to seriously engaging in that culture, both of which are detrimental to us, those we serve and the organization itself. Believe it or not, many answer "yes" to this question reflecting, once again, that a well-being focus is lacking.

Benefits of a Well-being, Wellness or Holistic Approach to Stress

Black (2017) wrote, "promoting healthy habits to employees is an effective way to benefit both employer and employee. Healthy, active employees incur lower health costs. Employees who take advantage of wellness programs are more productive. Physically active employees are healthier. Wellness programs inspire important behavior changes."

"Organizations now see well-being not just as an employee benefit or responsibility, but as a business performance strategy. . . . 43 percent believe that well-being reinforces their organization's mission and vision, 60 percent reported that it improves employee retention, and 61 percent said that it *improves employee productivity* and bottom-line business results" (Agarwai et al., 2018). There are a variety of apps now available to employees to assist with their well-being that are also making a difference, are inexpensive and easy to use. The VirginPulse app, for example, is used as frequently as Facebook. Its "users are 65 percent more engaged, have 32 percent lower turnover rates, and deliver 9 percent higher productivity than their peers" (Agarwai et al., 2018).

One study (Lowensteyn, Berberin, DaCosta, Joseph, & Grover, 2018) evaluated 730 employees to determine the benefit of their wellness program. They found significant reduction of systolic blood pressure, high emotional stress reduction and fatigue reduction. The study concluded that after one year the benefits included clinically important improvements in physical and mental health.

Note: Some refer to wellness/well-being programs as holistic wellness programs (Murphy, 2018). Regardless of the term used, "companies today are offering wellness benefits that go beyond their workforce's physical well-being to those that have a positive impact on employee's lifestyle and interests. The reason for this is that holistic wellness programs can help to drive recruiting and retention efforts, as well as productivity and employee engagement" (Turasi, 2015).

Question One: After reading about the focus of organizations on employee wellness and well-being and the benefits for doing so, how would you rate your organizations leadership demonstrated and continued effort to provide both onsite and offsite resources and assistance with your well-being in the six domains identified-financial, health, emotional (mental health), social, spiritual and professional growth? Limited____, Some focus/effort but inconsistent ____, A definite priority____.

Question Two: Of the six domains, which domains receive the least attention or provide the fewest resources _____, _____, _____, _____.

Please record your answers under the Post-Session Questions at the end of this session.

Well-being and Engagement Together: The Best Combination

Gallup has been a leader in the field of engagement for years. In 2006, they published the New York bestseller *12 Elements of Great Managing* (Wagner & Harter, 2006). In this resource they discuss the results of their Q 12 scale, which evaluates the level of engagement in an organization. The Q 12 has been tested over 30 years with 25 million employees throughout the world with the consistent result showing that engagement is critical to retention and performance. Research in education also clearly shows that the level of engagement is critical to teacher retention (Neason, 2014). In human services, mental health and other organizations responding to a traumatized population, the level of engagement employees experience with their managers and/or supervisors is also predictive of *retention and clinical efficacy with clients* (Mental Health America, 2017).

"Engagement" Is the Answer to Pre-session Question #12

Most answers to this question do not indicate engagement. Some indicate leadership, which is important only in so far as leaders themselves create a culture of engagement. Some mention supervision, which is also very critical but again only in so far as supervision engages supervisees.

"Gallup defines engaged employees as those who are involved in, enthusiastic about and committed to their work and workplace" (Gallup Daily, 2017). They have repeatedly shown worldwide that "Employee engagement strategies have proven to reduce staff turnover, improve productivity and efficiency. . . . Most importantly, engaged employees are happier, both at work and in their lives" (Gallup, 2016). Put simply, a happy employee is a valued employee. Engagement is an emotional commitment the we have to the well-being of the organization. It means we care about our work and our organization.

Engagement and Spiritual Wellness

Remember the spiritual wellness question I used as an example in the last section? In a recent survey of 250 employees within an organization funded to serve a trauma population, employees answered a similar question. Approximately 40% of frontline workers indicated they were doing things that went against their better judgment, 25% of supervisors indicated the same. The 40% doing things against their better judgment are certainly experiencing the stress of personal and psychological conflict. Such a conflict creates trust issues with leadership, fosters an adversarial attitude and restricts the level of engagement within the organization and interactions with clients.

I don't think it was surprising that 80% of these 250 employees also indicated they considered looking for another job in a 12-month period and 50% thought about leaving every week. Yes, there were other organizational factors contributing to their stress, however, research clearly shows that low engagement is a key factor in poor retention and performance.

This is good news as Gallup has shown that when levels of engagement go up so too does employee satisfaction, performance and retention. But here is even better news.

Reality: *When high levels of well-being co-exist with high levels of engagement, everything changes for the better*.

Employees who are engaged and who have high well-being in at least four of the five well-being areas are:

> 30% more likely not to miss any workdays because of poor health in any given month, and miss 70% fewer workdays because of poor health over the course of a year,
> 27% more likely to report "excellent" performance in their own job at work,
> 27% more likely to report "excellent" performance by their organization,
> 45% more likely to report high levels of adaptability in the presence of change,
> 59% less likely to look for a job with a different organization in the next 12 months,
> 18% less likely to change employers in a 12-month period, and
> 42% more likely to evaluate their overall lives highly.

(Engagement Multiplier, 2014)

Unfortunately, many organizations invest their resources in well-being programs and stop there, thinking this singular focus will make a difference. It does to some extent, but not to the degree when they also invest in engagement practices. Doubling up creates a much more successful outcome. When used together employees are more productive, happier and healthier – and as result, so too is the organization.

Reality: *If I am not engaged and experience STS, I am not likely to follow-up on STS intervention/ treatment recommendations*.

Consider the following: disengaged employees will

- make excuses,
- make careless mistakes,
- have trouble getting work done or completing records accurately,
- not assertively participate in supervision and meetings,
- resist change,
- not respond appropriately or timely to clients calls/work emails,
- use up all their sick time often on Mondays and Fridays,

- show up late, spend too much time on breaks and lunch, leave early, and
- not engage in self-care.

Reality: *The more engaged I am, the more passionate I am about the quality of my relationship/intervention with clients and the more committed I am to my organization. Therefore, if I experience STS, I will do what is needed to resolve it.*

Sustaining High Levels of Employee Engagement

Developing high levels of engagement among employees is not difficult but does take *effective ongoing effort.* Let's look at a few of the ways high levels of employee engagement are sustained.

Leaders, inclusive of managers and supervisors, must demonstrate that they care about the well-being of their employees by regularly connecting with them. According to Harter and Adkins (Gallup Workplace, 2015), managers (and supervisors) account for up to 70% of variance in engagement. Consistent communication is clearly connected to higher engagement. There are several excellent engagement surveys recommended in the Assessment Session but keep in mind that, as good as they may be, assessments are faceless. To get at "why" specific areas of engagement are low, we need to engage employees for the answers. This is best accomplished with face-to-face conversations with employees following assessment. I recommend the following after engagement surveys are completed and scored.

1. Sit down with staff in small groups and go through each item on the survey and ask for their feedback and opinions.
2. Anonymously report each group's comments and then indicate the actions leadership will be taking to improve engagement at all levels.
3. Conduct monthly follow-up sessions, as adjustments will be needed (this further demonstrates how serious leaders are about supporting employees).
4. Identify problem areas and then assign small groups to discuss and provide possible solutions. Report all solutions and then get to work initiating solutions until the problem is resolved.
5. Continue to meet in small groups and/or via supervision for "engagement reviews" that allow employees to identify what is important to them, what makes their day, their week, what makes them feel appreciated, checking to see if they are clear as to what is expected of them and what they would like to learn.

What matters most is that leadership take time to sit down with staff to have these conversations, to hear what they are thinking about the work they do, the clients they serve, what's required of them, the resources and artificial intelligence support available to them, why they remain with the organization, what they find meaningful about the work they do, what excites them.

Note: In some respects, engagement begins in the hiring process. Applicants must be made aware of the type of clients they will be assisting, the trauma they have endured, the unavoidable stress that comes from exposure to trauma victims and/or trauma incidents as well as the demands of the job. This is best accomplished via video segments involving workers talking about their experiences, the stress they experience and the ways the organization assists them with managing this stress. Obviously, they also need to be exposed to the rewards of the job as described by current workers. This provides for a much more realistic and a better-informed applicant, who will be much better prepared should they be ask to join the organization. This format is referred to as Realistic Job Previews (RJPs). Simply Google "Realistic Job Previews in Health and Human Services/Mental Health" for more detailed information.

Okay. Let's get back to what encourages high levels of engagement.

Employees will engage when leaders:

- encourage collaboration, working together as a team, being respectful and considerate of each other and giving and seeking useful feedback from one another as needed,
- stress the importance of quality service and provide ongoing resources that support service quality,
- demonstrate their passion for quality at all levels,
- keep employees informed about what is occurring in the organization and consistently report on its strengths, what is being accomplished with clients and in the community (To be engaged employees need to feel proud of their organization and that they are part of something larger than themselves),
- have the tough conversations about employees taking responsibility for resolving conflict among themselves rather than shifting blame or complaining to others and to always be proactive, so when mistakes are made to immediately bring them to the attention of their supervisor/manager so they can be corrected quickly but also become teachable moments for all to learn from. (Being proactive also includes encouraging employees to share their ideas, seek new experiences within the organization and taking the initiative to improve skills), and
- develop a culture where employees feel safe (physically and emotionally) and connected to the mission, values and beliefs of the organization. (More on safety in our next session.)

Employees will engage when their supervisor/manager:

- identifies problem areas and possible ways to correct those problems, for example time management techniques, completing written records (it's amazing how many employees can verbalize client interactions but find it difficult to translate those interactions in writing. Knowing that a written record reflects knowledge and skill levels can be threatening. It takes practice and support for some to become comfortable and confident with preparing written documents),
- establishes monthly progress goals,
- provides information and resources related to the work they do but also help enhance their professional growth, and
- assists them with their self-care/well-being needs and strategies.

Employees will engage when they:

- hear weekly from their supervisors/managers via face-to-face, email or text or through the organization's social network, and
- their universal needs are consistently acknowledged.

Note: We all have four universal brain-based needs (Brendtro & Mitchell, 2015; van Bockern & McDonald, 2015). These needs are belonging, mastery, independence and generosity. When these are acknowledged, we connect with and feel cared for by those who take the time to meet our needs. These needs can be easily addressed on a regular basis and clearly let the recipient know that their qualities are noticed. For example,

Mary:	It is always good to see you. (Belonging)
Lorenzo:	I didn't realize how much you know about . . . (Mastery)
Juanita:	I really appreciated the way you took the initiative to . . . (Independence)
Chris:	That was really nice, the way you helped out Susan yesterday . . . (Generosity)

Employees engage when their supervisor/manager:

- addresses their strengths,
- helps them find ways to improve on those strengths, and
- helps them find ways to utilize those strengths in the work place. (Opportunities might include mentoring newer employees, writing and presenting reports about new trends, what other similar organizations have found helpful, preparing YouTube segments, conduct trainings, completing certification training; the opportunities are endless. Employees will have suggestions of their own that, when allowed to pursue, will further enhances their level of engagement.)

Remaining Resilient

More than ever, in this ever-changing global world, remaining resilient, regardless of the stress of the work we do or the environment we are in, dictates that we focus on connecting with and caring for one another, that we engage. Focusing on the well-being and wellness of employees, connecting and demonstrating care for them is smart because it supports high levels of engagement, which leads to greater retention, improved performance and quality service and overall resilience. It is also an ethical responsibility of organizations serving a trauma population because the greater the well-being and engagement experienced by staff, the higher the quality of service provided to clients.

Question Three: After reading about the ways that leaders, managers and supervisors promote engagement, how would you rate the level of engagement in your work setting?

Poor_____ Minimal_____ Limited_____ Somewhat good_____ Very good_____

Please record your response under the Post-session Questions at the end of this session.

Summary

We've seen that it has taken years for organizations to actively respond to STS among its staff, even after abundant research showing its prevalence. The CDC says that "One-fourth of employees view their jobs as the number one stressor in their lives" (ESI EAP, Nov. 14, 2016). Remember the California study in Session One about child welfare worker stress and the large number of staff reporting they had more health issues than their peers working in other professions. The fact is, in high stress work environments and occupations, inclusive of TSO settings, employees visit physicians 26 more times than those in low stress jobs (Azagba & Sharaf, 2011). Stress hurts, period.

The impact of stress on our cognitive processes, behavior, performance, engagement with others and within the organization where we provide trauma service, leads to numerous performance, engagement and retention issues, whose improvement will be limited if our focus on employee well-being is limited to STS and placing the primary responsibility for well-being and self-care on employees. The focus on well-being must be inclusive of STS but also on the other domains of employee's lives we've addressed, and the organization must support a culture of *onsite* well-being assistance and services that go beyond STS.

Organizational Mindset Recommendations

Consider adopting the following growth-oriented mindsets:

- As much as it is needed today, the focus on STS is a fixed mindset rather than the more expansive well-being growth mindset focusing on multiple sources of employee stress inclusive of STS.
- Stress is stress. Regardless of its source, stress affects our bodies, our emotions, cognitive processes and performance even when sources such as STS are not significant sources of stress. Stressed employees, regardless of the source of that stress, struggle with performance, consistency, engagement, maintaining a positive work place culture; their stress becomes the stress of their peers (Tyler, 2012).
- Helpers bring their own personal life stress into the work place and these sources also influence performance, engagement and the care of others and present additional risk for or vulnerability to CF/STS/BO.
- An organizational growth mindset focuses efforts at reducing/managing employee stress as a comprehensive *onsite* well-being approach that assists and support staff in the emotional (mental health), physical (health), social (connections), spiritual (purpose, meaning, values, community), career development and financial domains.
- When high levels of well-being co-exist with high levels of engagement, everything changes for the better-performance consistency, professional growth, quality of care, productivity, employee engagement and satisfaction, retention and organizational well-being.
- Productive and positive relationships throughout an organization are dependent upon and nourished by leaders who are visibly caring for and connecting with all staff.
- To successfully enhance the well-being of staff in TSOs, leaders need to practice the characteristics of transformational leadership - walk the talk (idealized influence), inspire and motivate, give personal attention (individualized consideration) and provide intellectual stimulation (how well-being efforts are beneficial).

Recommendations for Well-being Initiation

1. **Invite and advocate**—Leaders do not want to force well-being activities and programs on employees but first advocate their benefits through education of employees via articles, existing well-being programs, YouTube discussions etc., followed by an invitation to provide their feedback as to what well-being means for them in the six domains identified in this session. Following this, employees can be invited to on site well-being activities.
2. **Model well-being**—If leaders in an organization do not model well-being efforts, employees will simply not engage. Modeling can be done through discussion and example.
3. **Demonstrate care and connect**—Leaders must help, encourage employees to set well-being goals and then consistently follow up with them to see how they are doing and problem solve together the barriers that may get in the way or the need to look at other activities that better fit individual well-being needs.
4. **Research**—There are numerous well-being sources and resources available (see Appendix). For example, Gallup has numerous resources such as, "How Millennials Want to Live and Work, Women in America: Work and Life Well-Lived," in addition to multiple surveys, guidelines, etc. Present as much as you can to staff (not all at once) for their feedback as to what fits for them. The well-being interest of every group will vary and topics/interest will change over time making this an ongoing process.
5. **Demonstrated effort matters**—Developing a comprehensive well-being program across the six domains will take time. It doesn't have to happen all at once. If there is a visible and consistent sincere effort by leadership to make the change, engagement and well-being and the many benefits we've identified will begin to improve.

Our Next Session

In our next session we are going to examine a few critical issues associated with being a trauma-informed organization and providing trauma-informed services. The remainder of the session will then focus on the key issues regarding supervision as it relates to secondary trauma, the responsibility of employees related to supervision and the unavoidable stress supervisors must also learn to manage.

Post-session Questions

Write down your answers to the following questions. Keep these responses, as they will be used later when detailing self-care practices.

Questions

1. Of all that you have read and experienced up to this point, what surprises you the most?

    _____

    _____

2. Of all that you have read and experienced up to this point, what one thought stands out the most for you?

    _____

    _____

3. As you think about the one thought that stands out the most for you, how might it change the way you think about CF, secondary stress and BO?

    _____

    _____

4. How has this changed what you feel you need to do about the unavoidable stress of what you do?

    _____

    _____

Record answers here to the three questions asked during this session.

Question One: After reading about the focus of organizations on employee wellness and well-being and the benefits for doing so, how would you rate your organizations leadership demonstrated and continued effort to provide both onsite and offsite resources and assistance with your well-being in the six domains identified-financial, health, emotional (mental health), social, spiritual and professional growth? Limited____, Some focus/effort but inconsistent ____, A definite priority____.

Question Two: Of the six domains, which domains receive the least attention or provide the fewest resources _____, _____, _____, _____.

Question Three: After reading about the ways that leaders, managers and supervisors promote engagement, how would you rate the level of engagement in your work setting?

Poor____, Minimal____, Limited____, Somewhat good____, Very good____.

Note: Keep your answers in mind when considering the sources of workplace stress and how much your workplace practices are contributing to your stress versus the actual work you do.

References

Agarwai, D., Bersin, J., Lahri, G., Schwartz, J., & Volini, E. (2018). Well-being: A strategy and a responsibility: 2018 global human capital trends. Retrieved September 24, 2018, from www.centreforleadershipadvantage. com/2018/ . . . /the-wellness-revolution-3-thin

APA. (2018). *APA's organizational excellence award*. Retrieved October 4, 2018, from www.apaexcellence.org/ awards/national/

Azagba, S., & Sharaf, M. (2011, August 11). Psychosocial working conditions and the utilization of health care services. *BMC Public Health*, 642.

Bevacqua, J. (2018). *The sum of success: Workplace holistic health & wellness programs*. Retrieved October 27, 2018, from https://risepeople.com/blog/workplace-holistic-health-wellness-programs/

Black, A. (2017). *Five reasons employee wellness is worth the investment*. Retrieved September 13, from, https:// health.gov/news/ . . . /2017/ . . . /five-reasons-employee-wellness-is-worth-the-invest. . .

Bloom, S. (2006). *Human service systems and organizational stress*. Retrieved July 14, 2018, from sanctuary- web.com/. . ./Bloom%20Pubs/2006%20Bloom%20Human%20Service%20Sy. . .

Bloom, S., & Sreedhar, S. Y. (2008). The sanctuary model of trauma-informed organizational change. *Reclaiming Children and Youth, 17*(3), 48–53.

Brendtro, L., & Mitchell, M. (2015). *Deep brain learning: Evidence-based essentials in education, treatment, and youth development*. Albion, MI: Starr Commonwealth.

Brown, B. (2018). *dare to lead: Brave work, tough conversations, whole hearts*. New York: Random House.

Engagement Multiplier. (2014, December 16). *Employee engagement vs. employee well-being*. Retrieved from www.engagementmultiplier.com/blog/employee-engagement-vs-employee-well/

ESI EAP. (2016). *The many benefits of corporate wellness programs*. Retrieved July 2018, from www.theeap. com/wellness/many-benefits-corporate-wellness-programs

Faulkner, A. (2017, March 1). *Wellness programs are out, well-being initiatives are in*. Retrieved October 4, 2018, from www.adp.com/ . . . /2017/ . . . /wellness-programs-are-out-wellbeing-initiatives-are-i. . .

Gallup. (2016). *Why is employee engagement so important?* Retrieved July 11, 2017, from www.engagement multiplier.com/blog/why-is-employee-engagement-so-important/

Gallup Daily: U.S. Employee Engagement. (2017). *Gallup Daily*.

Gerrity, E., & Folcarelli, C. (2008). *Child traumatic stress: What every policymaker should know*. Durham, NC and Los Angeles, CA: National Center for Child Traumatic Stress. Retrieved October 11, 2018, from www.nctsn. org/ . . . //child_traumatic_stress_what_policymakers_should_know.p

Governing. (2016). *Where are all the social workers going?* Retrieved March 7, 2018, from www.governing.com/ columns/smart-mgmt/gov-social-workers-turnover.html

Hoge, M. A., Morris, J. A., Daniels, A. S., Stuart, G. W., Huey, L. Y., & Adams, N. (2007). *An action plan for behavioral health workforce development: A framework for discussion*. Rockville, MD: Substance Abuse and Mental Health Services Administration, p. 58.

Kohll, A. (2017, December 06). *Is there a difference between employee wellness and employee well-being?* Retrieved October 10, 2018, from www.huffingtonpost.com/ . . . kohll/is-there-a-difference-bet_2_b_11112402.htm.

KU. (2018). *Seven ways to improve your spiritual health*. Retrieved October 27, 2018, from https://wellness. ku.edu/seven-ways-improve-your-spiritual-health

LaMontagne, A. D., Keegel, T., Louie, A. M., Ostry, A., & Landsbergis, P. A. (2007). A systematic review of the job-stress intervention evaluation literature, 1990–2005. *International Journal of Occupational and Environmental Health, 13*, 268–280.

Lowensteyn, I., Berberin, V., DaCosta, D., Joseph, L., & Grover, S. A. (2018, March). The measurable benefits of a workplace wellness program in Canada: Results after one year. *Journal of Occupational and Environmental Medicine, 60*(3), 211–216.

Mental Health America. (2017). *Mind the workplace*. Retrieved August 15, 2018, from www.mentalhealth america.net

Murphy, P. (2018). *Holistic wellness programs incorporate a 360 degree view of health*. Retrieved October 5, 2018, from www.hni.com/ . . . /holistic-wellness-programs-incorporate-a-360-degree-view-of. . .

National Child Traumatic Stress Network. (2012). *Creating trauma-informed child- and family-serving systems: A definition*. Retrieved January 15, 2013, from www.nctsn.org/trauma-informed-care/creating-trauma-informed-systems

NCTSN Resources. (2011). *Secondary traumatic stress: A fact sheet for child serving professionals*. Retrieved from, www.nctsn.org/resources/secondary-traumatic-stress-fact-sheet-child-serving-pr

NCTSN. (2018). *Secondary traumatic stress*. Retrieved July 28, 2018, from https://www.nctsn.org/trauma-informed-care/secondary-traumatic-stress

Neason, A. (2014). *Half of teachers leave the job after five years: Here's what to do about it*. Retrieved May 15, 2015, from http://hechingerreport.org/half-teachers-leave-job-five-years-heres/

Pinsker, B. (2018). *The next frontier in workplace wellness: Financial health*. Retrieved September 29, 2018, from www.reuters.com/ . . . financialwellness/the-next-frontier-in-workplace-wellness-fi. . .

Prudential's Comprehensive Approach to Supporting Health. (2018). Retrieved October 29, 2018, from www.workplacementalhealth.org/Case-Studies/Prudential-Financial-Inc

Rath, T., & Harter, J. (2010). *Wellbeing: The five essential elements*. New York: Gallup Press.

Sharp, S. (2013). Trauma-informed care: Behavioral health overview. *National Council for Community Behavioral Health*. Retrieved January 23, 2013, from www.thenationalcouncil.org/areas-of . . . / trauma-informed-behavioral-healthcare

Srivastava, R. (2018). *Spiritual wellbeing at work: How to do it right*. Retrieved October 27, 2018, from www.hrzone.com/lead/culture/spiritual-wellbeing-at-work-how-to-do-it-right

Tyler, T. A. (2012). The limbic model of systemic trauma. *Journal of Social Work Practice: Psychotherapeutic Approaches in Health, Welfare and the Community, 26*(1), 125–138.

Turasi, L. (2015). *9 holistic wellness initiatives employees appreciate*. Retrieved July 7, 2018, from workplace.care.com/9-holistic-wellness-initiatives-employees-appreciate

van Bockern, S., & McDonald, T. (2015). Creating circle of courage schools. *Reclaiming Children and Youth, 20*(4), 13–17.

Wagner, R., & Harter, J. (2006). *12 elements of great managing*. New York: Gallup Press.

WHO. (2018). *ICD-10-CM diagnosis code Z73.0: Burnout*. Retrieved October 4, 2018, from www.icd10data.com/ICD10CM/Codes/Z00-Z99/Z69-Z76/Z73-/Z73.0

Wilson, C., Pence, D. M., & Conradi, L. (2013). *Trauma informed care*. Retrieved October 17, 2018, from oxfordindex.oup.com/view/10.1093/acrefore/9780199975839.013.1063

5 Trauma-informed Organizations, Leadership, Secondary Traumatic Stress and Supervision

Pre-session Questions

Answer all questions as best you can. If you seem to have no answer, give it your best effort as this will help reinforce what is learned throughout this session.

1. When an organization indicates they are trauma-informed, what is the first question you want to explore?

   _____

   _____

2. List the six principles of trauma-informed care.

   _____, _____,

   _____, _____,

   _____, _____.

3. If you were a supervisor in a trauma-informed environment pursuing the principle of safety in the supervisory process, what four questions should you be able to answer regarding safety?

   (a) _____

   (b) _____

   (c) _____

   (d) _____

4. Although there is no formal definition, describe what you consider to be the difference between being trauma-informed versus trauma-sensitive.

   _____

   _____

   _____

5. List two factors that enhance resilience, performance, compassion satisfaction and staff retention.

   _____, _____.

6. Identify the four characteristics of transformational leaders.

   _____, _____,

   _____, _____.

7.   You are going to be meeting your assigned supervisor/manager for the first time. As we all know, not all supervisors or managers are helpful. Write down the concerns you have about entering into this relationship with your assigned supervisor or manager.

_____

_____

_____

8.   If you are a trauma-informed supervisor, use a separate sheet of paper to write out what you would say in your first session with a new supervisee. If you are a supervisee, write down what you would hope to hear from your assigned supervisor in your first session.

9.   What 10 processes help make supervision safe and effective? (Both supervisees and supervisors should try to answer this.)

_____, _____,

_____, _____,

_____, _____,

_____, _____,

_____, _____.

10. If you are a supervisor, list as best you can the 9 core competencies of trauma-informed supervision.

_____, _____,

_____, _____,

_____, _____,

_____, _____,

_____.

Session Five

Trauma-informed Organizations, Leadership, STS and Supervision

Opening Statement

We spent our last session talking about the importance of well-being and engagement as critical factors related to high levels of performance, quality service, retention, the well-being of the organization and most importantly the minimization and sustained containment of work-related stress inclusive of CF/STS. If you recall high levels of engagement indicate that all levels of leadership are consistently connecting with and demonstrating their care for the well-being of all members in the organization. Common sense tells us then that, if an organization is providing services to trauma populations, those involved in trauma incidents and/or to those presenting with emotionally challenging situations, an engaged leadership will be very concerned about its staff and the impact of the stress they are exposed to because of the service they provide.

Reality: *Leaders in TSOs who value the well-being of their employees and the role engagement plays in minimizing the stress of the work they do, will also support a culture that is trauma-informed and, in particular, actively pursue their ethical responsibility to assist staff with STS/CF.*

Making an effort to become a trauma-informed organization says, "We now recognize and understand the impact trauma has on our clients, their everyday lives, their relationships and their efforts to survive and succeed. Knowing what we now know about trauma, we are working on policies, procedures and practices in order to now bring our clients trauma specific services and resources, to present them with a variety of ways to heal and to give them a voice in our organization and in the community."

It should go on to say, "The well-being of all our employees is also of utmost concern. What we do is very stressful. Those providing direct services to our clients/consumers face the additional stress of working with those in trauma and being exposed to trauma inducing situations. We consider it our responsibility to help support all our employee's efforts to manage the stress of what we do. We understand that the more effective we are in supporting our employee's well-being, the more effective we will be in the service we provide. We also understand that this focus on employee well-being supports our efforts to engage employees in building a resilient environment where we all can flourish."

However ...

The effort at being trauma-informed is of value for everyone involved. However, we must be careful about the assumptions we make about organizations that do refer to themselves as trauma-informed. Over the last 10 years I have consulted with and provided trauma-focused training to numerous organizations and staff, who identified themselves as trauma-informed, yet further questioning revealed they were only somewhat informed and not engaging in those actions that support the principles of trauma-informed care. What those experiences taught me is that being informed does not necessarily constitute an understanding of trauma in ways that translate into trauma-sensitive practices.

Why This Discussion?

Reality: *If you are new to the field and are going to be assisting those in trauma, responding to trauma situations and/or to those presenting emotionally challenging situations, you want to be with an organization that demonstrates it understands the stressful impact of the work you will be doing by providing you the appropriate support.*

The issues we are about to cover can be used to help you evaluate the support you will or will not be provided. If you are in an organization that is in the process of becoming trauma-informed or identified as informed, then these issues are ones you want to make sure are addressed. And of course, even if you have been working at your organization for some time, you want to know you are receiving the most up to date recommended trauma related support possible.

The purposes of this session are to

1. cite a number of practical issues around being trauma-informed to demonstrate that being informed is not the same as being trauma-sensitive. This is important because it addresses how an organization's overall understanding of trauma dictates the depth of their actively caring for their employee's well-being, inclusive of minimizing the impact of their stress. It demonstrates that having a body of knowledge is not the same as knowing how to apply that knowledge,
2. conclude our focus on organizational efforts to respond to and enhance employee well-being, inclusive of managing the stress they bring into the workplace as well as the stress of the work they do,
3. look specifically at supervisory practices and strategies for minimizing STS among staff, which is a responsibility often assigned to supervisors. Keep in mind that supervisors are also vulnerable to STS and their need for the same care given employees is also critical.

Let's get started.

Non-informed Yet Supportive

I have conducted training for a number of organizations that were not formally identified as trauma-informed yet supported the six guiding principles of trauma-informed care (SAMSHA News, 2014) (*Answer to Pre-session Question #2*). These include:

- *safety* of clients and staff physically and psychologically,
- *trustworthiness and transparency* with staff, clients, families and community,
- *peer support* and mutuality recognizing that healing happens through relationships,
- *collaboration and mutuality* across the agency recognizing that everyone plays a role in a trauma-informed approach,
- *empowerment, voice and choice* again across staff, clients and families, recognizing that each individual's situation is unique and all staff need to be encouraged to contribute to decision making, and
- *being sensitive to cultural norms and practices, historical trauma and gender issues.*

From an organizational standpoint, these principles need to be supported by the policies, procedures and practices of organizations; beliefs, values and mission will also reflect and support the same principles. The key here is to be truly trauma-informed organizations and staff must pursue these principles through a trauma-informed lens. For example, if you are a supervisor attempting to support the trauma-informed principle of safety with supervisees, you should be able to answer the following questions (*Answer to Pre-session Question #3*):

- As a trauma-informed supervisor, how do I present myself as someone who is safe?
- What is it that my supervisees need in order to feel safe about the supervisory process?
- What 10 processes help make supervision safe and effective?

These are questions that we will answer in the second part of this session. I just wanted to point out that we might be informed that safety is a trauma-informed principle, yet not really understand how we translate that understanding into the way we practice our specific role in the organization.

Becoming a Trauma-informed Organization

Obviously TSOs are encouraged to become trauma-informed to help ensure clients are receiving trauma-specific care and, in our case that organizations are actively supporting the well-being of their staff. Stated specifically, "A program, organization, or system that is trauma-informed realizes the widespread impact of trauma and understands potential paths for recovery; recognizes the signs and symptoms of trauma in clients, families, staff, and others involved with the system; and respond by fully integrating knowledge about trauma into policies, procedures, and practices, and seeks to actively resist re-traumatization" (SAMSHA, 2014, p. 9).

There are numerous toolkits and resources available for agencies that wish to become trauma-informed. For example, Trauma-Informed Organizations TIP 57 from SAMHSA's Treatment Improvement Protocol (TIP) Series, No. 57 (2014) is available online. It is an excellent resource. Besides extensive information about trauma, understanding its impact, screening and assessment, clinical issues and trauma-specific services, it covers all aspects of building a trauma-informed organization and workforce.

Reality: *The real question that needs to be pursued when organizations say they are trauma-informed is "How well informed?" (Answer to Pre-session Question #1.)*

A while back I conducted trauma training for a group of 50 clinical professionals from the same organization; they indicated they were trauma-informed. I presented this group with 10 book titles by leading authors in the field of trauma (Bessel van der Kolk, Bruce Perry, Peter Levine, Babette Rothchild, Daniel Siegel, Cathy Malchiodi, Eliana Gil, Judith Herman, Pat Ogden, Charles Figley). I asked which of these books they had read. Only three staff had read two or more of these authors. From my perspective this group was not trauma-informed.

Systematic Exposure

Completing a trauma-informed organizational assessment and using that information to rewrite policies and practices is an effort that needs to be applauded; however, the hard work is translating that information into practices that support an informed approach to care. It is important to also appreciate that three or four days of presentations on trauma do not make one trauma-informed, perhaps trauma aware but not trauma-informed or trauma-sensitive. Actually, research on the effectiveness of single-session didactic and/or skill-building workshops demonstrates that immediate gains in counselor knowledge and skills diminish quickly after the training event (Martino, Canning-Ball, Carrol, & Rounsaville, 2011).

Reality: *Becoming trauma-informed has to be a systematic process of repeated exposure to the abundance of information that is available through books, training, webinars, online courses and certification programs; not simply hearing about it but also reading about it, having discussions about it and applying that knowledge to everyday interactions with those we are caring for, in order to discover what works best, what matters most to them and also what we feel comfortable providing.*

This effort to consume all we can learn about trauma and best practices and then to practice what we are learning, evaluating the outcomes of our efforts and making necessary adjustments to improve outcomes, will help us feel more confident about what we do and certainly much less stressed about what we do. This kind of systematic approach strengthens our resilience to stress; it is both preventative and restorative. Most importantly, those we serve will better benefit from our growing range of expertise and knowledge. Staff who feel that they are increasing competency in job skills, especially if they are employing evidence-based practices, also generally experience less STS (Craig & Sprang, 2010).

Reality: (*Pre-session Answer to Question #5*) *Being good at what I do and feeling good about what I do are not only ingredients of resilience but also compassion satisfaction; both enhance resilience, performance, compassion satisfaction and retention.*

Trauma-informed Care: Beyond Being Informed

What then constitutes trauma-informed care? Trauma-informed care refers to the practices provided, as well one's approach to the intervention and/or interaction with clients. Recently I met with another group of professionals who, compared to others, did have a good knowledge base about trauma; however, when I asked the clinical staff if they could describe how they integrate self-regulation into their intervention sessions, other than recommending clients take yoga or try meditation and use breathing techniques, they could not. All clinical staff had been trained in Trauma Focused-Cognitive Behavioral Therapy (TF-CBT). No one was trained in treatments like Eye Movement Desensitization and Reprocessing (EMDR), Somatic Experiencing, Narrative Exposure Therapy or Neuro-counseling. There were no certified art therapist and only one licensed play therapist; both interventions play a critical role in the processing of trauma as do other expressive therapies (Malchiodi, 2011; Foa, Keane, Friedman, & Cohen, 2008; Gil, 2006). As no one intervention fits every individual, how can one say they deliver trauma-informed care when clients do not have a choice and clinicians are not collectively trained in various techniques so they too have choices to help clients when one method is not working? *From my perspective this staff was not engaging the trauma-informed care principle of choice nor sensitive to the unique needs of trauma victims.*

Let me say right now what I mean by trauma-sensitive and then move forward with our discussion. Call it a mini-debriefing of my frustration at times of the failure to translate trauma information into practice.

Trauma-informed and Trauma Sensitive

Many of your peers define trauma-sensitive as being attuned to the individual needs of clients but rarely add any further specifics. This is correct in part. Although there is no formal definition of what constitutes being trauma-sensitive, I made the distinction between trauma-informed and trauma-sensitive several years ago after repeatedly hearing from administrators and professionals that they were trauma-informed. However, when I asked a number of very specific questions of staff to evaluate their knowledge and skill level, inclusive of those I just presented you, I found that practice knowledge was lacking. The term "sensitive" says more to me than the term "informed."

The definition of sensitive is "quick to detect or respond to slight changes, signals, or influences and having or displaying a quick and delicate appreciation of others' feelings" (Oxford Dictionary, 2018). I define trauma-informed as being aware of the many aspects of trauma. I define trauma-sensitive (*Pre-session Answer to Question #4*) as being engaged in supporting the principles a trauma-informed approach and using those informed practices based on a comprehensive trauma assessment that helps us direct efforts at sensitively addressing the neuro-biological needs of victims, being alert to the subjective ways they are experiencing themselves, their environment and the people in the environments they are navigating every day, and being sensitive to the fact that behaviors of victims are fear driven and an effort to protect themselves from perceived and/or real threat and further pain.

All trauma-sensitive approaches to intervention need to be framed in safety and choice, with an understanding that no one intervention fits every individual, that trauma is a mind-body experience and as much attention needs to be paid to the physiological/neurological aspects of trauma as is paid to the psychological impact. Approaches also need to understand that non-cognitive, sensory/expressive based approaches are as important as cognitive approaches and that intervention is approached developmentally and provided through a culturally sensitive lens. *Trauma-informed care is not necessarily sensitive care when these elements are missing.*

Debriefing: A Case in Point

Note: Staff working for organizations serving trauma victims and/or responding to trauma situations are often required to detail what they were exposed to and how they responded as a way to insure their responses meet legal responsibilities organizations are required to fulfill to maintain licensing and funding. This is understandable as the first responsibility is to the safety of those they serve. However, many organizations continue to use Critical Incident Stress Debriefing (CISD) processes: a talking process with staff following critical situations. Research documents that this process can and has placed participants at risk for STS and a prolonged recovery from their reactions to the traumatic situation they experienced.

CISD was not voluntary and assumed that everyone exposed needed the same treatment. It saw normal distress as pathological. Furthermore, victims were debriefed within three days following exposure, which for many was not time enough to allow for the regulation of nervous system arousal to all the stimuli it experienced. It was also a process that encouraged victims to share the details of what happened causing re-exposure to that trauma. It was not a trauma-sensitive approach as it ignored issues of safety, choice, arousal and resilience science documenting that many do better not talking about what happened. The fact is neither the National Institute for Mental Health (NIMH) or the World Health Organization (WHO), which oversees the International Classification of Diseases (ICD), supports this process (Bledsoe, 2003). Psychological First Aid (PFA) is now the recommended approach (NCTSN, 2018a). This is just one example of what I mean when I say that organizations responding to trauma victims must not only be trauma-informed, they also need to be trauma-sensitive in their practices. Okay. Thanks for giving me that moment. Let's move on to organizations who themselves are traumatized.

When TSOs Are Traumatized

There are trauma-serving organizations that are themselves traumatized. This is often reflected by authoritative, inflexible, punitive leadership practices, driven by crises, being conflict avoidant, having an unclear mission, giving little attention to values, and having an emotionally and/or physically unsafe environment. The work of Sandra Bloom (2006) and colleagues, who developed The Sanctuary Model, define sanctuary as a place where shared knowledge, values, language and practices are in place. The model has provided many traumatized organizations a blueprint for change. It's about developing or fostering a culture of communication, engagement and collaboration. Organizations who have initiated the processes of the model realized decreases in STS/BO, reduced violence and restraint use among clients and fewer workman comp issues. However, there are implementation issues to overcome for any organization attempting to build a trauma-informed environment.

Issues to Overcome

In an excellent report, Dubay, Burton, and Epstein (2018) point to outcome efforts by six organizations that initiated The Sanctuary Model. All found that it was a long-term investment, not all staff felt empowered by the process and leadership "buy in" was problematic. *This pretty much sums up the challenges any effort at organizational change encounters*. I could not help but think of Dr. Brown's TED Talk on vulnerability as I was reading this report. *Vulnerability*, which is the foundation for change, is too much of a risk for some.

Their Approaches to Self-care

What I did find interesting in this report were their approaches to employee self-care. Across the six programs, meditation, minute meditations before staff meetings, use of a quiet room, yoga, encouraging staff to take lunch breaks, access to a relaxation hot line with pre-recorded deep breathing exercises, peer-to-peer support and encouragement to practice self-care outside of the workplace were the primary efforts to help staff with self-care. Once again there was no mention or focus of efforts addressing the six domains of well-being we've addressed in the previous session. I think this further illustrates that what constitutes self-care in TSOs as it relates to reducing and/or effectively managing stress inclusive of STS remains more of a limited, if not fixed mindset rather than the growth-oriented mindset of focusing on the overall well-being of employees.

After reading this report my immediate thought was, *So, even if I am in agreement with the organizations efforts to change to being trauma-informed, how are you assisting me with the ongoing life stressors in my life that also impact my performance and the service I provide clients?*

TSO's Self-care Ethical Responsibility: 2014 SAMSHA Self-care Guidelines

The ethical responsibility of organizations toward the care of staff in trauma-informed organizations is specifically stated in SAMSHA (2014) guidelines. I will summarize this for you. The following information is adapted from the SAMSHA document. *Let me state clearly that this document provides rich and specific information regarding self-care. For many TSOs and those who indicate they are trauma-informed, this remains an excellent document to use as a checklist to evaluate the comprehensiveness of current practices. As you review it, I think you will find areas in your organization needing some improvement.*

Self-care

This document indicates that it is important to help staff develop a comprehensive personal and professional self-care plan to prevent and/or resolve secondary stress. At the same time, it makes it very clear that counselors are responsible for being aware of their own STS identification and management, countertransference reactions and seeking help as needed. *The problem with this is that often those with STS and other stress reactions are often the last to identify, acknowledge and act on these reactions without being made aware of them via education, assessment and supervision.*

It does mention one study showing that a workplace mindfulness group helped to reduce stress and likely encouraged workers to practice mindfulness at work (McGarrigle & Walsh, 2011). As an aside, meditation is also a form of stress regulation demonstrating great gains in schools. "Four schools in the San Francisco School District experiencing high levels of violence, poor attendance and academic performance initiated two fifteen-minute periods per day for students to be guided in mindful meditation. Introducing calm and reflection into the school day had amazing results. There was a 75% reduction in suspensions and a 40-point improvement on API scoring the first year" (Steele, 2017, p. 17). *It is interesting to note that the less frequent use of meditation/mindfulness in the analysis of those six agencies previously mentioned did not see the same results.* Remember our discussion on rewiring our brain? Repetition/frequency is critical for successful rewiring.

This TIC document also mentions developing a daily work schedule that included rest breaks, exercise and connection with workers, which are excellent recommendations and ones we'll review more extensively when addressing self-care. It does mention self-care to be inclusive of physical, psychological (cognitive and mental), emotional (includes relational) and spiritual factors. It does not stress financial or career development. It does provide a helpful worksheet comprised of questions to help employees develop their self-care plans in the areas identified. However, other than mentioning meditation and exercise at the workplace, this document does little to emphasize that organizations take responsibility for *providing onsite support in the six domains* we've discussed. Over all it addresses many of the critical areas of self-care yet is less specific about the importance of well-being as it relates to remaining resilient, not only in the face of the unavoidable stress of caring for trauma victims but the stress induced by both work and life conditions.

Question: Hearing about some of the issues, factors and practices associated with a trauma-informed organization how do rate your organization? Not informed____, Somewhat informed____, Informed with limited sensitivity____, informed and trauma sensitive____. (Please also post your answer under the post-session questions.)

Transformational Leadership

When it comes to successfully developing the well-being of staff in TSOs, leaders need to practice the engaging characteristics of transformational leadership (Caprino, 2018; Wikipedia, 2018) (*Pre-session Answer to Question #6*) – walk the talk (idealized influence), inspire and motivate, provide personal attention (individualized consideration) and intellectual stimulation (how well-being efforts are beneficial). Here are a few examples.

Question: *Has the leader, CEO of your organization had multiple conversations with you and peers about the importance of your well-being and talked about what he/she has found beneficial in helping with not only the stress of leading but remaining resilient in the midst of ever-changing demands and challenges of sustaining the organizations well-being?* Most answer "no" to this question.

Question: *Has your organization presented you with a self-care resource/toolkit that provides questions across the six domains we've identified to help you define the goals and the actions needed to realize the goals you set in each domain outside the workplace as well as in the workplace?*

You are not alone if your answer is "no." If the answer is "yes" can you answer "yes" to this next question?

Question: *Has your supervisor/manager consistently addressed your workplace goals and self-care efforts in these domains in the supervisory process-checking progress, identifying roadblocks, problem solving with you, identifying resources needed and possible alternative approaches?*

Often those who answer "yes" to the previous question, answer "no" to this second question reflecting the mindset that self-care is considered more of an individual responsibility versus an organizational responsibility. Being trauma-informed means that leadership is actively engaged in your being as trauma-informed as possible in order to bring the best of care to those you serve. It also means, or should mean, they outwardly demonstrate their care for your well-being, inclusive of your professional growth.

Question: *If you were a trauma-informed transformational leader of a TSO, wouldn't you, from a well-being, as well as a trauma-informed perspective, want your entire staff to read several highly endorsed books about trauma that go more in depth than a one- or two-day training?*

Three good reads are, and there are many others, Bessel van der Kolk's (2015) *The Body Keeps the Score: Brain, Mind, and Body in the Healing of Trauma*, Perry and Szalavitz's (2006) *The Boy Who Was Raised as a Dog: And Other Stories*, and Babette Rothchild's (2006) *Helping the Helper*. Keep in mind that there are going to be a number of employees in any TSO who are already experiencing STS as a result of what they do and other staff are likely to have had their own personal trauma experience. Reading these three books alone would be personally helpful to readers. Yes, for some any one of these could be a tough read yet they would at least finish with a deeper appreciation of the work their organization does as well as be more sensitive to the difficulties and challenges clients bring to the organization. This type of staff engagement benefits everyone.

Different Learning Styles

Allow me to digress for a minute and say a bit more about the power of books. These examples speak to organization being sensitive to the different learning styles of their staff; some learn most effectively by listening, some through visual presentations, some through hands on work (kinesthetic) and others by reading (Nakano, 2014; Steele, 2017). *Supervisors need to keep this mind as well. The more they can engage supervisees in these four learning styles the more effective the outcomes.*

Let me give you several examples related to the power of reading.

In response to a request to write a forward for the book I had written about helping traumatized children (Steele & Malchiodi, 2012), my colleague, Lenny Echterling, professor of psychology at James Madison University, wrote about one of his remarkable experiences with trauma survivors. He was overseas co-leading an intensive seven-day training for adult survivors of land mind explosions that were killing and maiming so many in Iraq, Lebanon, Jordan and other areas. The training was designed to promote resilience among these survivors and prepare them to do the same to help their fellow victims back home. Participants were asked to introduce themselves. One participant's introduction immediately revealed both his character and resilience. After identifying himself, he said,

"I am not a victim of a landmine. The landmine is a victim of me. I survived, the landmine did not."

What a great story, simple yet profound, a blueprint for responding to the personal challenges we face in our lives. This story connects us to the spirit and the courage of a man we will never meet, yet feel as if there is little distance between us, as if we are standing right next to him.

Reality: *Books can bring us much closer to the experience of trauma and ways others survive and thrive than do many presentations.*

There is no better place to discover what others have discovered, in their efforts to overcome the worst of challenges they experienced, than in the stories they share with us about those experiences. Presenting employees with books that would enhance their responses to victims is one of those well-being, *dare-to-lead* practices that would demonstrate leadership's care for and efforts to connect with *staff, especially when following up with an open discussion about the many examples and information provided in each book and what employees found to be the most helpful.*

Managers'/Supervisors' Involvement

It demands repeating: "A company's executive leaders can believe in the importance of good health as it relates to performance on and off the job, but if the front-line managers don't share this belief or, if the work environment isn't supportive of healthy behaviors, then companies will fail to see the results and long-term benefits" (Miller, 2015). Because managers/supervisors play a central role in employees' professional and overall lives, their dedication to employee well-being initiatives is pivotal for success (Wood & Nelson, 2017). For TSOs this means that the organization provides education about STS and its symptoms, normalizes STS as an unavoidable part of the work they do and provides the necessary on and off-site resources to help staff manage and/or recover from STS.

We often find today that supervisors are given the primary responsibility for managing the STS of employees. They certainly play a key role. However, if the managers, the supervisors of the supervisors, and the leader of all staff are not also actively involved in *attending to, caring for and connecting with staff* around the alleviation of stress, inclusive of supervisor STS, then efforts at supporting staff well-being and developing a culture of well-being are significantly diminished. Returning to the initial Prudential story, leadership simply stated, "If we don't include the manager and team as participants, it's less likely that employees will feel supported and flourish."

You Are Encouraged

I encourage all trauma-serving organizations to pursue and engage the process of becoming trauma-informed. The National Center for Trauma-Informed Care provides excellent resources and trainers. If already trauma-informed, then I would hope leadership is transformational, actively connecting with employees and involved in supporting (a) ongoing learning related to trauma practices,

(b) conducting periodic assessments throughout the year, (c) taking corrective actions as needed and (d) engaged in promoting and sustaining the well-being of all staff (not just responding to STS).

I've addressed what I have frequently found with organizations and the areas that need closer attention and evaluation in order to answer the question, "How well informed?" Hopefully, I've pointed out the crucial role leadership plays in supporting the well-being of staff and the organization and that being trauma-informed and sensitive has to be an ongoing systematic process of learning, evaluating and adjusting.

The good news is there is an abundance of excellent resources to help accomplish this. When this effort is also accompanied by efforts to provide on-site well-being resources and enhance engagement at all levels, performance, work quality, stress reduction, professional growth and retention will all improve. And when these organizational efforts are then combined with supervisory efforts to assist staff specifically with the stress of the work they do, the environment, the culture will become one where all can flourish. It is truly worth the effort.

Now, given that supervision is so critical to all these efforts, we need to detail critical factors and competencies related to trauma-informed, trauma-sensitive supervision.

Supervision: Mitigating the Effects of STS, Core Competencies

Assisting employees who experience STS dictates that supervisors meet core competencies for assisting with STS. The Secondary Traumatic Stress Core Competencies in Trauma-Informed Supervision (NCTSN, 2018b) (also found in the Appendix) lists nine core supervisory competency areas. Under each competency is an operational definition that details what a trauma-informed supervisor ought to be knowledgeable about and able to accomplish. This is designed as an evaluation tool, a very good one at that. In organizations serving and/or responding to trauma victims and/or situations, all supervisors have an ethical responsibility to practice and be efficient in these competencies. Given the prevalence of STS and the ethical responsibility regarding self-care, organizations also have the responsibility to provide the resources and training for its supervisors to establish competency across all nine core competency areas.

Activity

If you are a supervisor, use the NCTSN Supervisor Core Competency tool in the Appendix (Answer to Pre-session Activity #10) to move through each core competency and check those activities you practice. Also highlight those areas that you feel you need to know more about and/or receive more training to become efficient in that process and, then pursue what is needed to improve your competency in those areas. (Note: If you are a supervisee, you can use the Competency Checklist to evaluate the level of STS competency of your supervisor. Instructions are provided in the Appendix copy.)

If, from all the recommendations provided, this were the only recommendation you accepted, your efforts to help reduce the impact of STS on employees would realize a good deal of success.

Reality: *This said, being competent does not necessarily translate into an effective supervisory relationship.*

What Matters Most

Reality: *Effective supervision does involve knowledge and competency; however, ultimately the effectiveness of the relationship and what the supervisor is hoping to accomplish is based on how the supervisee experiences that relationship.*

From a trauma-informed perspective, supervision must first of all be experienced as safe. Why is this? Beginning a new supervisory relationship creates anxiety for the supervisee. In the *Pre-session Activity #7* you were asked to list concerns you might have with being assigned a supervisor. Following are the concerns others have identified.

Supervisee's Initial Mindset: What We Really Think About Our New Supervisor

I've combined the concerns expressed by many of your peers to reflect the mindset that many have entering into a relationship with their new supervisor or manager. How do these compare with what you listed? (*This is the answer to Pre-session Question #7.*)

"You are assigned to me as my supervisor. Even though I may have had a good supervisory relationship in the past, I still have no choice in this, so yes that makes me a bit anxious. You'll be watching me, evaluating my performance, so yes, I'm definitely a bit nervous about how you will react, what you are going to think about me and about my work. Even though I've already heard some good things about you, there may be something about me that hits you the wrong way, so yes, I'll be tentative. There may be something about the way you present yourself, your demeanor, your tone of voice that reminds me of someone in my past that made my life difficult or even hurt me, so yes, I'm anxious and may be somewhat protective in my responses to you initially. Maybe my idea of supervision is not the way you think about supervision, so not knowing that makes me concerned. What if I really need this job and it turns out I have a hard time with you, then what, so yes that makes me anxious. What kind of relationship is this going to be; will it be helpful, encouraging, a really good learning experience or just the opposite? I know, because my colleagues have experienced it, that even if I am quite competent, a lousy supervisor can make life very stressful, so yes I am going to be cautious."

Why This Anxiety?

As supervisees we enter into the supervisory process vulnerable because of any one of the unknowns cited above. Harvey (2015) reports that 60% of supervisees do not communicate personal issues with their supervisor and that 40%–60% do not disclose clinical (intervention) mistakes and that 40% distort clinical information about clients to supervisors. Furthermore 90% of supervisees do not disclose negative reactions to their supervisor. These responses are fear based. Let's face it: there is a power imbalance in the supervisory relationship. Supervisees enter into the supervisory relationship with anxieties that must be addressed immediately to help alleviate at least some of their fears.

Reality: *To reduce their anxiety and start the process of developing this relationship into an effective, collaborative, supportive and developmentally enriching one, the supervisee must first be made to feel safe with the relationship and the process by addressing some of the unknowns.*

This takes us back to the questions I raised earlier in the session.

- As a trauma-informed supervisor, how do I present myself as someone who is safe?
- What 10 processes help to make supervision safe and effective?

Keep in mind that "safety" is a primary principle of trauma-informed care related to staff as well as clients.

Safety: Structuring the Process

Imagine being in a surgical waiting room while a loved one is going through a difficult surgery, what do you need to reduce your anxiety? Information. You need to hear from the doctor that the surgery was successful and that your loved one is doing well. Imagine meeting your supervisor for the first time, a person that has been assigned to you because you have no choice over who supervises you. What do you need to calm some of your concerns? You'll want information in a structured format that addresses some of those concerns.

Reality: *Information presented in a timely, structured format reduces anxiety.*

How then do supervisors need to introduce themselves, their responsibilities and the supervisory process in a way that helps alleviate some of the fear, anxiety and concerns supervisees bring into their supervisory session? This is accomplished by structuring the first meeting to address supervisee anxiety about the relationship and the process.

Response to Pre-session Task #8

Pre-session Task #8 could be answered as a supervisor or as a supervisee. So as a supervisor how did you describe what you would say to your supervisee? If you are about to enter into a supervisory relationship as a supervisee, what did you indicate you would need to hear as a supervisee in your first session to answer your questions and address some of the anxieties you might have with this mandatory relationship? Compare what I present with what you wrote down.

The following is what trauma-informed supervisors ought to acknowledge in order to initiate an alliance that begins with a focus on the supervisory relationship being a safe one. It is also a process that communicates that you, the supervisor, are in "sync" with the concerns of the supervisee. When a supervisee experiences that you know some of what they are experiencing and thinking, they begin to feel safe enough to become more emotionally present and vulnerable. For supervisors, this example becomes a template for positioning yourself as someone who is sensitive to the needs and fears of supervisees. It also structures the relationship in a way that will make it safer for supervisees to later become more comfortable in engaging in self-reflection especially in the area of STS and self-care.

If you are a supervisee, you can check off what you indicated you would want to hear from your supervisor with what is addressed in this example. This provides you with a checklist to use to evaluate how well informed and sensitive your supervisor is to your needs.

Once you have completed reading these structuring statements, I'll ask you to take a minute to focus on your emotional response and then your thoughts about what you read. *I suggest reading this out load as hearing it combined with seeing it on paper will have a different impact on you than simply reading it silently.*

Structuring Statement

After initial greeting, welcoming to the organization, engaging in some small talk, for example, where they went to school, what interests them about working in this field, or what previous experiences they may have had, inform the supervisee that you want to take a few minutes to cover several important issues about the supervisory process and then begin:

There are several aspects about supervision I want to address that hopefully answer some of your questions and concerns. Please stop me at any time if you have questions or would like some clarification. In this first session I want to provide you with information about how I approach supervision.

I've written my comments down for you so you can take them with you. I also wrote them down for myself as there are a number of very important things to mention, so I want to be sure I do not miss anything. First of all, you have no choice as to my being your supervisor. It's not the best way to start a relationship and I'm sure it has you wandering how it will work out, how we will work out; if it will be a helpful experience, a positive and productive one that gives you the support you'll need, especially when confronted with challenging situations with clients, your peers or the demands of the job. Those are my concerns as well. My priority is to help you do your best and certainly to do what I can to make this a positive learning experience.

Supervisor Responsibilities and Roles

Teacher/Educator

I have three primary responsibilities as your supervisor. One is as a teacher/educator. There will be a lot of procedures to learn especially in these first few months. You'll need my support. There will likely be a few areas we need to problem solve together as well. If there are issues for which I do not have the answers, I will let you know and then go to my supporters for possible solutions.

Learning all you can about how trauma impacts individuals, our clients, is also critical to your effectiveness in helping them. This will take time but I certainly will help you with this. Now when it comes to working with traumatized clients and/or responding to trauma situations, it will be a learning process and at times very stressful. In fact, in our first few sessions, I want to make sure you are aware of the stressors you will face and the symptoms you might experience such as secondary stress. These stressors and symptoms are for the most part very normal responses to the work we do. In many cases they are unavoidable yet can still become problematic if we don't work together to develop ways to manage that stress. In this regard your self-care is very important to your overall well-being, as well as to the quality of your interactions with those you are trying to help; self-care is an area we'll spend time developing and reviewing as well.

As a teacher, I also believe that it is important to make this a somewhat predictable process so at the beginning of every session, I will be asking you what positive experiences you've enjoyed. At the end of the session I'll ask you of all that we covered, talked about, read or viewed, as I do use video segments, what stood out the most for you and how that might change or reinforce the way you are interacting or approaching different issues. And, before we end the session, we will agree on what we will pursue in the next session. In between will process what you want to focus on and what we might need to work on, learn about or think about.

Administrative Role

I also have an administrative responsibility to help you complete mandatory tasks that neither of us have a choice about, such as record keeping, paper work, certain behaviors related to policies and procedures. We are both accountable, you to me and the organization and I to my manager and the organization. Some requirements simply are not negotiable. However, should there be problems, it is my responsibility to bring your attention to the problem and then together agree on ways we can fix and/or resolve the issue. I approach problems as an opportunity to learn, to develop new coping skills, to strengthen resilience. Hopefully you approach them in the same way. In this regard, if a problem has occurred or a conflict has emerged, and they will, just please let me know immediately so we can work at a resolving them before they get out of hand. This will make it easier on both of us.

Supervisory Support

Finally, I have the responsibility to provide or direct you to whatever support you may need to do the work you will be doing as effectively as possible. If there are issues, I cannot help you with, I will do my best to connect you to those who can. If there are resources you feel will be helpful to you and the work you're doing, I will do my best to make those accessible. If there are situations outside the work environment that are hindering your effectiveness or your performance, I will do what I can to connect you with resources in those areas as well, because your well-being directly correlates with the quality of your work. This is important because we have an ethical responsibility to provide our clients with the best possible service. Hopefully you will feel comfortable enough to let me know if you are experiencing outside stress so I can help connect you with outside resources.

Supervisee Responsibility

Obviously, trusting this relationship will take a little time. You'll need to get a feel for what I think, how I feel about and respond to different issues. That's okay. However, you also have some responsibilities. You need to let me know when you don't understand something, so hopefully I can find a different way to explain it. If what I am asking you to do or talk about makes you uncomfortable, please let me know. There are numbers of ways to approach issues, and I will need your feed-back to know that I am not creating more stress or conflict for you. If it is, it is my responsibility to help you find ways to manage that stress and for us to resolve the conflict as best we can. Hopefully you'll feel comfortable to discuss any conflicts you might experience so we can work together to arrive at a solution that works best for you. Any questions so far?

Availability

Finally, I'm not going to micro-manage you; that's not how you learn. It's not how I supervise. You need some space to explore different ways to be as effective as you can. At the same time, if you want more direction, just ask. In this regard, especially in your first few months, I will respond as quickly and as often as needed to your questions, concerns and efforts to adjust to the various aspects of your job. If I don't get back to you right away, I am probably dealing with a crisis situation of some kind. I'll try to send a quick text to you if I am. When you do try to contact me, please just leave a voicemail or text me and briefly describe the issue and whether it is an emergency. If it is an emergency and I can't get back to you, I'll get you connected to one of my peers as we work as a team.

Summary

I know I've given you plenty to think about but I'm curious about a few things.

   Note: There is no need to say much in response to their answers to these first two questions. In response to the final question, simply acknowledge their concern and that you are confident that you can help them with that concern. Follow this with the final comments below.

1.   I'm am kind of curious as to what your first impressions are with your overall experience so far this week?
2.   What's been the most positive experience for you?
3.   Every one responds a little different to this question. I'm curious as to what makes you the most anxious about the job?

Okay. Let's set up a time for our next visit. I'll let you decide what you want to cover but we'll also begin to identify short-term goals for now so your clear about what is expected of you. Please contact me before then if you need to. It doesn't have to be an emergency; it can be a question about record keeping, a procedure or a policy. It doesn't matter.

Activity: Pause for a minute and then write down your emotional reaction to what you just read and only after identify your thoughts.

In workshops, I'll ask participants to think for a minute about the concerns they have about entering into a relationship with a new supervisor/manager. I'll then ask them to sit quietly while I read the above structuring statement. The four primary reactions participants have to this introduction are (a) "It seemed a bit long and yet I could feel my body just calm down and relax; it made me comfortable with you." (b) "I appreciated the amount of time spent on what you felt was most important about the process, so much so you wrote those out for yourself as well. It let me know you cared about making this relationship a helpful one." (c) "It really touched on the concerns I've had (as a supervisee). It made me feel you were able to tap into my concerns, which made me feel like you were really supportive and would be helpful."

Almost everyone cites one specific point that either put them at ease or give them a sense that this was going to be a positive experience. Examples include, "I liked the way you describe how each session would start and end . . . what you said about how you approach accountability . . . that you would not be micro managing . . . the way you described your role . . . the fact that it would take time to trust you."

In essence this process helps to establish you as someone who is safe.

Note: Use your own words. It is important to use your own words in structuring the supervisory process. It's important to express or identify the concerns you can imagine a supervise is bringing with them to the supervisory process, to clearly define your roles and responsibilities as well as the responsibilities of the supervisee, to acknowledge and normalize the stress of the work they will be doing and the importance of self-care. It's important initially to be curious as to how they are experiencing the work environment, what has been positive and what might be causing some anxiety, and to structure your availability, how you can be reached and what you need to know when they are trying to reach you.

Making Supervisory Interactions Safe and Effective

(*Answer to Pre-session Activity #9*) In many ways, establishing interactions between supervisee and supervisor as safe and effective is no different than the elements that help make interventions with traumatized individuals as safe and effective as possible. These are my recommendations.

1. *Always provide choice.* Supervisees must have the choice to say "yes" or "no" to what you are asking them to talk about or do, such as self-reflect. There may be some days when self-reflection creates too much anxiety to be helpful. Even in addressing the tasks and behaviors that are not negotiable, there will be choices available as to how they will attempt to correct the problem in the designated time frame. Choice gives us a sense of empowerment, which supports a sense of safety.

2. *Be curious rather than analytical or judgmental.* Rather than asking, "Why did you do this?" ask, "What happened?' Curiosity is actually the cornerstone of empathy (Hughes, 2009). Empathetic

people have an insatiable curiosity as to how others are experiencing their world. Being curious says, "You matter, what you are experiencing matters to me." Curiosity is also essential for successful self-reflection. Self-reflection is a core competency and matters greatly when attempting to help others with the stress they are experiencing.

3. *Ask open-ended questions.* Olafson and Kenniston (2008) indicated that open-ended questions are far more productive and allow even the most reluctant to respond more fully to questions (p. 77). Instead of asking, "How did that session with that difficult client go?" ask instead questions like, "What was the best part of that session, what was the worst part, what stands out the most about . . . ?" Open-ended questions facilitate curiosity.

4. *Teach and engage supervisees in self-regulation practices* especially when addressing or confronting difficult challenges with trauma clients and/or situations. This also is a core competency requirement related to STS and applies to managing all forms of stress. It is also important to stress that this goes beyond meditation, exercising, etc. It's about teaching how to resource the body while experiencing stressful emotional and physiological reactions when responding to and/or interacting with clients or situations triggering intense reactions.

5. *Structure sessions so they are predictable.* Begin with a focus on positive aspects; end in a positive way by reiterating what was learned, reframing their experience as a resource, reflecting on overall progress and/or the supervisee's strengths. Always identify what the focus of the next session will be so supervisees have the opportunity to prepare. Be predictable in this regard as predictability reinforces a sense of safety and supports regulation.

6. *Utilize multidimensional learning styles.* Although little is written about this from a supervisory perspective, supervision is a learning experience and as such supervisors need to engage multiple learning styles. This will help improve overall effectiveness of interactions and enhance the supervisee's development. Multidimensional approaches that include auditory, kinesthetic and visual approaches significantly enhance the learning experience. *Note*: Research does not show that learning improves by teaching to the individual's specific learning style; it improves when multiple learning styles are used (Bozarth, 2018).

7. *Initiate informal brief connections.* Luest (2018) documents that having a connection to another strengthens our resilience. Cheever and Hardin (1999) also found that those who have a connection with another or others did better following exposure to trauma than those who did not have a significant connection to at least one other person. Supervisors have the ability to enhance the effectiveness of their supervisory relationship and the resilience of their supervisees by briefly connecting with them outside of the formal supervisory session. There are a number of ways to accomplish this.

- *A brief text:* "Just thinking about you. If you have any questions just let me know."
- *An email* with a brief note and an attached article. "Saw this and thought you might be interested."
- *Making "purposeful rounds."* By this I mean taking a minute to make a face-to-face contact with the intent of addressing one of the four universal needs I addressed earlier (belonging, mastery, independence and generosity). When employees feel valued, they do better than those who do not.
- *Saying you matter, matters.* Once you identify their interests, what they do for leisure, etc., it is so easy to connect. For example, "Did you watch that game last night? "Have you read . . . latest novel; you'd like it." "I came across this app and thought you might want to grab it." These are very simple ways to say to the supervisee "You matter." As I said earlier, *those who*

report feeling valued by their employer are significantly more likely to be motivated to do their very best (93% vs. 33%) (APA, 2012).

- *Modeling self-care.* Working with supervisees to develop self-care plans that include practices during the workday is an ethical responsibility as is evaluating those efforts on a regular basis. It is equally important that supervisors model self-care practices in the work place. For example, how you protect and use your lunch hour says a lot to others about your commitment to self-care. It's hard to take any one serious who is not engaging in what they are presenting as necessary: more about this in our session on self-care.

8. *Remain accountable.* Establish clear measurable benchmarks to evaluate supervisee progress. Review these regularly to track progress and/or refocus efforts. Without accountability there is no progress or responsibility. This is an area of weakness for some supervisors who have a difficult time moving from their role as "supporter" to that of "administrator." Unfortunately, failure to hold supervisees accountable and confront conflicts and problems when they first emerge condones that behavior; it will only get worse. Even more critical is that others will perceive this avoidance as unfair and that if that employee's behavior has no consequence then there is no reason for others to meet requirements. It's contagious and often the reason good employees leave.

   Note: More organizations are now moving away from annual and quarterly reviews. The research clearly shows these are not helpful (Dickson, 2018 [an excellent article filled with research I encourage leaders and supervisors read]). They focus on past behaviors rather than current behaviors so small problems often become bigger problems. The solution many are turning to with great success is having regular conversations about current performance referred to as "continuous performance management" (Hearn, 2018). This means having regular conversations even daily until issues are resolved when necessary, which supports what was just said about the importance of brief connections. It's really about staying focused on those daily activities and interactions that present an opportunity for a "teachable moment" (Chandler, 2016). We also know that this approach enhances engagement. A strong level of engagement enhances performance and retention (Kirkland, 2018) so it is a win/win for all.

9. *Read and view.* No single book or document can cover all the issues around supervision. No one person in a sense is an expert. Reading expands your knowledge, keeps you current with practices and evidence-based research. As part of your professional development, take one day to spend just 15–30 minutes to surf the Internet. One search can yield multiple topics to pursue learning more about. Knowledge keeps us current, interesting and viable. It allows us to pass on the benefits of what we learn to others. Having an article every now and then to discuss in the supervisory process is another way to connect to supervisees as well as reinforce that there are several ways to think about and approach an issue. Given that we have become a very visual society, bringing YouTube segments into the supervisory process can also be very beneficial to the learning process especially around topics of trauma and self-care. Also keep in mind that human nature is such that you are not an expert in your own community no matter the value of what you have to share. However, using third-party references to communicate what you believe is important will encourage others to listen and hopefully encourage them to pursue what you believe is important.

10. *Do not go it alone.* Most will agree that managers are not trained to assist supervisors with their stress and risk for STS. Often management is about meeting contract requirements,

licensing and other liability issues especially around client services. Support to assist supervisors with STS/stress is limited, as managers are not often trained in managing the stress of their supervisors much less STS (Collins-Camargo & Millar, 2012). This is understandable yet leaves supervisors to fend for their own well-being, self-care and professional development. It is important for supervisors to meet regularly for peer support. Being part of a trauma-informed supervisor learning community provides a rich cross section of expertise, experiences and support often not afforded supervisors within their own organizations.

To Supervisees

You now have the kind of information to determine if you are receiving the kind of trauma-informed supervision to best help mitigate the stress of the trauma-related work you are or will be doing.

  Question: Given this information how would you rate your supervisory relationship? Poor____, somewhat supportive____, trauma-informed/sensitive____, very supportive, trauma-informed and sensitive____.

  Please record your answer under the post-session questions.

To Supervisors

You now have the necessary guidelines to engage in trauma-informed supervision in ways that help make you and the process safe and effective. There are areas we haven't discussed that are aspects of supervision regardless of the population being served, for example, ethical issues, confidentiality and supervisee/supervisor boundaries. These should have been part of your education yet ought to be periodically reviewed as they relate to responding to staff experiencing CF/STS. The good news is that many leaders are now appreciating that supervisors are essential to the well-being and effectiveness of employees, their performance and retention and as a result are bringing more support, training and resources to supervisors and the supervisory process.

A Final Note About Debriefing

Earlier I mentioned that critical incident stress debriefing is not supported. In addition to being skilled in applying psychological First Aid as needed, it is understandable that obtaining the who, what, when, where information is necessary for everybody's protection as well as to determine the next course of action. Following this, the three questions I found helpful to ask those exposed to a traumatic situation are:

1. Of all that happened, what one thought stands out the most for you?
2. Of all the reactions you had or are having-thoughts, emotions, physical reactions, what on reaction surprises you the most you are even having?
3. Where are you feeling this the most in your body right now?"

Simply normalize their responses and then focus on helping them explore ways to discharge/regulate their physiological reactions (focus on breathing, moving, walking, etc.) and suggest ways to take care of themselves over the next several days (being self-compassionate, focusing on their strengths, spending time with those they trust with their feelings, etc.). Do not begin any self-reflection until the individual feels comfortable to explore their experience in an effort to learn from it. This may be the next day or several days later. Similarly, do not attempt to have the individual process their feelings until they have regained a sense of safety and control cognitively, physiologically and emotionally. This may take several days. In the weeks/months that follow periodically evaluate for possible STS/PTSD.

Another technique is called the *Hot Walk Talk Protocol* (in the Appendix) that follows a similar process and is initiated after exposure. It uses walking to help discharge physiological reactions while gathering critical information. Also remember that the individual must always be given a choice as to what they believe is best for them at that point in time.

The Final Test: Ultimately Who Decides?

The effectiveness and safety of any supervisory relationship is ultimately the result of the supervisee's subjective experience with that relationship. If experienced as supportive, helpful and safe, it is likely to be experienced as effective; if challenging and conflictual, it will be experienced as not effective. There are numerous variables that contribute to a supervisee's subjective experience including their own personal history. If that supervisor has traits and characteristics of people in the supervisee's past that were not safe, it may be difficult to engage significantly enough for the supervisee to experience the relationship as helpful and effective.

Supervisors must continually check with supervisees to evaluate how their interactions, how what is being communicated is experienced as well as heard. To do this the supervisor must convey that they are open to feedback, that they are not judgmental and that such feedback is necessary to be as helpful and supportive as possible as a supervisor. To accomplish this the following framing statement can be helpful; after that it is up to the supervisee to risk sharing their experience and for the supervisor to be thankful for the feedback.

> I will be the first to tell you that I do not have all the answers. I kind of approach supervision as a non-knowing supervisor, who is going to be curious as to whether what I am communicating, sharing or trying to teach you is helpful. We'll kind of learn together as to what is most helpful for you. However, for that to happen, I will need to know how you are experiencing my efforts so, when needed, I can change direction. It's really that simple. You need to help me as much as I try to help you. Does this sound workable?

In this respect, Kulkarni, Bell, Hartman and Herman-Smith (2013) consider it to be extremely important that staff perceptions or the subjective ways they experience the workplace culture, policies and practices, leadership and ultimately supervision are consistently evaluated so that necessary adjustments can be made to support performance, engagement, satisfaction and retention of staff. Eisenberger, Stinglhamber, Vandenberge, Sucharski, and Rhoades (2002) also found that positive perceptions of supervision were also associated with positive perceptions of the organization; both enhance engagement and support well-being.

It's All About Resilience and Compassion Satisfaction

All of what we covered in these sessions creates a foundation for strengthening your resilience against the stress you will not be able to avoid. It will also help enhance your compassion satisfaction, which is also a protector against the stress of this work and what makes you viable and valuable to those you are hoping to help. In the next session, we review several assessment tools that will also help you identify additional areas associated with self-care. Then in our final session, you will be guided in the use of the outcomes of those assessments and provided additional information to help you develop your personalized self-care plan.

Post-session Questions

Write down your answers to the following questions. Keep these responses, as they will be used later when detailing self-care practices.

Questions

1. Of all that you have read and experienced up to this point, what surprises you the most?
   _____
   _____

2. Of all that you have read and experienced up to this point, what one thought stands out the most for you?
   _____
   _____

3. As you think about the one thought that stands out the most for you, how might it change the way you think about CF, secondary stress and BO?
   _____
   _____

4. How has this changed what you feel you need to do about the unavoidable stress of what you do?
   _____
   _____

Please record your answers below to these two questions asked earlier in the session.

Question: Hearing this information about some of the factors associated with a trauma-informed organization how do rate your organization's? Not informed____, Somewhat informed ____, Informed with limited sensitivity____, informed and trauma sensitive____.

Question: Given this information how would you rate your supervisory relationship? Poor____, somewhat supportive____, trauma-informed/sensitive____, very supportive, trauma-informed and sensitive____.

References

APA. (2012). *APA survey finds feeling valued at work linked to well-being and performance.* Retrieved November 10, 2018, from www.apa.org/news/press/releases/phwa/workplace-survey.pdf

Bledsoe, B. X. (2003, December). EMS Myth #3: Critical Incident Stress Management (CISM) is effective in managing EMS-related stress. Retrieved from www.emsworld.com/article/10325074/ems-myth-3-critical-incident-stress-management-cism-effective-managing-ems-related-stress

Bloom, S. (2006). *Human service systems and organizational stress.* Retrieved July 14, 2018, from sanctuary-web.com/.../Bloom%20Pubs/2006%20Bloom%20Human%20Service%20Sy...

Bozarth, J. (2018). The truth about teaching to learning styles, and what to do instead. *The e Learning Guild.* Santa, Rosa, CA. Retrieved from www.elearningguild.com/.../the-truth-about-teaching-to-learning-styles-and-wh...

Caprino, K. (2018, February 3). *Transformational leaders: The trait that separates them from the rest.* Retrieved November 5, 2018 from www.forbes.com/.../kathycaprino/2018/.../transformational-leaders-the-top-trait...

Chandler, J. (2016). What's new in employee performance evaluations? Retrieved November 20, 2018, from www.councilofnonprofits.org/ . . . /what-s-new-employee-performance-evaluatio. . .

Cheever, K. H., & Hardin, S. B. (1999). Effects of traumatic events, social support, and self-efficacy on adolescents' self-health assessments. *Western Journal of Nursing Research, 21*(5), 673.

Collins-Camargo, C., & Millar, K. (2012). Promoting supervisory practice change in public child welfare: Lessons learned from university/agency collaborative research in four states. *Child Welfare, 91*(1), 101–124.

Craig, C. D., & Sprang, G. (2010). Compassion satisfaction, compassion fatigue, and burnout in a national sample of trauma treatment therapists. *Anxiety, Stress, & Coping, 23*(3), 319–339.

Dickson, G. (2018). *9 research-backed reasons to rethink your annual employee evaluation*. Retrieved November 12, 2018, from https://blog.bonus.ly/6-research-backed-reasons-rethink-annual-employee-evaluation

Dubay, L., Burton, R., & Epstein, M. (2018). *Early adopters of trauma-informed care: An implementation analysis of the advancing trauma-informed care grantees*. Retrieved from www.chcs.org/media/early_adopters_of_trauma-informed_care-evaluation.pdf

Eisenberger, R., Stinglhamber, F., Vandenberge, C., Sucharski, L., & Rhoades, L. (2002). Perceived supervisor support: Contributions to perceived organizational support and employee retention. *Journal of Applied Psychology, 87*(3), 565–573.

Foa, E. B., Keane, T. M., et al. (2008). *Effective treatments for PTSD: Practice guidelines from the international society for traumatic stress studies*. New York: Guilford Press.

Gil, E. (2006). *Helping abused and traumatized children: Integrating directive and nondirective approaches*. New York: Guilford Press.

Harvey, A. K. (2015). *Clinical supervision: Essentials for trauma therapy*. Retrieved November 2, 2018, from https://dhhr.wv.gov/bhhf/ibhc/Documents/ . . . /Clinical%20Supervision.pdf

Hearn, S. (2018). *5 game-changing performance management trends for 2018*. Retrieved November 2, 2018, from www.clearreview.com/5-performance-management-trends-2018/

Hughes, R. (2009). Attachment focused treatment for children. In M. Kerman (Ed.), *Clinical pearls of wisdom* (pp. 169–181). New York: Norton.

Kirkland, J. (2018). *Engaged supervisors set the tone for employee retention*. Retrieved October 10, 2018, from www.ems1.com/ . . . /392718048-Engaged-supervisors-set-the-tone-for-employee

Kulkarni, S., Bell, H., Hartman, J. L., & Herman-Smith, R. L. (2013). Exploring individual and organizational factors contributing to compassion satisfaction, secondary traumatic stress, and burnout in domestic violence service providers. *Journal of the Society for Social Work and Research, 4*(2), 114–130.

Luest, H. (2018). *Connection-the key to healing and resilience*. Retrieved December 9, 2018, from www.socialworker.com/feature-articles/ . . . /connection-key-to-healing-resilience/

Malchiodi, C. A. (2011a). Art therapy and the brain. In C. Malchiodi (Ed.), *Handbook of art therapy*. New York: Guilford Press.

Martino, S., Canning-Ball, M., Carroll, K. M., Rounsaville, B. J. (2011). A criterion-based stepwise approach for training counselors in motivational interviewing. *Journal of Substance Abuse Treatment, 40*, 357–365. [PMC free article] [PubMed].

McGarrigle, T., & Walsh, C. A. (2011). Mindfulness, self-care, and wellness in social work: Effects of contemplative training. *Journal of Religion & Spirituality in Social Work: Social Thought, 30*, 212–233.

Miller, S. (2015). *Employers see wellness link to productivity, performance*. Retrieved October 22, 2018, from www.shrm.org/resourcesandtools/hr-topics/ . . . /wellness-productivity-link-.aspx

Nakano, C. (2014). *The four different types of learners, and what they mean to your presentations*. Retrieved November 4, 2018, from https://blog.prezi.com/the-four-different-types-of-learners-and-what-they-mean-to-your- . . .

NCTSN. (2018a). *Psychological first aid*. Retrieved February 12, 2018, from www.nctsn.org/treatments . . . / psychological-first-aid . . . psychological. . . /about-pfa

NCTSN. (2018b). *The secondary traumatic stress core competencies in trauma-informed supervision*. Retrieved November 1, 2018, from www.nctsn.org/ . . . /using-secondary-traumatic-stress-core-competencies-trauma-i. . .

Olafson, E., & Kenniston, J. (2008). Obtaining information from children in the justice system. *Juvenile and Family Court Journal, 59*(4), 71–89.

Oxford Learner's Dictionary. (2018). *Sensitivity definition*. Retrieved November 2, 2018, from www.oxfordlearners dictionaries.com/us/definition/english/sensitivity

Perry, B., & Szalavitz, M. (2006). *The boy who was raised as a dog: And other stories*. New York: Basic Books.

Rothchild, B. (2006). *Help for the helper: The psychophysiology of compassion fatigue and vicarious trauma*. New York: W.W. Norton.

SAMSHA. (2014). Trauma-informed care in behavioral health services. Treatment Improvement Protocol (TIP) Series, No. 57. Center for Substance Abuse Treatment (US). Rockville (MD): *Substance Abuse and Mental Health Services Administration.*

SAMSHA News. (2014). Guiding principles of trauma-informed care. *SAMSHA News, 22*(2) (Spring). Retrieved July 24, 2016, from www.samhsa.gov/samhsaNewsLetter/Volume_22_Number_2/trauma . . . /guiding. . .

Steele, W. (2017). *Optimizing learning outcomes: Brain-centric, trauma-sensitive practices*. New York: Routledge, p. 17.

Steele, W., & Malchiodi, C. (2012). *Working with traumatized children and adolescents*. New York: Routledge.

Treatment Improvement Protocol (TIP) Series, No. 57; Center for Substance Abuse Treatment (US). Rockville (MD): *Substance Abuse and Mental Health Services Administration (US)*. (2014). Retrieved October 12, 2017, from www.ncbi.nlm.nih.gov/books/NBK207204/

van der Kolk, B. (2015). *The body keeps the score: Brain, mind, and body in the healing of trauma*. New York: Penguin Books.

Wikipedia. (2018). *Transformational leadership*. Retrieved October 5, 2018, from https://en.wikipedia.org/wiki/Transformational_leadership

Wood, J., & Nelson, B. (2017, November 29). The manager's role in employee well-being. *Gallup Workplace*. Retrieved October 10, 2018, from www.gallup.com/workplace/236249/manager-role-employee.aspx

6 Assessment

Opening Statement

When talking about stress management or discussing self-care, I'm sure most of you have read or have been told how important it is to have a work-life balance. There certainly is a plethora of resources available on the Internet. Simply Google "Wellness Self-care Plans," and you will be presented with hundreds of resources. Life coaches often use the *Wheel of Life* to help clients develop a balanced approach. There are a number of these available. Their authors use the spokes of the wheels to identify those areas that constitute balanced living. There are variations. For example, you may find one that identifies health, fun and recreation, significant other/romance, family and friends, career, finances, personal growth and physical environment. You may find another whose wheel spokes read physical/health, family/home, mental/education, social/cultural and financial/career.

In the field of psychology, social work and mental health, a recommended balanced approach might include a focus on family, career/education, mental health, spirituality, home/friends, finances and health. Another variation you'll find is physical, emotional, psychological, personal, professional and spiritual. You will have to read a bit to determine what each area includes. For example, the personal area might include relationships, social life, recreation and finances.

There is no doubt that many caregivers, those that assist and/or respond to trauma victims, have a poor work-life balance so these resources can be helpful in determining areas that may need attention.

However, Consider This

If I tend to be less than optimistic and you're recommending activities that you believe can help put my life in balance, how likely am I to pursue those activities? Not very likely. How I approach life, what I think, my mindsets, my perceptions, how I treat myself, the regulation of my emotions and behaviors all play a critical role in determining the degree to which I practice balanced self-care. Before embracing a self-care plan, we need to identify those thoughts, mindsets, beliefs, attitudes and characteristics that are counter-productive to minimizing CF, secondary trauma and BO. For example, when I make a mistake or fail at something and tend to be self-critical, judgmental and get down on myself, I'm not engaging in self-compassion. We know that low levels of self-compassion are linked to high levels of CF and BO (Durkin, Beaumont, Martin, & Carson, 2016). If when faced with conflict and/or challenges, I have a difficult time speaking up for myself, I'm not practicing self-efficacy, a characteristic of resilience. We know that resilience also supports compassion satisfaction and is an essential function in mitigating the effects of CF and BO (Burnett & Wahl, 2015). Obviously, you are encouraged to strive for balanced self-care, however spending time with family, friends, engaging in exercise and good nutrition alone, as necessary and as valuable as they are for our well-being, may not be doing the job. The fact remains that our thoughts, perceptions, beliefs, values, emotions and responses to everyday challenges must be in alignment with and supportive of the kind of self-care needed to mitigate the effects of all stress, inclusive of CF/STS/BO regardless of what we might do in other areas of our life.

This Assessment Series

For all these reasons, I recommend completing the series of assessments described in this section. The first series, *Overall Stress Outcomes*, evaluates many of the areas associated with a work-life balance. The second series examines BO, secondary trauma and CF. The third series, *Organizational Assessments*, helps to identify those organizational practices or lack of practices that place us at risk for CF/STS/BO. The final series, *Self-Efficacy*, examines self-compassion, resilience and spiritual intelligence, which are key preventative and recovery factors. Although I've mentioned the importance of spiritual intelligence several times, I feel obligated to do so once again because of a resistance and/or reluctance of organizations to incorporate spiritual intelligence into training as an effective process for increasing job satisfaction and reducing BO and CF (Newmeyer et al., 2014; Hassan, Nadeem, Akhtet, & Nisar, 2016).

In This Session

The purposes of this session are to

1.   review each survey/tool,
2.   explain why each is recommended and what it measures. The majority of tools can be found in the Appendix, the others are easily accessible on the Internet. I recommend completing these over a period of a week rather than trying to complete them all at one time. Most of the tools are brief so you could do 2-3 per day. Your results are to be recorded on the *Self-Care Checklist* (in the Appendix). This information will then be used in our final session to help you develop your personalized self-care plan. Remember this reality statement.

Reality: *Stress is stress. Regardless of its source, stress affects our bodies, our emotions, cognitive processes and performance even when sources such as CF/STS and BO are not significant sources of our stress. If other sources of stress exist, our emotions, cognitive process and performance (the care of clients) will likely remain problematic.*

For this reason, we want to evaluate our overall level of stress and those issues/situations that may be triggering that stress. Let me then review with you the surveys/tools. We'll begin by addressing your overall stress level that includes how you are approaching life as well as the work you are doing.

Overall Stress Assessment Series

Question: Given the accumulation of knowledge you now have about the various sources/symptoms/causes of stress, how do you now rate your stress level? Use an "x" to mark your current stress level %.

10%-20%____, 20%-30%____, 30%-40%____, 40%-60%____, 60%-70%____, 70%-100%____.

Record this answer on your Self-Care Checklist.

Note: Keep in mind that the following formal stress tools I recommend you take measure your over-all stress level. They ask a few questions about work but also about other areas of your life. Now, your general stress level may be fine; however, your work-related stress level high. For this reason, it is recommended that you complete all assessments. Approaching stress from this perspective is much more comprehensive and will yield the kind of valuable and specific information needed to guide your self-care planning and interventions specific to CF/STS/BO.

Now I'd like you to further evaluate your perception of your stress using a formal tool titled

Perceived Stress Inventory (PSS) (in the Appendix)

Why this tool?

a. no cost,
b. measures what others do not – our perception, which determines whether a situation/condition is stressful for us, and
c. measures our stress response to everyday life situations versus only the work environment.

The Perceived Stress Scale (Cohen, Kamarck, & Mermelstein, 1983) has been one of the more widely used psychological inventories for measuring one's perception of stress. It is not specific to working conditions nor focused on those who care for others. It is a brief 10-item inventory that measures how we are interpreting what we were exposed to day-to-day over the past month. What stresses one may not stress out another so this measure of perception is important for determining individual stress levels based on how we are experiencing life in general. The fact is if we perceive a situation to be stressful our nervous system, cognitive processes and performance levels respond accordingly.

The PSS measures how often we feel certain ways to determine stress levels. There are five frequency measures from "never" to "very often." One example includes, "In the last month, how often have you felt confident about your ability to handle your personal problems?" The scale has strong predictive measures related to health and well-being. Dr. Cohen, professor of psychology at Carnegie-Mellon University, is the author of the PSS. This scale can be used without permission for nonprofit academic research or nonprofit educational purposes. (Detailed information related to this tool can be accessed through https://www.cmu.edu/dietrich/psychology/people/core-training.../cohen-sheldon.html.)

Keep in mind that stress varies from one day to the next, one month to the next. This scale provides a general reference to your current perceived stress level. Your score will give you a general reference as to your stress level. Also keep in mind, you may be experiencing low stress level yet there are items that point to a potential trigger and/or area of concern that you want to consider when completing your self-care plan. Just as there will be certain clients that trigger a more intense stress reactions than others, there will be certain situations or conditions that do the same. The more we are aware of these triggers, the more effectively we can respond.

Record the appropriate information on your Self-Care Checklist.

The following scales also provide a reference of overall stress level by evaluating different aspects of our life/life style. I recommend completing these to obtain a more comprehensive view of your stress levels than any one tool can provide. They also provide recommendations in those areas where your stress may be elevated.

Stress 360 Assessment

Stress 360 evaluates elements of our lifestyle, occupation, attitude and diet to assess our overall stress load. I recommend that you take this survey. Simply Google "Self-Assessment-American Institute of Stress" and then click on Stress 360 (https://www.stress.org/self-assessment/).

Why this tool?

a.　no cost,
b.　evaluates life and work stressors,
c.　less than 10 minutes to complete, and
d.　Your score is sent in less than 60 seconds with a video message about the score, plus additional tools sent to your email such as a debriefing form to help identify where to place your focus.

Record the appropriate information on your Self-Care Checklist. After completing the assessment, they ask for your name and email and will send you your score in each of the 5 areas. If you click on the PDF at the bottom of the outcome record it will open and contain how you rated each question. Before clicking out and while still open be sure to print out the PDF of how you rated the questions so you can list on your Self-Care Checklist the areas causing the greatest stress. Your answers will also indicate what you may want to change or work on to lower your stress.

The Stress and Well-Being Survey

Why this tool?

a.　no cost,
b.　evaluates four well-being areas,
c.　measure five aspects of well-being, and
d.　provides immediate scoring and suggestions.

The *Stress and Well-Being Survey* helps to assess the state of our heart, mind and emotions at home, at work, in relationships and in relation to finances. It's helpful because it measures our stress management, adaptability, resilience, emotional vitality and total well-being levels and then compares these with five aspects of well-being. The scale then goes one step further and provides practical steps for achieving our Zone of Performance: when we are at our best. This tool is from the HeartMath Institute. Simply Google "Self-Assessment-American Institute of Stress" (www.stress.org/self-assessment/) and then click on Stress and Well-Being Survey.

StressCom (Optional)

Why this tool? It's

a.　comprehensive,
b.　measures how we approach work versus actual work stressors, which is critical to effective self-care,
c.　provides immediate calculation of our score and compares our score with others,
d.　provides bar charts and more,
e.　provides ways to effectively manage problem areas,

f.   allows us to print out the results and recommendations for approaching everyday life differently, and

g.   there is a minimal fee.

Note: A $12 fee allows you to take this assessment quarterly for one year. The results of the other three tools above will provide helpful information related to your overall stress; however, I do recommend this tool because it is quite comprehensive.

StressCom, also available via the American Institute of Stress (AIS), asks 60 questions about our stress level and provides instant results in the way of a bar chart, which helps us to identify areas that may need more of our attention. It compares your scores with those in our profession such as health professionals, fire fighters, police and educators. It evaluates how we respond to the following areas/issues: control, competition, task orientation, change, time and management of symptoms. Under each category it provides a checklist of the ways to manage that area effectively and then provides 11 stress management techniques. Cost: Being able to use this tool quarterly is an excellent feature as life situations/work situations change and, as they do, so too does our stress.

Record the appropriate outcomes on your Self-Care Checklist.

Summary

The four tools discussed in this section do a good job of evaluating our overall stress level as a result of the way we perceive and approach daily life. They provide us with very specific sources/causes of elevated stress and excellent strategies that can be incorporated into your self-care plan. The more aware we are of these, the more we can focus on mitigating their effects via our personalized self-care plan. From here we are going to evaluate stress specific to the work you do and the environment in which you do it. This will include BO conditions, CF, STS, trauma-informed supervisory competency, levels of engagement and leadership. Let's start with BO.

BO Scales

Of the very few free BO scales, I found the following two to be the most useful because of what they measure, the quick scoring and the posted suggestions.

Test-Stress.com

(*Note*: The ProQOL will also measure BO so I recommend just this one BO survey.)
   Why this tool?

a.   no cost,

b.   easy to access and use,

c.   evaluates the three primary symptoms of BO, and

d.   immediate automatic scoring results in each category with suggestions.

The 22-item BO Test-Stress (MBI-see description below) self-assessment test is available from Test-Stress.com. It's very helpful because it evaluates three primary areas of BO-emotional/physical exhaustion, depersonalization (cynicism/low compassion) and personal accomplishment (or diminished professional efficacy). These are the three most commonly cited and researched areas of BO. Results provide a breakdown of your BO level in each of the three areas and makes several recommendations. The assessment is accessible by Googling "Test-Stress.

com Are You in Burnout?" This will take you to several websites; click on the title *Burnout Test: Take the Burnout Test Are You In* . . . or go to https://www.test-stress.com/en/free-burnout-test. php. (Note at the end of the summary of your results, there is a link to free test you might want to explore.)

Gold Standard: The Maslach Burnout Inventory (MBI) (Optional)

The following tool has undergone years of research and is the most frequently "go to" BO assessment tool. The reasons are listed below.

Why this scale?

a.   provides very comprehensive coverage of BO factors,
b.   covers professionals in human services, education, medical field, general population,
c.   evaluates organizational strengths and weaknesses impacting BO,
d.   available to individuals or groups,
e.   a standard tool for 35 years, and
f.   can be taken and automatically scored on line. (There is a modest cost.)

The *Maslach Burnout Inventory (MBI)* has been a standard tool for some 35 years. Its Human Services Survey (MBI-HSS) is the most frequently used version as it applies to professionals across the human service field. It is comprised of 22 items and asks you to rate them based on how often you experience that specific symptom. There are six ratings from "every day" to "never." One example is, "I have accomplished many worthwhile things in this job."

For the medical field the MBI-HSS MP (Medical Personnel) addresses issues specific to a variety of medical roles. The MBI-Educator Survey (ES) covers those working in an education setting. There is a General Survey the MBI-GS for use with those not in education or human services as well as the MBI-GS(S) General Survey for College Students.

The MBI Burnout Tool Kit also comes with AWS-Area of Work-Life Survey that allows individuals to identify strengths and weaknesses in the workplace that impact BO. It evaluates responses to workload, control or involvement in decision making, reward/recognition, quality of relationship with managers, colleagues and those you serve; fairness related to how the organization treats all employees and values related to how consistent your values are with the organization's values. This combined inventory (BO and work-life) is a 50-item inventory. Inventories can be purchased for modest amounts at https://www.mindgarden.com/117-maslach-burnout-inventory. You can also Google "Mind Garden.com" for the above and additional information.

If the MBI is not an option know that the first two tools provide good information regarding the impact BO is having on you physically and emotionally, on your performance/behavior and professional satisfaction and growth. The free tool from Test-Stress.com is the 22-item scale from the MBI series of tools.

CF and STS

The Silencing Response Scale (in Appendix)

Why this tool?

a.   no cost,
b.   only 15 questions,
c.   researched,
d.   reveals potential triggers,

e.   evaluates those thought processes associated with CF and STS, and

f.   allows us to identify specific communication patterns with clients that are harmful to their efforts to heal and indicate we are at risk for CF/STS.

The *silencing response* is a characteristic of CF and/or STS. It evaluates thought processes associated with CF and STS. It is the result of being overexposed to trauma material to extent that the helper is overwhelmed by the exposure and must now shut down the traumatic stories and experiences of clients. By "shutting down" we mean redirecting the client to less traumatic material, remaining apathetic or otherwise finding a way to avoid client's traumatic material. This response is an attempt by the helper to avoid the fear, uneasiness and/or the pain the client may be causing them. It is a way that helpers protect themselves when feeling the most vulnerable. That vulnerability may have to do with reactions of STS, or an indication of CF (Baranowsky, 2002). The Silencing Response Scale inclusive of scoring can be found in the Appendix.

Record the appropriate outcomes on your Self-Care Checklist.

Note: This is a tool that is only as valuable as you are with the honesty of your responses. If honest, most professional exposed to trauma victims or situations will indicate experiencing any one or several of these reactions at some time. It is really a quick and easy way to let us know that it's time to step back for a minute to do some self-reflecting as to whether any of these reactions are specific to a particular client, overexposure or feeling incompetent and needing more trauma-specific training. Any one of these reasons dictate further exploration with a trauma-informed supervisor or professional in your community. The other factor is frequency. If any of these are experienced on a weekly or monthly basis versus once or twice a year, it would obviously indicate the need to process our reactions. Used this way this tool is very beneficial.

STS Checklist (in Appendix)

Why this survey?

a.   no cost,

b.   inclusive of DSM-5 criteria of alterations in cognition and mood, which in my opinion reflect symptoms associated with vicarious trauma/STS/CF, and

c.   it's ideal for determining the possible need for STS related intervention and/or evaluation for PTSD.

This is not a diagnostic tool. The items have been adapted from Bride's STS scale (Bride, Robinson, Yegidis, & Figley, 2004) and the most current DSM-5 (American Psychiatric Association, 2013) PTSD criteria for PTSD, which added criteria "D," alterations in cognitions and mood. It can be argued that those experiencing STS do experience cognitive and mood changes that have been associated with CF and vicarious trauma as discussed in the research mentioned in Session One. For this reason, they are included here in this adapted format.

Professional Quality of Life Scale (ProQOL 5; in Appendix)

Why this tool?

a.   no cost,

b.   measures CF/CS, STS and BO,

c.   most frequently used by human services, mental health, and

d.   scoring outcomes present critical decision-making information regarding continuing in profession, leaving the employer, identifying specific source of stress, etc.

This scale is the latest revision of the original Compassion Fatigue Self-Test (CFS), developed by Charles Figley in 1995. The first several versions of the ProQOL had unresolved psychometric issues that this latest version corrected. It is a widely used scale that can be used without permission and downloaded at no cost. Many prefer it over the Maslach Burnout Inventory because in addition to BO it evaluates levels of compassion satisfaction/CF and STS. In addition, scoring outcomes allow users to make informed decisions regarding self-care, based on the source of their stressors. For example, outcomes showing high compassion satisfaction (CS), low BO but high STS indicates that the individual will need support in addressing their STS reactions. If successful they are likely to continue their work given the high level of CS and low level of BO.

We know that advancing our understanding of STS, normalizing our reactions and providing ways to regulate tour fears will strengthen our resilience and minimize STS reactions to future exposure to trauma situations and materials. At the same time, we know that the presence of STS may lead to PTSD in which case additional treatment may be necessary.

The ProQOL is not a diagnostic tool but an inventory that helps identify potentially problematic areas. It stresses that it is not a measure of pathology but the natural consequences of working with a traumatized population. It provides five different combination outcomes of the three areas (BO, STS, CS) evaluated and what each means regarding decisions about continuing at that work place and/or continuing in the profession. The ProQOL is located in the Appendix and can also be downloaded at www.proqol.org/uploads/ProQOL_5_English_Self-Score_3-2012.pdf. This is the most recent version, Version 5. Once downloaded, you may print it out and use the printed copy to complete the inventory. Additional information about the ProQOL can be found at ProQOL.org. Record the appropriate outcomes on your *Self-Care Checklist*.

Organizational Assessments

Self-Engagement Survey (in Appendix)

Why this tool? It identifies:

a.   the level of engagement by peers, supervisors/managers,
b.   how well leaders demonstrate their care for employee well-being/wellness, and
c.   how well supported and recognized we feel about the work we are doing.

Measuring engagement today is big business. If you search for engagement assessment tools on the Internet, you will be immediately presented with a long list of ads promoting different companies that evaluate organizational engagement. Engagement can consist of employee's sense of engagement, the organizational culture, leadership practices, etc. For our purpose, how we feel about the way peers, supervisors, managers interact with us and how leadership demonstrates their concern for our well-being and professional growth is what matters significantly to the trauma related stress and BO factors we are exposed to because of the work we do. For this reason, I encourage you to complete the *Self-Engagement Survey* found in the Appendix. It covers the primary issues we have discussed throughout our sessions.

The critical issue is the degree to which we feel supported, valued and recognized in our work environment. When these are lacking or limited our level of engagement will be low, which negatively influences our stress levels, resilience, the work we are doing, performance, interactions with others and ultimately our desire to remain in that environment.

Record your responses to the Self-Engagement Survey on your Self-Care Checklist.

The Q12 (Optional Researched Organization-Wide Engagement Assessment Tool)

Why this tool? It has:

a. a long history of results with over 25 million employees, and
b. it addresses the number one factor associated with retention, job satisfaction and performance. (*Note*: Normally a tool to evaluate all employees, although individuals can review, answer the 12 questions and have a good sense as to the strength/weakness of engagement.)

This survey from Gallup is one of the most effective surveys measuring the level of engagement of employees. Gallup (2018) has tested this tool over 30 years with 25 million employees throughout the world and found engagement is critical to retention and performance. In human services, mental health and other organizations responding to a traumatized population, the level of engagement employees experience with their managers or supervisors is also predictive of retention and clinical efficacy with clients (Workplace Mental Health | Mental Health America, 2018). The Q12 survey can be taken on line for a minimal cost and all results tabulated by Gallup followed by meaningful reports that show strengths and weaknesses and recommendations for implementing higher levels of engagement as needed.

Individual Assessment of Organization

The following assessments help individuals identify how trauma-informed their organization is related to engaging in practices specific to STS and being trauma-informed.

Secondary Traumatic Stress Informed Organization Assessment (STSI-OA) (in Appendix)

Why this tool?

a. no cost,
b. developed by members of NCTSN,
c. researched (Sprang et al., 2014; Sprang, Ross, Miller, Blackshear, & Ascienzo, 2017),
d. specific to organizations assisting traumatized population,
e. evaluates ways organization is or is not addressing STS,
f. covers six domains which identify specific areas supporting or not supporting prevention of CF/STS, and
g. provides a measurement of improvement when used multiple times

This scale was designed to help organizations monitor and, as needed, change or develop practices and policies specific to STS that support workers impacted by their work with a traumatized population. I like it because individuals can use it to help identify the strengths/weaknesses of their organization when it comes to creating an environment that is proactive in its approach to helping employees minimize the impact of STS and CF. *Stated differently, organizations that promote the practices identified in this tool are demonstrating their care and concern for the well-being of their employees.* It is a 40-item questionnaire that covers six domains:

*   an organization's support of resilience-building practices (7 items),
*   practices related to physical and psychological safety (7 items),
*   presence of trauma-informed STS policies (6 items),
*   the use of trauma-informed leadership practices (9 items),

- the use of routine STS driven organizational practices (7 items), and
- how well the organization evaluates and monitors STS and STS policies and practices in the workplace (4 items).

It can be downloaded at no cost. It is a tool when used multiple times that can track progress toward implementation of trauma-informed organizational STS practices. *The Appendix version is designed for individuals to evaluate their organizations response to the prevention of and assistance with STS of employees as a result of working continuously with a trauma population. It is in a checklist format to which you can answer "yes," "sometimes" or "not at all." The outcome will provide an indication as to the organizations focus on your wellness.* (For organizational wide use go to the website www.uky.edu/CTAC/STSI-OA.) *Record the appropriate outcomes on your Self-Care Checklist.*

The free access STSI-OA tool is the most current, researched and NCTSN member developed tool at the time of this writing and I believe generic enough to be used by any organization serving or responding to a trauma population and/or situations.

In Session Five you were asked to rate the trauma-informed level of your organization. You record the answer in the post-session activity. The question was: Hearing this information about some of the factors associated with a trauma-informed organization how do you rate your organization? Not informed____, Somewhat informed____, Informed with limited sensitivity____, informed and trauma sensitive____.

(Please also post your answer under the post-session questions.) Record your answer here.

In Session Five you were also asked to rate the trauma-informed/STS-informed level of your supervisor. The question was: Given this information how would you rate your supervisory relationship? Poor____, somewhat supportive____, trauma-informed/sensitive____, very supportive, trauma-informed and sensitive____.

Record your answer here.

STS Supervisor Competency (in Appendix)

Why this survey?

a.   no cost,
b.   identifies specific behaviors/practices supervisors need to be competent to provide in addressing STS with supervisees, and
c.   it was developed by NCTSN members.

If you have not completed this survey, please do so as it provides valuable information related to your competency as a supervisor or, as a supervisee, it helps to identify the STS competency of your supervisor, which is critical to your well-being, performance and professional development.
Record areas of need on your Self-Care Checklist.

Wellness Oriented TI-Care Organizational Assessment Tool

Why this survey?

a.   easy to use and score,
b.   evaluates seven key domains of overall TI practices/polices, and
c.   the National Council on Behavioral Health provides consultation.

Our primary purpose in this work is to address what organizations ought to be doing related to STS/CF/BO. Being trauma-informed is critical to our well-being so we should be aware of how well our organization is working from a trauma-informed lens; the tool provides an excellent opportunity for you to do this as an individual or for the organization with all staff. The seven domains covered include:

1. screening and assessment,
2. consumer driven care and services,
3. wellness and TI educated and responsive work force,
4. use of TI evidenced-based and emerging best practices,
5. safety and security,
6. community outreach and partner building, and
7. organizational performance and evaluation

This tool was developed by The National Council for Behavioral Health. Permission to use agency wide can be obtained by emailing communications@thenationalcouncil.org or by calling (202) 684-7457. There is a cost involved.

The ARTIC Scale (Optional)

The ARTIC Scale is a psychometrically valid measures of trauma-informed care (TIC). It is a measure of professional and paraprofessional attitudes toward TIC. To date, the ARTIC has been used by over 150 entities in 10 countries, translated into four languages and administered to over 15,000 professionals. It was developed by the Traumatic Stress Institute of Klingberg Family Centers and Dr. Courtney Baker of Tulane University. Google "Traumatic Stress Institute" for more information (https://traumaticstressinstitute.org/the-artic-scale/).

Organizations and schools can use the ARTIC to assess readiness for TIC implementation. They can also use it to measure change as a result of TIC interventions. It can help monitor change over time, spurring organizations to deepen their commitment to TIC, and prevent the backsliding in TIC practice that can commonly occur. Finally, it can help determine what TIC messages need reinforcement in the system and which staff need additional training and supervision.

ARTIC Subscales

ARTIC sub-scales include:

Underlying Causes of Problem Behavior and Symptoms. Emphasizes behavior and symptoms as adaptations and malleable versus behavior and symptoms as intentional and fixed.

Responses to Problem Behavior and Symptoms. Emphasizes relationships, flexibility, kindness, and safety as the agent of behavior and symptom change versus rules, consequences, and accountability as the agent of change.

On-the-Job Behavior. Endorses empathy-focused staff behavior versus control-focused staff behavior.

Self-Efficacy at Work. Endorses feeling able to meet the demands of working with a traumatized population versus feeling unable to meet the demands.

Reactions to the Work. Endorses appreciating the effects of secondary trauma/vicarious traumatization and coping by seeking support versus minimizing the effects of secondary trauma/vicarious traumatization and coping by ignoring or hiding the impact. When you purchase the ARTIC Scale, you will receive detailed instructions about scoring.

The majority of other tools available at no cost evaluate multiple domains of trauma-informed organizational functioning, its policies and practices related to the community, consumers and staff. Many national associations such as the Children's Trust Fund provide their own tools to address the trauma-informed domains established by NCTSN. Given that our focus is specific to STS/CF/BO, the STSI-OA described is an excellent no-cost tool and is easily accessible.

Scales Related to Self-efficacy

Self-efficacy (Bandura, 1997; Fida, Laschinger, & Leiter, 2018) is the belief in our ability to manage life situations and succeed in all areas of life. It is strongly related with resilience (Schwarzer & Warner, 2013), bouncing back after a failure because we believe we can "find a way" to overcome challenges. Self-efficacy and effective effort go hand in hand. Even though a challenge becomes harder than we thought it would be, we keep at it until we succeed. Self-efficacy and self-compassion also go hand in hand (Souza & Hutz, 2016) as do self-efficacy and self-regulation (Alessandri, Vecchione, & Caprara, 2014); we can stay in control of our emotions because we know we can find solutions. Rahmanian and associates (2018) also found a high correlation between self-efficacy and spiritual intelligence, which, as we discussed earlier, comprises a set of beliefs that support our well-being. Following are assessments for self-compassion, resilience and spiritual intelligence. Possessing these beliefs and responses to life challenges constitutes self-efficacy which is necessary for the prevention and/or mitigation of stress inclusive of STS/CF/BO.

The Self-Compassion Scale (in Appendix)

Why this tool?

a. no cost, and
b. measures factors critical to effective self-care, minimization of CF.

The Self-Compassion Scale developed by Kristen Neff (2003) is a 26-item scale that evaluates behaviors associated with self-compassion. It can be downloaded and used without permission at self-compassion.org. Because self-compassion is a cornerstone of self-care, it is important to evaluate how well we are responding to our own needs when facing stress.

Spiritual Intelligence Self-Report Inventory (SISRI-24) (in Appendix)

Why this tool?

a. no cost,
b. measures cognitive processes in the face of stressful situations/conditions,
c. critical component of effective self-care, and
d. critical to self-fulfillment, work performance.

SIRI research shows that high levels of spiritual intelligence results in enhanced work performance, allows human beings to be creative, to change the rules and alter situations (Anbugeetha, 2015; Kumar & Pragadeeswaran, 2011). Spiritual intelligence is the key to personal fulfillment and good work performance and can lead to a more satisfying and productive work place. It is a component of self-care as it supports finding meaning and purpose in our lives, which in turn allows us to adapt to stressful situations. Another way to define spiritual intelligence is that its components foster the development of wisdom (King & DeCicco, 2009). The survey has 24 items that measure behaviors, thought processes and mental characteristics. It can be downloaded and used without permission from www.davidbking.net/sisri-24.pdf.

Record outcomes on your Self-Care Checklist.

Resilience Characteristics Survey (in Appendix)

Why this tool?

a. no cost,
b. addresses multiple characteristics associated with resilience,
c. identifies characteristics by category and optimal score for each category, and
d. reflects mindsets and behaviors associated with resilience.

Charney (2004) provides one of the most comprehensive lists of protective factors related to resilience reflected by several items in the checklist: optimism, altruism, having a moral compass, social supports, humor, role models, taking risk, mission/purpose and spirituality.

This survey also reflects characteristics reported by King and DeCicco (2009); Bonano (2010); Seligman (2011); and Diehl (2017).

Resilience Self-Assessment

Google "Mind Tools Resilience Self-Assessment" and click on "How Resilient Are You?" (https://www.mindtools.com; click on Career Skills › Dealing with Challenges).
Why this tool?

a. no cost,
b. 16 items,
c. measures confidence, social support, adaptability and purposefulness,
d. immediate scoring, and
e. provides multiple recommendations and additional resources.

Note: Be sure to print out the interpretations of your score.
Record outcome on your Self-Care Checklist.
This completes the listing of recommended tools.

About Surveys/Assessment Tools

- Unless otherwise indicated, scales are often time sensitive. You might score low on a STS scale one week and much higher on the same scale weeks later because of increased exposure and/or conditions not previously experienced. From this perspective, scales should be completed at least on two different occasions yearly.
- Scales are wonderful for becoming aware of which symptoms are associated with the different sources of stress. Once these symptoms are identified they become "alert markers" to watch throughout the year and address in your self-care plan.
- From an organizational perspective, it obviously helps to have a sense of the overall stress level among staff. It is even more helpful to know the source of that stress in order to proactively respond with practices proven to reduce that specific stress. Practices for reducing BO, for example, will be different from practices shown to reduce STS and those practices will be somewhat different from those used to assist individuals experiencing CF.

- The way scales and inventories are presented to employees is critical to obtaining helpful outcomes. Asking individuals to complete these scales generally raises immediate concerns as to how the information is going to be used. If those completing these scales fear that the results may be used in a less than positive way, they will not be truthful in which case no one benefits.
- Obviously, confidentiality is a must. In this work, the majority of tools are meant to be taken by individuals to determine areas needing attention in their efforts to manage the stress of the work they do. It is information they can share, if feeling comfortable and safe to do so, with their supervisor for assistance in developing strategies, coping skills, etc. to help develop their resilience, performance, compassion satisfaction while mitigating the stress induced by repeated exposure to trauma.
- When administering tools agency wide, such as those related to being trauma-informed, assessing for BO or STS, it is critical that identifying information conceals or eliminates any identification of outcomes with an individual. It is also important to make sure that you do not report results for very small groups of people. For example, if your intended report would break out responses by department, but only four people responded from one department, then reporting those responses could jeopardize the privacy of those respondents' answers.
- Keep in mind that total scores do not always provide the most helpful information. Identifying those items that reflect a problem area for an individual or group of individuals may be more helpful than a total score. I really recommend when reviewing results that individual items be identified that are potential problem areas. For example, your overall score for self-compassion is favorable, yet your category scores show you tend to "over identify" which you would then want to focus on changing.

Summary

Completing these tools will provide the information needed to focus your self-care efforts for developing your personalized self-care plan. Use the Self-Care Check list in the Appendix to record areas needing attention and any recommendations that were given to you when completing the online surveys. In the next and final session, we'll pull it altogether into one care plan as well as provide additional self-care practices.

References

Alessandri, G., Vecchione, M., & Caprara, G. V. (2014, October 6). Assessment of regulatory emotional self-efficacy beliefs: A review of the status of the art and some suggestions to move the field forward. *Journal of Psychoeducation Assessment, 33*(1), 24-32.

American Psychiatric Association. (2013). *Diagnostic and statistical manual of mental disorders* (5th ed.). Washington, DC: APA.

Anbugeetha, A. (2015). An analysis of the spiritual intelligence self-report inventory (SISRI). *International Journal of Management, 6*(7), 25-36.

Bandura, A. (1997). *Self-efficacy: The exercise of control*. New York: Worth Publishers.

Baranowsky, A. B. (2002). The silencing response in clinical practice: On the road to dialogue. In C. R. Figley (Ed.), *Treating compassion fatigue* (pp. 155-170). New York: Brunner-Routledge.

Bonano, G. (2010). *The other side of sadness: What the new science of bereavement tells us about life after loss*. New York: Basic Books.

Bride, B. E., Robinson, M. R., Yegidis, B., & Figley, C. R. (2004). Development and validation of the secondary traumatic stress scale. *Research on Social Work Practice, 14*, 27-35.

Burnett, H., & Wahl, K. (2015). The compassion fatigue and resilience connection: A survey of resilience, compassion fatigue, burnout, and compassion satisfaction among trauma responders. *International Journal of Emergency Mental Health and Human Resilience, 17*(1), 318-326.

Charney, D. S. (2004). Psychobiological mechanisms of resilience and vulnerability: Implications for successful adaptation to extreme stress. *American Journal of Psychiatry, 161*(2), 195-216.

Cohen, S., Kamarck, T., & Mermelstein, R. (1983, December). A global measure of perceived stress. *Journal of Health and Social Behavior, 24*(4), 385-396.

Diehl E. (2017). Growth Mindsets for Learning: Effective Effort. In W. Steele (Ed.). *Optimizing Learning Outcomes: Proven Brain-Centric, Trauma Sensitive Practices* (p. 122). New York: Routledge.

Durkin, M., Beaumont, E., Martin, C., & Carson, J. (2016). A pilot study exploring the relationship between self-compassion, self-judgement, self-kindness, compassion, professional quality of life and wellbeing among UK community nurses. *Nurse Education Today, 46*, 109-114.

Fida, R., Laschinger, H. K. S., & Leiter, M. (2018). The protective role of self-efficacy against workplace incivility and burnout in nursing: A time lagged study. *Health Care Management Review, 43*, 21-29.

Gallup. (2018). *Gallup Q12 employee engagement survey*. Retrieved August 15, 2018, from https://q12.gallup.com/public/en-us/Features

Hassan, M., Nadeem, A. B., Akhtet, A., & Nisar, T. (2016). Impact of workplace spirituality on job satisfaction: Mediating effect of trust. *Cogent Business & Management, 3*(1). doi:10.1080/23311975.2016.1189808

King, D. B., & DeCicco, T. L. (2009). A viable model and self-report measure of spiritual intelligence. *International Journal of Transpersonal Studies, 28*(1), 68-85.

Kumar, T., & Pragadeeswaran, S. (2011, August). Effects of occupational stress on spiritual quotient among executives. *International Journal of Trade, Economics and Finance, 2*(4).

Neff, K. D. (2003). Development and validation of a scale to measure self-compassion. *Self and Identity, 2*, 223-250.

Newmeyer, M., Keys, B., Gregory, S., et al. (2014). The Mother Teresa effect: The modulation of spirituality in using The CISM model with mental health service providers. *International Journal of Emergency Mental Health and Human Resilience, 16*(1), 13-19.

Rahmanian, M., Hojat, M., Jahromi, M., & Nabiolahi, A. (2018, August 2). The relationship between spiritual intelligence with self-efficacy in adolescents suffering type 1 diabetes. *Journal Educational Health Promotion, 7*, 100.

Schwarzer, R., & Warner, L. (2013). Perceived self-efficacy and its relationship to resilience: Resilience in children, adolescents, and adults. *The Springer Series on Human Exceptionality*, 139-150. doi:10.1007/978-1-4614-4939-3_10

Seligman, M. (2011). Flourish. New York, NY: Free Press. [Google Scholar]

Souza, L., & Hutz, C. (2016). Self-compassion in relation to self-esteem, self-efficacy and demographical aspects. *Paidéia, 26*, 181-188.

Sprang, G., Ross, L., Blackshear, K., Miller, B., Vrabel, C., Ham, J., . . . Caringi, J. (2014). *The secondary traumatic stress informed organization assessment (STSI-OA) tool*. Lexington, Kentucky: University of Kentucky Center on Trauma and Children, #14-STS001.

Sprang, G., Ross, L., Miller, B. C., Blackshear, K., & Ascienzo, S. (2017). The secondary traumatic stress informed organization assessment. *Traumatology, 23*(2), 165-171.

Workplace Mental Health | Mental Health America. (2018). Retrieved January 4, 2019, from www.mentalhealthamerica.net/workplace-mental-health

7 Putting It All Together

Opening Statement

Well, here we are at our final session. Given all the information you've received, what you learned from some of our activities and the assessments you completed, I'm sure some of you have already identified several mindsets and practices that need changing or developing.

The purposes of this session are to,

1. examine your thoughts regarding your assessment outcomes,
2. identify what needs your attention and what matters most to you,
3. support the essential and critical need to prioritize and reflect regularly,
4. identify what self-care is not,
5. discuss daily at work regulation practices, and
6. interventions specific to CF/STS and BO.

There will be additional aids and resources in the Appendix that will also support the effectiveness of your self-care efforts.

Focusing Down: What Matters Most

Outcomes of the completed assessments provide a great deal of information about how you approach life and its challenges, your thoughts, beliefs, emotional and behavioral reactions to the various life challenges and stressors you face, as well as symptoms you could be experiencing specific to CF/STS/BO. What is difficult to determine, without assessment, is how our thought processes, attitudes, behaviors, emotions and work environment are contributing to the overall negative impact stress may be having daily on the different areas of our lives. You began that process by completing the recommended assessments. It's now time to focus down to what you consider matters the most in your efforts to best manage those responses to the stress in your life inclusive of the stress related to CF/STS/BO. This process will help you focus on those areas and actions that will be most important to your professional and personal wellness and well-being, to mitigating the stress of the work you do, to help you engage in balanced self-care practices. You will need your completed *Self-Care Checklist* as we go through this next process and the *What Matters Most Worksheet* found in the Appendix.

There are four phases to this process:

1. reflecting on your assessment outcomes,
2. prioritizing what matters most,
3. identifying possible actions, and
4. taking action/accountability

Phase One: Reflecting on the Outcomes

I'll comment on each assessment tool and then provide time for you to reflect on your outcomes for each assessment in order to then identify what matters most to you given those outcomes. You can then transcribe what matters most on the *What Matters Most Worksheet*. Let's begin with your responses to Question #4 in each of the post-session series of questions and then go forward with your other outcomes.

Post-Session Reflection

As you reflect on your responses to question #4, which is, "How has this changed what you feel you need to do about the unavoidable stress of what you do?" in each of the Post-Session Questions, Sessions One through Five, ask yourself what you now consider matters most to you. How would you complete this sentence: "I need to . . ."? Be as specific as possible. (You may find that you need multiple actions.)

   Record your answer on the What Matters Most Worksheet in the Appendix.

Perceived Stress Scale (PSS)

How we perceive and think about the situations we face daily directly influences how we respond physiologically, emotionally and behaviorally. If we perceive a situation to be stressful, even when it may not be for others, our nervous system, cognitive processes and performance levels will respond accordingly. Think of your perceptions as being either a fixed mindset or a growth mindset, one that is limiting and negative or one that is flexible and optimistic. If your PSS score is mild, your mindsets are likely to be growth oriented and optimistic. Statements rated "very often" and those rated "somewhat" are more reflective of a fixed mindset. These are the ones you want to spend some time reflecting about as to what may be causing you to be so fixed and negative in your thinking and, of course, how you can rescript these to reflect optimism, adaptability and self-regulation.

   As you now reflect on your PSS outcomes, what matters most for you? How would you complete this sentence: "I need to . . ."? Be as specific as possible. (You may find that you need multiple actions.)

   List your response on your What Matters Most Worksheet found in the Appendix.

Stress 360 Outcomes

These outcomes provide a focus as to which area of your life may be experiencing the most stress. Outcomes from the other tools you completed will likely support these outcomes. For example, if on this scale your attitude appears to be problematic, you may find the same reflected under the Self-Compassion and Resilience Characteristics outcomes. If, for example, your outcomes show occupational stress, your Test-Stress.com BO assessment outcomes and the BO level on the ProQOL may reflect outcomes similar to the Stress 360 outcomes. In addition, results of the *Self-Engagement Survey* may indicate low levels or problematic issues with engagement. The value of completing several tools is that outcomes are generally more comprehensive and provide more specific information as to the sources of that stress. These combined results make it easier to prioritize areas needing attention.

   As you now reflect on your Stress 360 outcomes, what stands out as a priority for you? How would you complete this sentence: "I need to . . ."? Be as specific as possible.

   List your response(s) on the What Matters Most Worksheet.

The Stress and Well-Being Survey

Adaptability is a characteristic of being resilient, being optimistic and having an *effective effort* growth mindset. If your adaptability outcome is not favorable, it may also be reflective of the scope of your coping/problem solving skills or reflect a need for more knowledge and skill development training related to the work you are doing. If your emotional vitality score is low, it may be tied to BO, limited self-regulation and self-compassion and overall poor self-care across the six domains we discussed in earlier sessions. Once again as you reflect on all the outcomes of these tools, patterns and sources of stress will emerge.

As you now reflect on your Stress and Well-being outcomes, what stands out as a priority for you? How would you complete this sentence: "I need to . . ."? Be as specific as possible.

List your response(s) on the What Matters Most Worksheet.

StressCom (Optional)

This tool identifies your wellness in six different areas that help to further isolate issues that may need to be targeted as priorities in your self-care plan. They may also reinforce other findings. For example, your rating regarding *control* and *change* may reflect issues with control revealed on the PSS or under adaptability on the *Stress and Well-Being Survey* or under the *Resilience Characteristics* survey. As you consider the outcomes on this tool, reflect on the recommendations related to the high stress areas that are provided with your scores.

Now as you review the outcomes of the *StressCom* survey, what stands out as a priority for you? How would you complete this sentence: "I need to . . ."? Be as specific as possible.

List your response(s) on the What Matters Most Worksheet.

Let's now focus down on BO, secondary trauma and CF.

Test-Stress.com

This BO assessment tool has been well researched and provides evaluation of the three symptoms of BO. These symptoms are also evaluated on the ProQOL but with less detailed information. The ProQOL indicates the level of BO as does the Test-Stress.com scale; however, the Test-Stress outcomes provide a breakout as to which of the three symptom areas are the most stressful. This allows you to focus on your change efforts in the area needing the most attention. BO is a serious issue and, as we've discussed multiple times, leaves us more at risk for CF and STS. If we are emotionally and physically exhausted and walk into another traumatic situation, we will be more at risk. We're also more likely to make a major mistake or interact in ways that create greater risk and stress for our clients as well as ourselves and the organization that employs us. BO symptoms need to be addressed.

As you now reflect on your Stress and Well-Being outcomes, what stands out as a priority for you? How would you complete this sentence: "I need to . . ."? Be as specific as possible.

List your response(s) on the What Matters Most Worksheet.

Silencing Response Scale

Reviewing your responses to this tool what surprises you the most about your responses, what stands out the most for you? After reflecting on your responses, how would you complete this sentence: "I need to . . ."? Be as specific as possible. (You may have multiple actions that are needed.)

Record your response(s) on the What Matters Most Worksheet.

STS Checklist

All professionals experience one or more STS reactions at some point. However, when experiencing STS, you will experience at least one reaction within each category. Your reactions may follow inter-action with one client or they may be a result of assisting and/or responding to multiple clients/situa-tions over time. Even if you are not experiencing at least one reaction in each category, the reactions you are experiencing serve as a red flag. It will be important in supervision to further evaluate who or what those reactions are associated with so you can process them appropriately. A supervisor who meets the core competency requirements for STS supervision should be able to help you learn from theses reactions as well as resolve them. If this is not available to you, you may want to consult with a trauma specialist outside of the organization.

As you now reflect on your STS outcomes, what stands out as a priority for you? How would you complete this sentence: "I need to . . ."? Be as specific as possible.

List your response(s) on the What Matters Most Worksheet.

The ProQOL

This tool is a "go to" for many organizations and caregivers. What is most helpful is that it provides a number of possible combinations of outcomes and provides suggestions regarding possible action needed for each combination. However, do keep in mind that even if your score for BO and STS is average, not a high risk, do consider the outcome of the *STS Checklist* and the Test-Stress outcomes as they are more specific as to which reactions are creating the most stress. Even though results may not be indicative of high BO or STS levels, they are red flags that should be addressed in super-vision before they lead to other reactions.

As you now reflect on your ProQOL outcomes, what stands out as a priority for you? How would you complete this sentence: "I need to . . ."? Be as specific as possible.

List your response(s) on the What Matters Most Worksheet.

Self-Engagement Survey

Positive engagement ("yes" answers) generally supports retention, higher levels of performance and engaging in activities that support the organization. "Somewhat" engagement will be reflected in more sporadic performance and attendance, less involvement in support of the organization, more frequent thoughts about/searches for another job. A high score "rarely engaged" is indicative of a very poor fit with the organization. Poor engagement, even "somewhat" engagement, sug-gests that this culture, its policies and practices may not be a very good fit for you. If you stay in an environment without sufficient engagement, you will experience BO and the stress associated with a lack of professional accomplishment, the frequent conflicts, crises, favoritism and other factors associated with low engagement environments. Keep in mind that this low level of engagement is not necessarily about you but also about the absence of transformational leadership at all levels.

As you now reflect on your Self-Engagement outcomes, what stands out for you? How would you complete this sentence: "I need to . . ."? Be as specific as possible.

List your response(s) on the What Matters Most Worksheet.

Secondary Traumatic Stress Informed Organization Assessment (STSI-OA)

Your well-being is as dependent on what your organization provides as it is on your self-care prac-tices. This is why it is important to evaluate how your organization may be contributing to your stress. As previously indicated, if engagement levels are low, your stress will be high and will impact your performance and desire to remain with that organization. If the organization is also lacking in STS practices, you are far more vulnerable to not only STS but also CF and likely BO. Trauma-sensitive organizations generally engage practices to reduce stress in all these areas. You need to consider this when thinking about sources that are causing you undue stress, whether you need to consider changing environments and/or your current role.

As you now reflect on your STSI-OA outcomes, what stands out as a priority for you? How would you complete this sentence: "I need to . . ."? Be as specific as possible.

List your response(s) on the What Matters Most Worksheet.

STS Competency Survey

By all means if you are assisting victims of trauma, you definitely need to be in a supervisory relationship in which the supervisor meets the core competencies related to STS. If this is not the case, then you are far more vulnerable to STS and CF.

If you are a supervisee, review your answers to the three questions regarding your supervisory relationship and the STS competency of your supervisor. As you reflect on your answers, what matters most for you? How would you complete this sentence: "I need to . . ."? Be as specific as possible.

List your response(s) on the What Matters Most Worksheet.

As a supervisor, review the core competency outcomes and those areas you identified as needing your attention. As you reflect on your responses, what stands out as a priority for you? How would you complete this sentence: "I need to . . ."? Be as specific as possible.

List your response(s) on the What Matters Most Worksheet.

Self-compassion

If you are having difficulty with self-compassion, you may also find that your resilience and attempts at self-efficacy are limited and need your attention. The three are inter-related; when one is weak, the others will also be limited in helping you manage the negative impact of the stress you are experiencing inclusive of CF/STS and BO. In reality you need to be doing well in each of the six self-compassion categories. Do give your attention to any one of these that are not supportive of compassion toward yourself as you will want to work toward changing them. Without self-compassion, CF presents a much greater risk.

As you reflect on your Self-Compassion outcomes, what stands out as a priority for you? How would you complete this sentence: "I need to . . ."? Be as specific as possible.

List your response(s) on the What Matters Most Worksheet.

Spiritual Intelligence Self-Report Inventory (SISRI-24)

This is the one area that many do not consider when thinking about self-care. The fact that the mindsets and practices that make up our spiritual intelligence are referred to as spiritual simply turn some people away, but they support the best in us, our empathy, resilience, gratitude and emotional regulation. Spiritual mindsets and practices help us lead purposeful/meaningful lives, make decisions based on that purpose and meaning and support a good greater than ourselves. These are the mindsets and practices that lead to compassion satisfaction and life satisfaction.

As you reflect on your SISRI outcomes, what stands out as a priority for you? How would you complete this sentence: "I need to . . ."? Be as specific as possible.

List your response(s) on the What Matters Most Worksheet.

Mind Tool Resilience Self-Assessment

This tool exams confidence, social support, adaptability and purposefulness to determine the level of resilience. These outcomes should be similar to previous tool outcomes related to optimism (confidence) and adaptability. Its measurement of purposefulness is not as comprehensive as the SISRI spiritual assessment; however, it does provide a good measure of social support, a willingness to seek help from others, value others.

    As you reflect on the Mind Tool Resilience Self-Assessment outcomes, what stands out as a priority for you? How would you complete this sentence: "I need to . . ."? Be as specific as possible.

    List your response(s) on the What Matters Most Worksheet.

Resilience Characteristics Survey

Many of the resilience tools found on the Internet do not cover resilient factors reported in the literature and supported by the research. For this reason, I developed this survey to encompass the factors discussed in our sessions and supported by research. The free Mind Tool assessment for resilience does not address effective effort, self-care/wellness, spiritual intelligence beyond purpose. This survey evaluates these areas in addition to the areas of the Mind Tool; however, I recommend completing both.

    As you now reflect on your Resilience Characteristics outcomes, what stands out as a priority for you? How would you complete this sentence: "I need to . . ."? Be as specific as possible.

    List your response(s) on the What Matters Most Worksheet.

Final Reflection

To complete Phase One, review the *Reflective Questionnaires* in the Appendix. Reviewing and beginning with the *IQ Matrix Questionnaire* is recommended. The other questionnaires cover various areas. Select those that apply to you and then record your responses as directed on the *What Matters Most Worksheet*.

Phase Two: Prioritizing Your "To-do's"

Your "to-do's" are now your self-care priorities. Some will be more important than others for you. It's critical that you now take a minute to order your priorities by their importance. If, for example, you are in the midst of experiencing BO, there are negative consequences for everyone. You need to focus on caring for your physiological and psychological well-being. Perhaps taking that five-minute break every hour, taking a walk during your lunch and reframing your thoughts will help. Perhaps you will need to do more and seek help from an outside source. What matters is that this becomes a priority because of the consequences involved in doing nothing.

Why Set Priorities?

Why prioritize? It reduces stress and increases productivity. It gives you a sense of pride and control. It motivates you, gives you a sense of empowerment. Our self-care efforts will need to be integrated with those other priorities we have such as driving the kids to baseball or gymnastics practice, changing the oil in the car, paying bills, returning phone calls, getting to that doctor's appointment on time. Life is busy. If we do not keep our self-care priorities in our sights, it's very easy to be pulled in other directions. Workplaces today demand multi-tasking and responding to unrelenting demands, day-to-day crises. Under these stressful conditions it is very easy to lose sight of what is important, to get sucked into what others want, even when it is not pertinent to our work or our responsibilities; that makes for lost time, energy and performance efficiency.

Keeping our self-care priorities in view helps to counter these demands and the stress they induce. Focusing on our priorities also helps avoid physical and emotional fatigue, especially in organizations engaged in practices associated with BO.

Ultimately, prioritizing gives us more time to relax, to mitigate the stress of what we do, to be valued and remain of value to others especially those we are caring for and responding to on a daily basis. However, for this to happen, we need to daily remind ourselves of those priorities. Writing down our priorities externalizes them into something real, concrete and tangible. Looking at those written priorities on a regular basis reinforces our efforts and commitment to be at our best, our most effective and our healthiest physically, psychologically, emotionally and socially, and in our relationships and in the work we do.

Setting and Ordering Your Self-care Priorities

Let me recommend the following method to order your priorities. When looking at to-do list, first ask yourself the following question for each to-do:

1. Which to-do's do I consider important and needing my immediate attention?
2. What might be the negative consequences for me if I do not pursue these?
3. Who will suffer the most from my not attending to these to-do's?
4. Which of these to-do's promises the greatest benefit?

Your answers to these four questions will help you determine your top priorities. Record these on your *What Matters Most Worksheet* in the order you consider most important. You may find that there are two or three top priorities you consider equally important. This is okay because you can often combine your efforts and work on these at the same time. For example, let's say you discovered that you need to do more in the areas of engagement, regulating your physiological responses to the stress you're experiencing and practicing daily gratitude. When you take your five-minute break (we'll discuss this in a minute), you could also visit one of your colleagues, engage in small talk and express appreciation for their taking a break with you: for example, "Thanks for taking a break with me. I needed it."

Secondary Priorities

The remaining to-do's become those priorities you consider important but not as urgent as your top priorities. This does not mean that they are ignored only that they do not have the same negative consequences as your top priorities if no action is taken immediately. However, in many cases, you'll find that working on a top priority benefits some of your secondary priorities. For example, while working on reframing your thoughts to be more optimistic, you may find that you are also improving the regulation of negative emotions as well as more effectively regulating your nervous systems response to stress and also finding that you are physically and emotionally less exhausted at the end of the day.

Phase Three: Identifying Possible Actions

If you feel you need to identify specific activities or direction for any of your priorities, the Internet is a wonderful "how-to" resource. For example, if you want a little more direction on how to reframe your thoughts simply Google "How to Reframe My Thoughts." For actions related to self-efficacy simply Google "How to Improve My Self-efficacy"; the same goes for improving your "resilience," "emotional regulation skills" or "how to enhance your environment" in ways that address not only the physical aspects but also neurological aspects associated with performance, concentration, etc. When searching, you'll generally find what you need on the first page of sources; information will also generally be presented by business and psychology sources. I'm always curious so I'll check out the second page of resources. This takes no more than 5-10 minutes of your time and can yield wonderful help. The suggestions you find can then be added to the *My Priorities, My Action Plan Worksheet* in the Appendix.

Following are additional sources that identify specific practices and activities to support many of the aspects we've discussed and you evaluated when completing the assessment series. These will provide much of what you need to support your self-care efforts. Simply Google the titles as indicated:

- The Only Guide You'll Need for Reframing Your Thoughts Using NLP.
- 17 Ways to Take Care of Yourself.
- Resilience Practices.
- Self-efficacy Practices.
- Self-compassion Strategies.
- Overcoming BO in the Workplace.
- Finding Purpose Strategies.
- Changing Our Perceptions.
- 6 Reasons Why You Should Use a Daily Planner.
- Stop Fighting Your Negative Thoughts.
- How to Talk to Yourself.
- Speak to Yourself Using Words that Soothe and Heal.
- 10 Reasons to Stop Judging People.
- 20 Expert Tactics for Dealing With Difficult People.
- 8 Easy Meditation Tips for Beginners.
- 7 Things NOT to Do When Practicing Mindfulness Meditation.
- Mindfulness Practices at Work.

List the actions you determined could be helpful under each priority on your *My Priorities, My Action Plan Worksheet*.

Phase Four: Taking Action/Accountability

Accountability, in this case, means taking ownership of our day. It means identifying what is in our best interest, what will help us be the person we want to be and accomplish what we hope to accomplish. It means making a commitment to do what it takes to sustain our effectiveness in our interactions with those we are caring for and responding to. It means embracing self-care practices daily while at work and outside of work and then holding ourselves accountable for our overall well-being. One of the best ways to remain accountable is to regularly practice self-reflection. Let me talk a bit about the value and benefits of reflection.

Know What You Need to Be More Resilient: Reflect

Why reflect? If we are serious about being the best we can, realizing our potential in all areas of our life, mitigating the effects of stress and CF we must focus on self-awareness and self-regulation. Self-reflection strengthens both self-awareness and self-regulation. Reflection is the practice of looking inward, which helps us learn to tap into and develop our strengths, our values and our well-being (Morin, 2011). Reflection also helps identify how what we do and say affects others, which is essential for empathy. By identifying how we might approach the daily challenges in our relationships, personal life and work life differently, we are actually regulating our responses to those challenges (Baumeister & Vohs, 2003; Heatherton, Krendl, Macrae, & Kelley, 2007); we become far more responsive than reactive. Self-reflection (awareness) is about keeping control of our life rather than allowing others and/or the conditions we face to control our responses. It improves critical thinking and decision-making; enriches emotional intelligence; and strengthens empathy, listening skills, effective communications and relationships (Morin, 2011; Avolio & Gardner, 2005; Diggins, 2004; Furnham & Stringfield, 1994). It's important to note that transformational leaders exercise reflection, and research shows they have high levels of self-awareness (Barling, Slater, & Kelloway, 2000). Also, keep in mind our discussion about supervision and the importance of the reflective process—becoming aware of our reactions, our thoughts, our beliefs and our emotions regarding client interactions. If you remember, reflective supervision is a core competency (Greene, 2017; Anghel, Amas, & Hicks, 2010; Urdang, 2010) especially related to mitigating STS/CF/BO.

Reality: *Failure to practice self-reflection is like being stuck on life's treadmill, always moving but going nowhere.*

Focused and Balanced

There are two forms of self-reflection: focused and balanced (see self-reflection questions in the Appendix). The self-compassion survey you completed is an example of a focused reflection on those reactions that either support your compassion or drain it. Reflecting on your reactions to clients in supervision is a focused reflection. Reflecting on a particular incident that occurred is a focused reflection. These end-of-day reflections are encouraged as they help to

- reinforce your strengths,
- regulate your emotions,
- learn from your mistakes, failures,
- discover potential problems and opportunities in advance,
- fine tune your effective effort strategies to move toward accomplishing what matters most to you,
- reset your focus and adjust your next day priorities as needed,
- feel better prepared and confident to start fresh the following day, and
- empty your mind to "let go" of the day.

Some days it's a five-minute practice and other days, because of the challenges of the day, it may need more of your time. Daily reflection is more of a focused reflection on what stood out the most to us that day. Once you are done with reflecting about the day, it's then time to engage in those sensory activities that allow you to relax and prepare for a good night sleep.

Balanced Reflection

A balanced reflection covers the major areas of our lives: health, family/personal relationships, social relationships/activities, spirituality, as we have defined it; personal and professional growth and finances. The time needed is between 15 and 30 minutes, depending on range of experiences for the week, especially those that were challenging and created some difficulty. If you Google "Wheel of Life," you'll find several models that life coaches use to help individuals reflect on all these life areas, what is important to them and what needs their attention. Others focus on reflecting on our thoughts, behaviors, emotions, interactions, attitudes, beliefs and health. Evaluating these areas and using that information to update your priorities is how we integrate our priorities between life and work; it's the essence of effective self-care.

Reality: *Reflecting and setting priorities practices are mutually inclusive.*

If I want to become less reactive to trauma reminders and/or trauma situations, I need to reflect on what triggers these unwanted reactions as well what can help me better regulate them. These actions then become my priority. Let's say I work for child protective services. One of my primary tasks is to complete case records in a timely fashion and meet all the requirements of what needs to be included in those records. The consequences of not doing so places my clients, the organization and myself at risk, yet I am falling behind and my records are incomplete. I need to reflect on what is happening that prevents me from meeting these requirements, determine what has to change and then make those efforts a priority. Completing my records and reflecting on what I need to do to accomplish this are mutually inclusive. Let's say after reflecting, I realize that I need to change my mindset, to reframe my thoughts to be more optimistic or far less self-critical. In order to accomplish this, I need to make reframing a priority. The two are mutually inclusive.

Self-reflective Questions

Because self-reflection is such a powerful change agent, several self-reflection questionnaires are included in the Appendix. They address many of the areas addressed in the assessments you completed such as our thoughts and thought processes, emotions, attitudes, beliefs, physical and spiritual self-care, our interactions/engagement with others, the knowledge we gained, behavior and interactions. There is a series of self-reflective questions related to your interactions with clients and one related to record keeping, which gives many caregivers a challenge. There is a *Brief End-of-Day Reflection* that can be used when prioritizing as well as an end of week one to help with organizing the upcoming week.

Reality: *Self-reflection brings out the best in us in all aspects of life.*

At the End of the Day/End of the Week

Progress, growth, resilience, self-efficacy, self-compassion, compassion satisfaction, mitigating the stress of the work you do, sustaining and improving your effectiveness as caregivers and responders demands self-reflection. Now that you have identified your self-care priorities, I strongly recommend that you take time at the end of every day to briefly reflect on your efforts. Simply use the *Brief End-of-Day Reflection* questionnaire in the Appendix. After reflecting, I then recommend that you look at priorities for the following day (assuming you set priorities for the week) and adjust these as needed. At the end of the week, I recommend that you use the *IQ Matrix Questionnaire* or Dr. Marway's *Self-Care Assessment Questions* (in Appendix) to review the week, all that you learned and encountered and then use this information to establish your priorities for the following week. This keeps you focused and accelerates success. It keeps you accountable. It will make a significant difference.

Immediate Interventions

If you are currently in the midst of experiencing CF/STS and/or BO, immediate intervention is necessary. Following are several recommendations.

BO

The majority of studies show that organizational directed interventions have a greater effect at reducing BO than do individually directed interventions (Panagioti, Panagopoulou, & Bower, 2017; Ahola, Tanner, & Sappanen, 2017). These interventions include flexible scheduling, varied caseload, no after-hours e-mails or texts (except for those on call), transitional leadership at all levels, a focus on staff engagement, provision of wellness and well-being resources especially with on-site availability.

If you are experiencing BO, you can manage some of the symptoms through direct interventions such as meditation, cognitive behavioral intervention, EMDR, Writing Exposure Therapy, skill training, etc.; however, these will not significantly diminish those BO symptoms that are related to known organizational driven practices associated with BO. If the organization is unable to take responsibility for changing these practices, looking for a different organization with the qualities just identified is the best intervention.

CF

The primary interventions recommended for CF are self-care and a work-life balance. The key obviously is to determine the specific areas needing attention, which you have already identified. Most have found that focusing efforts on resilience building, which involves self-efficacy, self-compassion and emotional regulation to be of significant help. Meditation is mentioned frequently. Keep in mind our earlier review of several programs who discovered that to be effective, meditation had to be practiced frequently. Also keep in mind the organizational factors discussed in previous sessions, those that support a culture that is trauma-informed and trauma-sensitive, a high level of engagement and has a leadership that demonstrates its concern for your wellness and well-being. If these are missing, your individual efforts may help but be offset by a less than supportive workplace culture.

If your individual efforts are not helping, you may want to bring your concerns into supervision if you feel emotionally safe doing so; if not, then you need to connect with a trauma specialist outside of the work environment. This is especially important when struggling with countertransference issues and/or a personal past trauma that is being activated by your clients. When searching, look for someone who practices and is certified in several trauma specific interventions such as EMDR, Somatic Experiencing, the use of art therapy, journaling and other practice-based, evidence-based trauma interventions.

STS

If in the midst of experiencing STS, take your concerns to your supervisor if, as discussed earlier, that supervisor is STS competent otherwise seek help from an outside trauma specialist. A number of the interventions effective with PTSD will likely also be effective with alleviating the symptoms of STS. That specialist should also evaluate your self-care efforts and work-life balance and, as previously mentioned, be certified in several trauma specific approaches.

Safety

Interventions for CF and STS are generally brief. There is no one intervention that is necessarily better than another; it's what fits best for you, who you feel safest with and what you feel safest doing. Review the potential trauma specialist's credentials; ask about their approaches and what they consider most important. Pay attention to your subjective experience as you listen. Ask yourself: Am I feeling comfortable with this person? What is my "gut" saying to me? Are they too "matter of fact"?

Are they focused only on my symptoms or curious about the subjective thoughts and feelings, fears or anxiety I am experiencing about what is happening to me? And once again, ask yourself if you feel safe in their presence? If you do fine; if not seek out someone else until you find that person who seems to connect with you in a way that allows you to feel safe with them.

Necessary at Work Daily Self-care Practices

Reality: *Self-care is not what we try to cram into a weekend to cut loose or come down; it's what we do every day at work and outside of the work setting that keeps the brakes on stress.*

Regulating the accumulation of negative stress and its impact on your performance, interactions with clients, the effectiveness of your responses and mitigating CF/STS BO cannot be accomplished on the weekends. The fact is by the time we get to the weekend, the stress that has accumulated has already negatively impacted our mood, thoughts, behaviors and biology. Following are several daily practices that are brief yet make a world of difference.

Move

In Session Three you were asked to focus on a current stressful issue and then asked to take several poses. During each pose you focused on how that pose changed what you were thinking about that stressor and what you felt. All agreed that just a brief change in posture altered thoughts and feelings. Actually, after sitting, any movement will change not only our cognitive and emotional responses but also our biology.

Reality: *Simply changing your posture for two minutes reduces the stress hormone cortisol by 20%* (Cuddy, Wilmuth, & Carney, 2012).

Based on research about sitting for more than 30 minutes at a time and its association with health risk, associate research scientist at Columbia University Medical Center, Keith Diaz (Reynolds, 2017) recommends, that every 30 minutes we simply take 1 minute to get up from the desk to move, stretch or walk around the office. That may seem too frequent; however, there is ample research (Bergouignan, 2016) to support this. There is also research that shows that 5 minutes of walking (moving) every hour has the positive benefits of enhancing our mood, energy, concentration and focus. Moving for brief periods, whether it be for a minute every 30 minutes or 5 minutes every hour, makes a definite difference by keeping our response to the stressors of our work and working environment regulated. Any movement, even the briefest, has well-being benefits. Do make it a priority, if sitting for 30 minutes or more to get up and move. It's easy to set an alert on your phone, computer or smartwatch to remind you.

Know Your Regulators

When unwanted reactions are triggered, it is important to regulate these reactions via a brief action such as focusing on your breathing, on a specific thought, walking around, pulling out your iPhone and looking at photographs that remind you of what is important and help put the breaks on your nervous system response; viewing a funny YouTube you have saved to relax for a minute, playing a favorite song, changing scenery for a few minutes or checking in briefly with a colleague. Have several options available as what works one day may not work the next day.

If you are anticipating a difficult situation, know beforehand what you will try to do to regulate those reactions. In this situation, it is helpful if you can practice beforehand top-down regulation by identifying those cognitive thoughts you want to stay focused on during that anticipated situation. With practice this can be very helpful.

Sensory Closure and Transition

When the workday is over, it is important to shut it down at a sensory level and then use a sensory cue to transition into life outside of work. By sensory cue I mean a sound, a visual, something tactile. Make this a daily practice. For example, pay attention to the feel and sound as you close your office door or as you close the car door to leave the parking lot or as you listen to a favorite song you've programed for the drive home. To actually transition to your non-work environment, your life outside of work, also focus on a sensory trigger that lets your nervous system know you are in hopefully a less stressful environment. That trigger may be hugging a loved one or petting your pet; maybe it's when you put on your favorite slacks, jeans, sweats or go to the fridge for a favorite snack, some good old comfort food. Remember our nervous system often responds faster to sensory cues than cognitive cues although if a cognitive cue works for you, use it. Make these sensory transitions from work to home a daily routine as repetition rewires our brain; soon these transitions will become automatic.

Before the Day Is Over

Practice Gratitude

Reality: *People who practice gratitude cope better with stress, recover more quickly from illness, and enjoy more robust physical health, including lower blood pressure and better immune function* (Emmons, 2013).

More than any other personality trait, gratitude is strongly linked to mental health and life satisfaction. Not only is gratitude a warm and uplifting way to feel, it benefits the body as well. Gratitude reduces lifetime risk for depression, anxiety and substance abuse disorders, and it helps people entangled with those and other problems to heal and find closure (Emmons, 2013). Gratitude also "fortifies our bonds with other people" (Bergland, 2015), which allows us to do better when exposed to trauma than those who do not have significant connections with others. In other words, gratitude strengthens our resilience. As far as gratitude being "the parent of all other virtues," it is also associated with optimism and generosity, which are also essential to sustaining resilience. Gratitude, optimism and generosity have all been neurologically mapped to show how they actually alter our brains responses in positive ways (Zahn et al., 2009; Kini, Wong, Mcinnis, Gabana, & Brown, 2016). *The Five Minute Journal,* by Intelligent Change (there is also an app), comes highly recommended with a five-star rating and endorsed as a daily resource for practicing gratitude. It makes practicing gratitude daily quite easy. Gratitude consists of identifying what we are personally grateful for each day and also expressing gratitude to others through appreciation, recognition and acts of kindness. This needs to be a daily priority. It takes only minutes but the benefits are long lasting.

Prepare for Tomorrow

End the day, every day, with a few minutes of reflection and setting your priorities for the next day. This keeps you accountable but also signals your nervous system and your psyche that the day is over, and you are ready for tomorrow so now you can relax. *It only takes a few minutes.* I simply write down each day of the week as headings and then under those headings list all that I hope to do each day or complete by the time one of the days rolls around. I then mark those items in each list that are a must do that day; the others I know can be moved to the next day or so if I don't get to them as planned. Throughout the week I update the entire list. At the end of each day (and the end of the week) I do some brief reflecting on what I did or did not accomplish, how I did with what

I encountered and then I reprioritize the next day as needed. All this takes less than 10 minutes. It works for me; however, there are a number of apps that you may find fit best for you. These apps include Remember the Milk, Toodle do, Nozbe, Lazy Meter or Things on the Mac. I'm basically a paper and pencil person when it comes to setting priorities. For me, writing produces more sensory, kinesthetic involvement and reinforcement than digital processes at least when it comes to setting priorities. Experiment and do what works best for you.

Renew Your Energy: Avoid Blue Light

Try to go at least 30 minutes before going to bed avoiding all blue light sources such as the television, iPhone, computer, video games. This is a great time to meditate or reflect on the day. Blue light stimulates the brain making it more difficult to fall into a restorative sleep. The research is quite strong as to the negative impact of blue light on sleep patterns. This 30 minutes without blue light stimulation before bed will also help slow down the nervous system, help remove tension and ready your body and brain for deep restorative sleep. In reference to blue light, keep the bedroom dark. If you are with a partner who needs to sleep with the television on, get yourself a sleep mask to block out the light. You will be surprised by how much easier you fall asleep and enjoy a more restful and restorative sleep. This is an important factor in fighting stress. Results from the world's largest sleep study (Wild, Nichols, Battista, Stojanoski, & Owen, 2018) have shown that people who sleep on average between 7 to 8 hours per night performed better cognitively than those who slept less, or more, than this amount. The stronger our cognitive functioning, the more effective our efforts to mitigate the cognitive deficiencies resulting from ongoing stress (Crum, Akinila, Martin, & Fath, 2017).

That's It

You've been presented a wealth of information and a number of strategies to select from. You will also find additional self-care practices and resources in the Appendix. Let me leave you with this quote: William James, the father of American psychology, wrote (2019): "If you can change your mind, you can change your life."

References

Ahola, K., Tanner, S., & Sappanen, J. (2017, March). Interventions to alleviate burnout symptoms and to support return to work among employees with burnout: Systematic review and meta-analysis. *Burnout Research, 4*, 1-1.

Anghel, R., Amas, D., & Hicks, J. (2010). Self-awareness and personal development in social work education: A pilot programme of experiential workshops. *Networks, 13*.

Avolio, B. J., & Gardner, W. L. (2005). Authentic leadership development: Getting to the root of positive forms of leadership. *The Leadership Quarterly, 16*(3), 315-338.

Barling, J., Slater, F., & Kevin Kelloway, E. (2000). Transformational leadership and emotional intelligence: An exploratory study. *Leadership & Organization Development Journal, 21*(3), 157-161.

Baumeister, R. F., & Vohs, K. D. (2003). Self-regulation and the executive function of the self. In M. R. Leary & J. P. Tangney (Eds.), *Handbook of self and identity* (pp. 197-217). New York: Guildford Press.

Bergland, C. (2015). *Small acts of generosity and the neuroscience of gratitude: Brain scans can map the neural mechanisms of gratitude activated by generosity*. Retrieved January 27, 2018, from https://www.psychology today.com/us/blog/the-athletes-way/201510/small-acts-generosity-and-the-neuroscience-gratitude

Bergouignan, A., Legget, T., De Jong, N., Kealey, E., Nikolovski, J., Groppel, J., . . . Bessesen, D. (2016). Effect of frequent interruptions of prolonged sitting on self-perceived levels of energy, mood, food cravings and cognitive function. *International Journal of Behavioral Nutrition and Physical, 13*, 113.

Crum, A., Akinila, M., Martin, A., & Fath, S. (2017). The role of stress mindset in shaping cognitive, emotional, and physiological responses to challenging and threatening stress. *Anxiety, Stress, & Coping.* http://dx.doi.org/10.1080/10615806.2016.1275585

Cuddy, A. J. C., Wilmuth, C. A., & Carney, D. R. (2012, September). The benefit of power posing before a high-stakes social evaluation. *Harvard Business School Working Paper, No. 13-027.*

Diggins, C. (2004). Emotional intelligence: The key to effective performance. *Human Resource Management, 12*(1), 33-35.

Emmons, R. (2013). Gratitude as a Psychotherapeutic Intervention. *Journal of Clinical Psychology, 69*(8), 846-855.

Furnham, A., & Stringfield, P. (1994). Correlates of self and subordinate ratings of managerial practices as a correlate of supervisor evaluation. *Journal of Occupational and Organizational Psychology, 67*(1), 57-67.

Greene, A. (2017). The role of self-awareness and reflection in social care practice. *Journal of Social Care, 1*(1), Article 3.

Heatherton, T. F., Krendl, A. C., Macrae, C. N., & Kelley, W. M. (2007). A social brain sciences approach to understanding self. *The Self,* 4-16.

James, W. (2019). Quote. Retrieved February 18, 2019, from https://everydaypowerblog.com/inner-strength-quotes/

Kini, P., Wong, J., Mcinnis, S., Gabana, N., & Brown, J. W. (2016). The effects of gratitude expression on neural activity. *NeuroImage, 128,* 1-10.

Morin, A. (2011). Self-awareness part 1: Definition, measures, effects, functions, and antecedents. *Social and Personality Psychology Compass, 5*(10), 807-823.

Panagioti, M., Panagopoulou, E., & Bower, P. (2017). Controlled Interventions to reduce burnout in physicians: A systematic review and meta-analysis. *JAMA Internal Medicine, 177*(2), 195-205.

Reynolds, G. (2017, September 13). Get up, stand up! (Phys. ed.). *New York Times.*

Urdang, E. (2010). Awareness of self: A critical tool. *Social Work Education, 29*(5), 523-538.

Wild, C. J., Nichols, E. S., Battista, M. E., Stojanoski, B., & Owen, A. M. (2018). Dissociable effects of self-reported daily sleep duration on high-level cognitive abilities. *Sleep.* doi:10.1093/sleep/zsy182

Zahn, R., Moll, J., Paiva, M., Garrido, G., Krueger, F., Huey, E., & Grafman, J. (2009). The neural basis of human social values: Evidence from functional MRI. *Cerebral Cortex, 19*(2), 276-283.

Appendices

A. Assessments

A1   Perceived Stress Scale–10 item

The PSS Scale is reprinted with permission of the American Sociological Association, from Cohen, S., Kamarck, T., and Mermelstein, R. (1983). A global measure of perceived stress. *Journal of Health and Social Behavior,* Vol 24; No 4, 386-396.

The questions in this scale ask you about your feelings and thoughts during the last month. In each case, please indicate with a check how often you felt or thought a certain way.

1. In the last month, how often have you been upset because of something that happened unexpectedly?

    ___0=never   ___1=almost never   ___2=sometimes ___3=fairly often   ___4=very often

2. In the last month, how often have you felt that you were unable to control the important things in your life?

    ___0=never   ___1=almost never   ___2=sometimes ___3=fairly often   ___4=very often

3. In the last month, how often have you felt nervous and "stressed"?

    ___0=never   ___1=almost never   ___2=sometimes ___3=fairly often   ___4=very often

4. In the last month, how often have you felt confident about your ability to handle your personal problems?

    ___0=never   ___1=almost never   ___2=sometimes ___3=fairly often   ___4=very often

5. In the last month, how often have you felt that things were going your way?

    ___0=never   ___1=almost never   ___2=sometimes ___3=fairly often   ___4=very often

6. In the last month, how often have you found that you could not cope with all the things that you had to do?

    ___0=never   ___1=almost never   ___2=sometimes ___3=fairly often   ___4=very often

7. In the last month, how often have you been able to control irritations in your life?

    ___0=never   ___1=almost never   ___2=sometimes ___3=fairly often   ___4=very often

8. In the last month, how often have you felt that you were on top of things?

    ___0=never   ___1=almost never   ___2=sometimes ___3=fairly often   ___4=very often

9. In the last month, how often have you been angered because of things that were outside of your control?

    ___0=never   ___1=almost never   ___2=sometimes ___3=fairly often   ___4=very often

10. In the last month, how often have you felt difficulties were piling up so high that you could not overcome them?

    ___0=never   ___1=almost never   ___2=sometimes ___3=fairly often   ___4=very often

Scoring: Reverse the scoring for the following questions before adding your total score.

Appendix A1

Reversed Items: 4, 5, 7, 8–The scoring value of these 4 positive items are reversed so 0 = 4; 1 = 3; 2 = 2; 3 = 1 and 4 = 0.

The total possible score is 40.

Scores ranging from 0-13 are considered mild; from 14-26 moderate and 27-40 high.

Note: The scoring does not reflect any kind of diagnosis or recommendation for treatment. However, it does reflect that certain life situations are or are not creating stress in your life that may trigger further reflection as to how you might respond differently and/or what you may need to do more of in the way of self-care.

I also suggest the following use. Questions 2, 5, 7 & 8andaddress being able to (or not able to) control things in your life/be on top of things; questions 4, 6, and 10 address how well you are coping; questions 1, 3 and 9 address your emotional reactions. If you scored 2-4 on these questions you want to consider placing these categories on your *Self-Care Checklist*. When preparing your self-care plan you can then do some self-reflecting about these areas and ways you might respond differently or be aware that these may become periodically stressful and need immediate attention.

This scale can be found and downloaded at PSS Mind Garden or in Cohen, S., Kamarck, T., Mermelstein, R. (1983). A global measure of perceived stress. *Journal of Health and Social Behavior, 24*, 385-396.

A2   Silencing Response Scale

Silencing Response Scale, Baranowski, 2002 (© 2011, Routledge)
Reprinted with permission from Routledge, Taylor and Francis

Instructions: This scale was developed to help caregivers identify specific communication struggles in their work. Choose the number that best reflects your experience. Answer all items to the best of your ability as they reflect your feelings. Use the following rating system,

0 = rarely or never___ 1___2___3___4___5___6___7___8___9___10 = very often

1. ____ Are there times when you believe your client is repeating emotional issues you feel were already covered?
2. ____ Do you get angry with client(s)?
3. ____ Are there times when you react with sarcasm toward your client(s)?
4. ____ Are there times when you fake interest?
5. ____ Do you feel that listening to certain experiences of your client(s) will not help?
6. ____ Do you feel that letting your client talk about their trauma will hurt them?
7. ____ Do you feel that listening to your client's experiences will hurt you?
8. ____ Are there times that you blame your client for the bad things that have happened to them?
9. ____ Are there times when you are unable to believe what your client is telling you because what they are describing seems overly traumatic?
10. ____ Are there times when you feel numb, avoidant or apathetic before meeting with certain clients?
11. ____ Do you consistently support certain clients in avoiding important therapeutic material despite ample time to address their concerns?
12. ____ Are there times when sessions do not seem to be going well or the client's treatment progress appears to be blocked?
13. ____ Do you become negatively aroused when a client is angry with you?
14. ____ Are there times when you cannot remember what a client has just said?
15. ____ Are there times when you cannot focus on what a client is saying?

Scoring:

Total all scores to arrive at the sum total.

TOTAL _____

95-150 = high risk; 41-94 = moderate risk; 21-40 some risk; and 0-20 = little risk

Suggestion (my opinion): Experiencing any one of the responses in this scale strongly suggests that you need to discuss your response(s) with a trauma-informed supervisor. Your response may be indicative of emerging STS reactions such as #s 2, 3, 4, 7, 8, 10, 13, 14 and 15. Other responses may indicate a need for additional supervision re: particular clients who's responses you are struggling with or those that may be activating you such as in #s 9, 11 and 12; or your responses could indicate a need for more trauma-specific training such as #s 1, 5 and 6. Some responses may indicate several possibilities such as #11, which could indicate avoidant responses on your part or that you need more training in ways to respond to trauma. In essence these statements reflect symptoms of CF inclusive of STS and/or trauma competency issues.

Appendix A2

Note: Keep in mind even seasoned professionals will occasionally experience any one of these responses. The difference is that seasoned, trauma-informed professionals will engage in self-reflection as to the possible meaning/source of their response rather than ignore or minimize that response.

Baranowsky, A. B. (2002). The silencing response in clinical practice: On the road to dialogue. In C. R. Figley (Ed.), *Treating compassion fatigue* (pp. 155–170). New York: Routledge.

A3   Secondary Traumatic Stress (STS) Checklist

Prepared 2019 by Dr. William Steele

The criteria for STS consist of symptoms of intrusion, avoidance and arousal; and, as of 2013 and the publication of the DSM-5 and Criteria "D," it is my opinion that alterations in cognitions and mood (Criteria "D") ought to be included.

   The following statements are related to what you directly experienced with a client or when responding to a situation that was traumatic, or as a result of your efforts to assist clients, who were directly traumatized. (Client can refer to victims of traumatic incidents and/or persons in your care.) This is not a diagnostic tool. The items have been adapted from Bride's STS scale (Bride, Robinson, Yegidis, & Figley, 2004) and the most current DSM-5 (American Psychiatric Association, 2013) PTSD criteria for PTSD which added criteria "D," alterations in cognitions and mood. It can be argued that those experiencing STS do experience cognitive and mood changes that have been associated with CF and vicarious trauma in past literature and research mentioned in Session One. For this reason, they are included here in this adapted format.

   Directions: Simply check those reactions under each category that you are experiencing and then review scoring instructions for results.

Intrusion

____I have unexpected upsetting thoughts/memories/images of what happened with/to clients.

____At times it feels like I am experiencing what my client experienced.

____I think about what happened to some clients even when I do not want to.

____I sometimes have disturbing dreams related to client situations/materials.

____I have unwanted, strong physical reactions (heart pounding, sweating, etc.) when something or someone reminds of that traumatic situation.

____Things that remind me of that situation causes me unwanted, strong distress.

Avoidance

____I am avoiding people, places, situations, reading of material that reminds me of traumatic client situations.

____I avoid certain clients/client conditions that remind me of that trauma situation.

____I find I am not socializing as much as I used to.

____I find I'm not as active as I have been in the past.

____There are times when I try to move clients away from talking about what happened because I do not want to hear it.

____I'm drinking more and/or using other substances to get me through.

Arousal

____I'm more jumpy, easily startled.

____I'm irritated more often.

____I'm having trouble sleeping.

____It feels like I'm constantly ready or waiting for something bad to happen.

____It's harder to concentrate, to focus.

Cognitive/Mood Alterations

____I find that at times I'm numb, detached.

____I have a more negative thoughts about myself, others or life since this happened.

____It's harder to be positive about people, places, things.

____I'm not doing the things I once enjoyed doing.

____There are things I can't remember about what happened in that case/with that client.

____I'm blaming myself or others for what happened.

Scoring:

Record number of items checked under each category.

Intrusion ____, Avoidance ____, Arousal ____, Cognitive/Mood Alterations ____.

If you are experiencing at least one reaction in intrusion, avoidance arousal category and two or more under alterations in cognitions and mood, further screening is recommended to determine if you may be also experiencing PTSD. Keep in mind that there remains a great deal of discussion as to what constitutes STS and the gap between STS and PTSD. *What matters* is that you take whatever reactions you checked seriously and discuss them with your supervisor or an outside trauma specialist if you do not feel comfortable bringing them to your supervisor. In most cases brief intervention can help resolve STS reactions if present, additional efforts may be needed to treat PTSD.

All professionals experience the reactions listed above at some point. If you are having a stressful time in your personal life, it certainly will be harder to deal with client traumas or situations. There will be some clients who call that cause you, on a stressful day, to say "not today." However, when experiencing STS you will have multiple reactions across the above categories. Your reactions may follow interaction with one client or they be as a result of assisting and/or responding to multiple clients/situations over time.

American Psychiatric Association. (2013). *Diagnostic and statistical manual of mental disorders* (5th ed.). Washington, DC: APA.

Bride, B. E., Robinson, M. R., Yegidis, B., & Figley, C. R. (2004). Development and validation of the STS scale. *Research on Social Work Practice, 14*, 27-35.

A4 Professional Quality of Life Scale 5 (ProQOL)

Reprinted with permission from ProQOL.org © *B. Hudnall Stamm, 2009-2012. Professional Quality of Life: Compassion Satisfaction and Fatigue Version 5 (ProQOL). www.proqol.org*

Compassion Satisfaction and CF (ProQOL) Version 2009

When you *[help]* people you have direct contact with their lives. As you may have found, your compassion for those you *[help]* can affect you in positive and negative ways. Below are some questions about your experiences, both positive and negative, as a *[helper]*. Consider each of the following questions about you and your current work situation. Select the number that honestly reflects how frequently you experienced these things in the *last 30 days*.

　　1=Never 2=Rarely 3=Sometimes 4=Often 5=Very Often

1.　＿＿I am happy.
2.　＿＿I am preoccupied with more than one person I *[help]*
3.　＿＿I get satisfaction from being able to *[help]* people.
4.　＿＿I feel connected to others.
5.　＿＿I jump or am startled by unexpected sounds.
6.　＿＿I feel invigorated after working with those I *[help]*.
7.　＿＿I find it difficult to separate my personal life from my life as a *[helper]*.
8.　＿＿I am not as productive at work because I am losing sleep over traumatic experiences of a person I *[help]*.
9.　＿＿I think that I might have been affected by the traumatic stress of those I *[help]*.
10.　＿＿I feel trapped by my job as a *[helper]*.
11.　＿＿Because of my *[helping]*, I have felt "on edge" about various things.
12.　＿＿I like my work as a *[helper]*.
13.　＿＿I feel depressed because of the traumatic experiences of the people I *[help]*.
14.　＿＿I feel as though I am experiencing the trauma of someone I have *[helped]*.
15.　＿＿I have beliefs that sustain me.
16.　＿＿I am pleased with how I am able to keep up with *[helping]* techniques and protocols.
17.　＿＿I am the person I always wanted to be.
18.　＿＿My work makes me feel satisfied.
19.　＿＿I feel worn out because of my work as a *[helper]*.
20.　＿＿I have happy thoughts and feelings about those I *[help]* and how I could help them.
21.　＿＿I feel overwhelmed because my case [work] load seems endless.
22.　＿＿I believe I can make a difference through my work.
23.　＿＿I avoid certain activities or situations because they remind me of frightening experiences of the people I *[help]*.
24.　＿＿I am proud of what I can do to *[help]*.
25.　＿＿As a result of my *[helping]*, I have intrusive, frightening thoughts.
26.　＿＿I feel "bogged down" by the system.

27. _____ I have thoughts that I am a "success" as a [helper].
28. _____ I can't recall important parts of my work with trauma victims.
29. _____ I am a very caring person.
30. _____ I am happy that I chose to do this work.

What Is My Score and What Does It Mean?

Compassion Satisfaction Scale

In this section, you will score your test so you understand the interpretation for you. To find your Compassion satisfaction score total the questions listed below and then find your score in the table below.

3. ___ 6. ____ 12. ____ 16. ____ 18. ____ 20. ____ 22. ____ 24. ____ 27. ____ 30. ____

Total (Sum): _____

Identifying Your Compassion Satisfaction (CS) Score

My sum is 22 or less, therefore my score = 43 or less, therefore my CS level is LOW

My sum is between 23 and 24 therefore my score =, 50, therefore my CS level is AVERAGE

My sum is 42 or more therefore my score is = 57 or more, therefore my CS level is HIGH

MY CS Score: _____ (My Level:_____)

Note: Once you have identified your scores, you can read the detailed interpretations below.

The BO Scale

On the BO Scale you will need to take an extra step. Starred items below are reverse scored. *If your initial score was 1 change it to 5; initial score of 2 becomes 4; initial score of 3 remains 3; initial score of 4 becomes 2 and an initial score of 5 becomes 1.* The reason we ask you to reverse the scores is because scientifically the measure works better when these questions are asked in a positive way though they can tell us more about their negative form. For example, question 1. "I am happy" tells us more about the effects of helping when you are *not* happy so you reverse the score.

*1. (Original score) ____ = (New Changed Score) _____ *4. ____ = ____ *8. ____ = ____

*10. ____ = ____ *15. ____ = ____ *17. ____ = ____ 19. ____ 21. ____ 26. ____

*29. ____ = ____

Total (Sum): _____

BO Scoring

My sum is 22 or less, therefore my score = 43 or less, therefore my BO level is LOW

My sum is between 23 and 41, therefore my score = 50, therefore my BO level is AVERAGE

My sum is 42 or more, therefore my score = 57 or more, therefore my BO level is HIGH

My BO Score: ___(My Level:_____)

STS Scale

Just like you did on Compassion Satisfaction, copy your rating on each of these questions on this table and add them up. When you have added them up you can find your score on the table below.

2. ____ 5. ____ 7. ____ 9. ____ 11. ____ 13. ____ 14. ____ 23. ____ 25. ____ 28. ____

Total (Sum): ____

Secondary Trauma (ST) Scoring

My sum is 22 or less, therefore my score = 43 or less, therefore my ST level is LOW

My sum is between 23 and 41, therefore my score = 50, therefore my ST level is AVERAGE

My sum is 42 or more, therefore my score = 57 or more, therefore my ST level is HIGH

My ST Score: ____(My Level:____)

Your Scores on the ProQOL: Professional Quality of Life

Based on your responses, place your personal scores below. If you have any concerns, you should discuss them with a mental health care professional.

Compassion Satisfaction _____

Compassion satisfaction is about the pleasure you derive from being able to do your work well. For example, you may feel like it is a pleasure to help others through your work. You may feel positively about your colleagues or your ability to contribute to the work setting or even the greater good of society. Higher scores on this scale represent a greater satisfaction related to your ability to be an effective caregiver in your job.

The average score is 50 (SD 10; alpha scale reliability .88). About 25% of people score higher than 57 and about 25% of people score below 43. If you are in the higher range, you probably derive a good deal of professional satisfaction from your position. If your scores are below 40, you may either find problems with your job, or there may be some other reason - for example, you might derive your satisfaction from activities other than your job.

BO_____

Most people have an intuitive idea of what BO is. From the research perspective, BO is one of the elements of CF. It is associated with feelings of hopelessness and difficulties in dealing with work or in doing your job effectively. These negative feelings usually have a gradual onset. They can reflect the feeling that your efforts make no difference, or they can be associated with a very high workload or a non-supportive work environment. Higher scores on this scale mean that you are at higher risk for BO.

The average score on the BO Scale is 50 (SD 10; alpha scale reliability .75). About 25% of people score above 57 and about 25% of people score below 43. If your score is below 43, this probably reflects positive feelings about your ability to be effective in your work. If you score above 57 you may wish to think about what at work makes you feel like you are not effective in your position. Your score may reflect your mood; perhaps you were having a "bad day" or are in need of some time off. If the high score persists or if it is reflective of other worries, it may be a cause for concern.

Secondary Traumatic Stress_____

The second component of CF is STS. It is about your work related, secondary exposure to extremely or traumatically stressful events. Developing problems due to exposure to other's trauma is somewhat rare but does happen to many people who care for those who have experienced extremely or traumatically stressful events. For example, you may repeatedly hear stories about the traumatic things that happen to other people, commonly called Vicarious Traumatization. If your work puts you directly in the path of danger, for example, field work in a war or area of civil violence, this is not secondary exposure; your exposure is primary. However, if you are exposed to others' traumatic events as a result of your work, for example, as a therapist or an emergency worker, this is secondary exposure. The symptoms of STS are usually rapid in onset and associated with a particular event. They may include being afraid, having difficulty sleeping, having images of the upsetting event pop into your mind, or avoiding things that remind you of the event.

The average score on this scale is 50 (SD 10; alpha scale reliability .81). About 25% of people score below 43 and about 25% of people score above 57. If your score is above 57, you may want to take some time to think about what at work may be frightening to you or if there is some other reason for the elevated score. While higher scores do not mean that you do have a problem, they are an indication that you may want to examine how you feel about your work and your work environment. You may wish to discuss this with your supervisor, a colleague, or a health care professional.

About the Scores

The best outcome is having high CS and low BO and CF. When STS is high while CS is high and BO low, usually brief intervention for STS will be beneficial. When both STS and BO are high intervention is recommended for STS and time away from work for BO. However, if the conditions causing BO are not changed, returning to that environment will likely not be beneficial.

Note: If interested in additional interpretation of scores you may download the 2010 Concise Pro-QOL Manual, 2nd Ed. at ProQOL.org.

A5   Self-Engagement Survey

© 2019 Dr. William Steele

The items in this scale reflect the items most frequently cited in sources identifying characteristics of engagement (Gallup, 2016; Engagement Multiplier, 2014; Pay Scale, 2018). It is not a diagnostic tool but an indicator of our level of engagement, which we know is associated with performance, retention and support of the organization. (See Session Four in this book.)

1.   Am I living up to the expectations of my job? Yes___ Somewhat ___ Rarely ___
2.   Am I supported by leadership/manager/supervisor to help meet these expectations? Yes___ Somewhat ___ Rarely___
3.   Is my progress, my efforts, the work I do discussed/reviewed at least every two weeks? Yes___ Somewhat___ Rarely___
4.   Am I given opportunities to enhance/develop my skills? Yes___ Somewhat___ Rarely___
5.   Are my peers supportive in helpful ways to me? Yes___ Somewhat___ Rarely___
6.   Do I feel my "voice," my comments and opinions are taken seriously? Yes___ Somewhat___ Rarely___
7.   My supervisor/manager connects/checks with me via email, text, phone, a brief note or brief visit regularly without micromanaging? Yes___ Somewhat___ Rarely___
8.   Leadership demonstrates its concern for my well-being? Yes___ Somewhat___ Rarely___
9.   I feel appreciated/recognized for the work I am doing? Yes___ Somewhat___ Rarely___
10. I enjoy working in this organization? Yes___ Somewhat___ Rarely___
11. I think about looking for another job ___Weekly___ Monthly___ Every few months ___Rarely

Scoring:

A.   Add the number of "Yes" responses to the first 10 statements. Total = ____ (Very engaged)
B.   Add the number of "Somewhat" responses to the first 10 statements. Total = ___ (Only somewhat engaged)
C.   Add the number of "Rarely" responses to the first 10 statements. Total = ___ (Rarely engaged)

#11. If you are thinking about looking for another job weekly add "4" to category "C" total; if monthly add "3" to total. If thinking about looking for another job every few months add "2" to category "B" total; if rarely thinking about another job add "2" to category "A."

  The highest total represents the level of engagement.

My level of engagement _____

Positive engagement generally supports retention, higher levels of performance and engaging in activities that support the organization. "Somewhat" engagement will be reflected in more sporadic performance and attendance, less involvement in support of the organization, more frequent thoughts/searches for another job.

Engagement Multiplier. (2014, December 16). *Employee engagement vs. employee well-being.* Retrieved from www.engagementmultiplier.com/blog/employee-engagement-vs-employee-well/

Appendix A5

Gallup. (2016). *Why is employee engagement so important?* Retrieved July 11, 2017, from www.engagement multiplier.com/ . . . /why-is-employee-engagement-so-important.

Pay Scale. (2018). *What you can do to improve employee engagement*. Retrieved January 4, 2019, from www. payscale.com/data/employee-engagement

A6 Secondary Traumatic Stress Informed-Organization Assessment (STSI)

Reprinted and adapted by permission from Dr. Ginny Sprang, Center on Trauma and Children University of Kentucky (see citation at the end of the assessment).

This tool identifies specific areas of strength and opportunities to implement STS-informed policies and practices. Developed by members of the NCTSN and available through the University of Kentucky Center on Trauma and Children, is an assessment tool that can be used by organizational representatives at any level to evaluate the degree to which their organization is STS-informed and able to respond to the impact of STS in the workplace. It can be downloaded at no cost by visiting www.uky.edu/CTAC/STSI-OA.

Directions: Simply check those items that you are currently aware are in place at your organization. If you do not know or are unsure use "u" to indicate further investigation is needed.

The organization promotes resilience building activities that enhance the following:

___Basic knowledge about STS

___Monitoring the impact of STS on professional wellbeing

___Maintaining positive focus on the core mission for which the organization exists

___A sense of hope, e.g., a belief in a clients' potential for trauma recovery, healing and personal growth

___Specific skills that enhance a worker's sense of professional competency

___Strong peer support among staff, supervisors and staff and/or outside consultants

___Healthy coping strategies to deal with the psychological demands of the job

To what degree does the organization promote a sense of safety?

___The organization protects the physical safety of staff using strategies or techniques to reduce risk (e.g., panic buttons, security alarms, multiple staff, etc.)

___Staff in the organization are encouraged to not share graphic details of trauma stories unnecessarily with coworkers

___Periodically, the organization conducts a safety survey or forum that assesses worker perceptions of psychological safety

___Periodically, the organization conducts a safety survey or forum that assesses worker perceptions of physical safety

___Organizational leaders manage risk appropriately and protect workers as much as possible from dangerous clients and/or situations

___The organization provides training on how to manage potentially dangerous situations (e.g., angry clients)

___The organization has a defined protocol for how to respond to staff when critical incidents occur

How STS-informed are organizational policies?

____ The organization has defined practices addressing the psychological safety of staff

____ The organization has defined practices addressing the physical safety of staff

____ The organization has a risk management policy in place to provide interventions to those who report high levels of STS

____ The organization has defined procedures to promote resiliencebuilding in staff (e.g., selfcare workshops)

____ The organization's strategic plan addresses ways to enhance staff resiliency

____ The organization's strategic plan addresses ways to enhance staff safety

How STS-informed are the practices of leaders (executive directors, CEOs, COOs, administration, etc.)?

____ Leadership actively encourages selfcare

____ Leadership models good selfcare

____ Supervisors promote safety and resilience to STS by routinely attending to the risks and signs of STS

____ Supervisors promote safety and resilience to STS by offering consistent supervision that includes discussion of the effect of the work on the worker

____ Supervisors promote safety and resilience to STS by intentionally managing caseloads and case assignments with the dose of indirect trauma exposure in mind

____ Staff provides input to leaders on ways the organization can improve its policies and practices regarding STS

____ Supervisors address STS by referring those with high levels of disturbance to trained mental health professionals

____ Supervisors promote safety and resilience to STS by offering additional supervision during times of high risk for STS

____ Leadership responds to STS as an occupational hazard and not a weakness

How STS-informed are other routine organizational practices?

____ The organization provides formal trainings on ways to enhance psychological safety

____ The organization provides formal trainings on ways to enhance physical safety

____ The organization provides formal trainings on enhancing resilience to STS

____ The organization offers activities (besides trainings) that promote resilience to STS

____ The organization discusses STS during new employee orientation

____ The organization has regular opportunities to provide team and peer support to individuals with high levels of exposure

___The organization provides release time to allow employees to attend trainings focused on resilience building or STS management

How well does the organization evaluate and monitor STS policies and practices?

___The organization assesses the level of STS in the workplace

___The organization routinely monitors workforce trends (e.g., attrition, absenteeism) that may signify a lack of safety or an increase in STS

___The organization responds to what it learns through evaluation, monitoring and/or feedback in ways that promote safety and resilience

___The organization routinely seeks feedback from the workforce regarding psychosocial trends that may signify an increase in STS (e.g., increased conflict, social isolation)

(*Note*: This survey has no scoring format but is used to identify areas needing attention.)

For our purposes only we simply want you to have a sense as to how well the organization is addressing STS, how well leadership is demonstrating concern for your well-being. There are 40 items. Total only the number of items checked and divide by 40 for a percentage. If 30 items were checked the % would = 75%. Do not count those items you marked as "u" for uncertain.

Score ___%

(*My opinion*) In a trauma-informed organization you should also expect that at least 75% compliance. Obviously, those items not checked or scored as "u" for uncertain/I don't know, need to be further pursued. It is not uncommon to find that some of these items may be in place yet the organization has not effectively communicated these are actually in place. In some cases, it reflects that supervisors/managers are not reviewing this information with supervisees. In either case, lack of awareness and/or not being informed has the potential to increases staff vulnerability to STS.

Sprang, G., Ross, L., Blackshear, K., Miller, B., Vrabel, C., Ham, J., Henry, J., & Caringi, J. (2014). *The Secondary Traumatic Stress-Informed Organization Assessment (STSI-OA) Tool*. Lexington, Kentucky: University of Kentucky Center on Trauma and Children, #14-STS001. Retrieved from www.uky.edu/CTAC/STSI-OA

A7   NCTSN Core Competencies for Secondary Trauma-Informed Supervisors

Reprinted with permission from NCTSN Core Competencies for Secondary Trauma-Informed Supervision
www.nctsn.org/ . . . /using-secondary-traumatic-stress-core-competencies-trauma-i. . .

Adapted as a checklist form retaining all original content.
Trauma-informed supervisors need to be competent in all nine areas.

Supervisees should expect their supervisor to initiate these practices and/or provide the information as described below.

Directions: As a supervisor, simply check those practices you are competent in providing. Those practices not checked become areas for competency training.

If you are a supervisee experiencing secondary trauma reactions (avoidance, arousal, intrusiveness), your supervisor ought to be assisting you using these core competencies. Under each competency category, check those your supervisor has introduced you too. Not all practices will apply directly to you. When finished, answer the two questions at the end of this checklist.

1. Knowledge of the signs, symptoms, and risk factors of STS and its impact on employees; Knowledge of agency support options, referral process for employee assistance, or external support resources for supervisees who are experiencing symptoms of STS.

The supervisor is able to do the following:

____Recognize the signs of STS in their supervisees.

____Address observed STS with symptomatic employees in a supportive manner that normalizes their responses, promotes resiliency, and is supportive of the supervisee and does not pathologize, demean, or threaten the supervisee.

____Delineate what the STS-informed services and support options are available from the organization.

____Facilitate the referral process for accessing available, quality services for symptomatic employees.

____Identify other resources that provide STS prevention or intervention services and is able to assist the employee into accessing those resources.

____Encourage the consistent use of organizational supports for the mitigation/prevention of STS symptoms as a normalized part of doing this work.

____Act as an advocate within the organization for STS supports, training, or other needed adjustments needed by supervisees indicated by supervisory monitoring of STS symptoms in supervisees.

____Differentiate STS, PTSD, and BO symptoms, and describe the differential varying responses to each condition.

____Identify how race, historical trauma, implicit bias, and/or culture impacts the way STS manifests at the individual and organizational levels.

2. Knowledge and capacity to self-assess, reflective capacity to monitor, and address the supervisor's own personal STS.

The supervisor is able to do the following:

___Recognize the effect of race, historical trauma, implicit bias, culture and/or other trauma exposure upon themselves him/herself and describe how it may manifest in the supervisory process.

___Self-assess for signs and symptoms of STS that is affecting their, his/her own functioning on a regular basis.

___Define a plan for regular reflection to identify and self-assess STS.

___Address STS signs and symptoms of STS when they arise in their own lives.

___Willingly seek support from peers or own supervisor.

3. Knowledge of how to encourage employees in sharing the emotional experience of doing trauma work in a safe and supportive manner.

The supervisor is able to do the following:

___Employ skills to enhance psychological safety of supervisees during supervision.

___Describe common emotional responses to trauma work.

___Skillfully employ reflective listening as part of supervisory practice.

___Identify and utilize supervisees' strengths in order to use data to increase supervisee self-awareness, competence, and resilience.

___Describe common emotional responses to trauma work and integrate these into discussions with supervisees.

___Normalize common emotional responses to trauma work during supervision.

___Provide emotional support to supervisees, and how to determine what method may be most helpful to supervisees.

4. Knowledge of skills to assist the employee in emotional re-regulation after difficult encounters; capacity to assess the effectiveness of intervention, monitor progress and make appropriate referrals, if necessary.

The supervisor is able to do the following:

Educate supervisees

___Define self-regulation;

___Teach self-regulation skills;

___Normalize emotional responses to difficult situations.

Assess supervisees

___Evaluate the immediate current well-being of the supervisee;

___Identify negative self-appraisals, cognitive distortions and ineffective coping behaviors that the supervisee may be demonstrating;

___Observe continuously and over time the emotional response of the supervisee over time to assess recovery and the potential need for added supports or referrals.

Coach and support supervisees

___Assist with self-regulation, including cognitive skills (e.g., thinking about a situation differently), and behavioral recovery (e.g., distraction, self-soothing, and physical relaxation and redirection of energy).

___Communicate concern and support.

___Support the supervisee toward the development of skills for managing intense affect, and to prompt supervisees to utilize these strategies when needed.

___Provide concrete suggestions regarding emotional regulation strategies, and emphasizes their importance by allowing supervisees the time needed to implement their chosen strategies.

5. Knowledge of basic Psychological First Aid (PFA) or other supportive approaches to assist staff after an emergency or crisis event.

The supervisor is able to do the following:

___Assure the psychological, physical, and emotional safety of staff following an emergency or crisis event incident, including a discussion of physical and psychological and emotional safety.

___Know the eight Core Actions of PFA approach.

___Recognize the different ways staff may respond to an emergency or crisis event.

___Invite questions from staff in a manner that supports individuals' need for emotional safety and by respecting individuals' choice to share or not share as they see fit.

___Provide accurate information regarding STS, signs to self-monitor the signs and symptoms, and strategies to enhance coping.

___Inquire about the immediate needs of staff following an event.

___Assist supervisees in the development of an action plan to address identified needs.

___Facilitate access to up-to-date information regarding on resources available to staff who have experienced direct/indirect trauma exposure, including EAP information, insurance empaneled providers, and specific recommendations related to referral sources familiar with STS.

6. Ability to both model and coach supervisees in using a trauma lens to guide case conceptualization and service delivery.

The supervisor is able to do the following:

___Educate supervisees regarding how trauma may alter functioning of a trauma-exposed client.

___Assure that the supervisee has formulated the role of trauma in the clinical presentation.

___Redirect the supervisee from focusing on what is wrong with a trauma-exposed client (i.e., diagnosis and symptoms) to what happened in the client's life (i.e., consideration of how behaviors/symptoms may make sense when the client's trauma exposure is assessed).

___Guide supervisees to a recognition of a client's trauma history and symptoms in a way that explains what the client may be experiencing and serves to guide service delivery.

___Redirect supervisees when they drift into attitudes/beliefs about clients that are inconsistent with the trauma-focused "lens."

___Educate supervisees about key trauma concepts, support them in incorporating these concepts into a trauma-informed case formulation, and in guiding the supervisee when they drift into an approach inconsistent with the trauma lens.

___Promote fidelity to trauma-responsive, and evidence-supported/based models in daily practice.

___Encourage supervisee to bring forth multiple perspectives of the presenting problem(s), priorities, focus, and goals of treatment by encouraging supervisee's active engagement of the client, the client's significant others/family, and extended supports in the assessment, intervention planning, and ongoing service delivery process.

7. Knowledge of resiliency factors and ability to structure resilience-building into individual and group supervisory activities.

The supervisor is able to do the following:

___Facilitate the supervisee's experience of a developing sense of mastery of the management of trauma-related issues with clients.

___Identify and develop supervisee's strengths and help supervisee him or her apply those strengths to job-related activities.

___Connect the individual to his or her team to guard against isolation and to develop a sense of shared ownership of difficult circumstances.

___Support the development of compassion satisfaction in the supervisee via the following:

___Assisting with the analysis of supervisee perceptions regarding complex case situations, and supporting acceptance of situations that cannot be changed.

___Assisting the supervisee to reframe situations to allow for the recognition of partial successes.

___Assisting the supervisee to adopt a positive view of him or herself and their skill level.

___Encouraging the supervisee to notice, acknowledge, and savor positive moments with clients.

___Reinforcing the benefits of engaging in pleasurable activities at work and off hours.

8. Ability to distinguish between expected changes in supervisee perspectives and cognitive distortions related to indirect trauma exposure.

The supervisor is able to do the following:

___Recognize when changes in a supervisee's perspectives occur.

___Successfully engage supervisee in discussion of observed changes and obtain supervisee's his or her perspectives thoughts regarding these changed views.

___Normalize that changes in worldview (e.g., bad things do happen to innocent children) that will naturally occur during trauma work.

___Assist supervisee by challenging unhelpful cognitive distortions about self, work, or the world; (e.g., thinking "This is useless," "The world is unsafe," "I'm the only one," or displaying hypervigilance).

___Provide support towards replacing cognitive distortions with more accurate assessments.

9. Ability to use appropriate self-disclosure in supervisory sessions to enhance the supervisees ability to recognize, acknowledge, and respond to the impact of indirect trauma.

The supervisor is able to do the following:

___Normalize STS responses through timely use of self-disclosure related to their, his or her own experiences dealing with trauma work.

___Employ self-disclosure as a tool to help supervisees recognize, acknowledge, and respond to the impact of indirect trauma.

___Willingly disclose when asked directly by a supervisee, thereby avoiding a posture of withholding, and facilitating emotional relatedness and equality in the relationship.

___Monitor their, his or her own motivation and intentions as a critical factor in weighing the ethical force of self-disclosure, particularly whether the goal of such disclosure is primarily for the supervisee's benefit.

Note: *There is no scoring for this tool. It is used to identify STS areas of supervisor competency.* However, supervisors should be expected to be competent in the majority of the above areas.

Scoring BY Supervisors. (Following scoring created by author to provide general reference only). There are 64 total items. Add the number of items checked and divide that number by 64 to arrive at a %. If you checked 39 items divided by 64 = 60% competency. You can do better. You need to do better. Seek out training and literature related to areas that need developing.

My Competency % = _____

STS supervision is critical to both prevention and recovery from STS. If not available within the organization then help should be sought from other competent sources.

Record areas of deficiency by category and/or item/practice on your Self-Care Checklist.

Scoring By Supervisees. Supervisees who are or may be experiencing STS should expect their supervisor to assist them using the above practices. As you review this checklist, what you did or did not check, answer the following two questions.

Record your answer here and on your Self-Care Checklist.

What is your immediate impression of your supervisor's STS competency?

_____

_____

Knowing what you know about supervisor STS competency, the effects of STS and the benefits of brief intervention, do you feel safe and confident that your supervisor can help? ___ Yes, ___No

Do you need to seek outside help from a trauma specialist? ___ Yes, ___No

A8   Self-Compassion Scale

How I Typically Act Towards Myself in Difficult Times

Please read each statement carefully before answering. To the left of each item, indicate how often you behave in the stated manner, using the following scale:

Almost never = 1 2 3 4 5 = Almost always

_____ 1.   I'm disapproving and judgmental about my own flaws and inadequacies.

_____ 2.   When I'm feeling down I tend to obsess and fixate on everything that's wrong.

_____ 3.   When things are going badly for me, I see the difficulties as part of life that everyone goes through.

_____ 4.   When I think about my inadequacies, it tends to make me feel more separate and cut off from the rest of the world.

_____ 5.   I try to be loving towards myself when I'm feeling emotional pain.

_____ 6.   When I fail at something important to me I become consumed by feelings of inadequacy.

_____ 7.   When I'm down and out, I remind myself that there are lots of other people in the world feeling like I am.

_____ 8.   When times are really difficult, I tend to be tough on myself.

_____ 9.   When something upsets me I try to keep my emotions in balance.

_____ 10. When I feel inadequate in some way, I try to remind myself that feelings of inadequacy are shared by most people.

_____ 11. I'm intolerant and impatient towards those aspects of my personality I don't like.

_____ 12. When I'm going through a very hard time, I give myself the caring and tenderness I need.

_____ 13. When I'm feeling down, I tend to feel like most other people are probably happier than I am.

_____ 14. When something painful happens I try to take a balanced view of the situation.

_____ 15. I try to see my failings as part of the human condition.

_____ 16. When I see aspects of myself that I don't like, I get down on myself.

_____ 17. When I fail at something important to me, I try to keep things in perspective.

_____ 18. When I'm really struggling, I tend to feel like other people must be having an easier time of it.

_____ 19. I'm kind to myself when I'm experiencing suffering.

_____ 20. When something upsets me I get carried away with my feelings.

_____ 21. I can be a bit cold-hearted towards myself when I'm experiencing suffering.

_____ 22. When I'm feeling down I try to approach my feelings with curiosity and openness.

_____ 23. I'm tolerant of my own flaws and inadequacies.

_____ 24. When something painful happens, I tend to blow the incident out of proportion.

_____ 25. When I fail at something that's important to me, I tend to feel alone in my failure.

_____ 26. I try to be understanding and patient towards those aspects of my personality I don't like.

Scoring

Self-Kindness Items: 5, 12, 19, 23, 26
**Self-Judgment Items: 1, 8, 11, 16, 21

Common Humanity Items: 3, 7, 10, 15
**Isolation Items: 4, 13, 18, 25

Mindfulness Items: 9, 14, 17, 22
**Over-identified Items: 2, 6, 20, 24

Subscale scores are computed by calculating the mean (average) of each subscale item responses by adding up the sum and then dividing the sum by the total number of items in that subscale. For example, if your sum total for Self-kindness is 20, divide it by the 5 items in that subscale for a mean/average of 4, meaning you are almost always kind to yourself during difficult times.

This scoring method provides you with very specific detail as to your mindset during stressful times. Remember it's our mindset that drives our behavior. *For ** categories (self-judgment, isolation & over-identified) you want an average score of 1–2, meaning you are not judgmental, do not isolate yourself when things are not good and that you are able to respond with appropriate emotions.* For the other three categories you want an average of 4–5 meaning you treat yourself with kindness, you compare yourself favorably with others who have setbacks and take your failures in stride (as a learning experience).

Being self-compassionate *is really about having those mindsets that direct compassionate behavior and help reduce stress and CF during difficult times. Approaching this tool from a mindset perspective makes it quite easy to identify mindsets in each statement that are counter-productive to compassion satisfaction or support self-compassion.*

Note: Research has shown that self-compassion is positively and significantly related to psychological health and well-being (e.g., happiness, optimism, positive affect, wisdom, personal initiative) beyond that which can be accounted for by personality (Neff, Rude, & Kirkpatrick, 2007; Neff, 2011). Vettese, Dyer, Li, and Wekerle (2011) found that self-reported levels of self-compassion mediated the link between childhood maltreatment and later emotional dysregulation. This suggests that people with trauma histories who have compassion for themselves are better able to deal with upsetting events in a productive manner.

Neff, K. D. (2003). Development and validation of a scale to measure self-compassion. *Self and Identity, 2,* 223–250.

Neff, K. D., Rude, S. S., & Kirkpatrick, K. L. (2007). An examination of self-compassion in relation to positive psychological functioning and personality traits. *Journal of Research in Personality, 41,* 908–916.

Neff, K. D. (2011). Self-compassion, self-esteem, and well-being. *Social and Personality Psychology Compass, 5,* 1–12.

Vettese, L. C., Dyer, C. E., Li, W. L., & Wekerle, C. (2011). Does self-compassion mitigate the association between childhood maltreatment and later emotional regulation difficulties? A preliminary investigation. *International Journal of Mental Health and Addiction, 9,* 480–491.

A9 Spiritual Intelligence Self-Report Inventory (SISRI)

The Spiritual Intelligence Self-Report Inventory © 2008 David King. Reprinted with permission from Dr. David B. King/ASA

Note: Why do you want to evaluate your spiritual intelligence? Those who have a higher level of spiritual intelligence are more flexible and self-conscious, and have a holistic attitude to existence and hardships of life (Emmons, 2000). Those with higher spiritual intelligence are benefiting from several capacities, for instance, they have *the power to cope with stress, change the threats of life into opportunities, and finally they have a better mental health status* (Wigglesworth, 2006). The SISRI is a researched, viable tool (King & DeCicco, 2009).

The following statements are designed to measure various behaviors, thought processes, and mental characteristics. Read each statement carefully and choose which one of the five possible responses best reflects you by checking the corresponding number. If you are not sure, or if a statement does not seem to apply to you, choose the answer that seems the best. Please answer honestly and make responses based on how you actually are rather than how you would like to be. The five possible responses are:

0—Not at all true of me, 1—Not very true of me, 2—Somewhat true of me, 3—Very true of me, 4—Completely true of me. For each item, check the one response that most accurately describes you.

1. I have often questioned or pondered the nature of reality. __0__1__2__3__4
2. I recognize aspects of myself that are deeper than my physical body. __0__1__2__3__4
3. I have spent time contemplating the purpose or reason for my existence. __0__1__2__3__4
4. I am able to enter higher states of consciousness or awareness. __0__1__2__3__4
5. I am able to deeply contemplate what happens after death. __0__1__2__3__4
6. It is difficult for me to sense anything other than the physical and material. __0__1__2__3__4
7. My ability to find meaning and purpose in life helps me adapt to stressful situations. __0__1__2__3__4
8. I can control when I enter higher states of consciousness or awareness. __0__1__2__3__4
9. I have developed my own theories about such things as life, death, reality, and existence. __0__1__2__3__4
10. I am aware of a deeper connection between myself and other people. __0__1__2__3__4
11. I am able to define a purpose or reason for my life. __0__1__2__3__4
12. I am able to move freely between levels of consciousness or awareness. __0__1__2__3__4
13. I frequently contemplate the meaning of events in my life. __0__1__2__3__4
14. I define myself by my deeper, non-physical self. __0__1__2__3__4
15. When I experience a failure, I am still able to find meaning in it. __0__1__2__3__4
16. I often see issues and choices more clearly while in higher states of consciousness/awareness. __0__1__2__3__4
17. I have often contemplated the relationship between human beings and the rest of the universe. __0__1__2__3__4
18. I am highly aware of the nonmaterial aspects of life. __0__1__2__3__4
19. I am able to make decisions according to my purpose in life. __0__1__2__3__4

20. I recognize qualities in people, which are more meaningful than their body, personality, or emotions. ___0___1___2___3___4
21. I have deeply contemplated whether or not there is some greater power or force (e.g., god, goddess, divine being, higher energy, etc.). ___0___1___2___3___4
22. Recognizing the nonmaterial aspects of life helps me feel centered. ___0___1___2___3___4
23. I am able to find meaning and purpose in my everyday experiences. ___0___1___2___3___4
24. I have developed my own techniques for entering higher states of consciousness or awareness. ___0___1___2___3___4

Total Spiritual Intelligence Score and examples of subscale meaning

Sum all item responses or subscale scores (after accounting for *reverse-coded item/question #6). A score of 0 now = 5; 1 = 4; 2 = 3; 3 = 1; 4 = 0.

24 items in total; range: 0-96; mid - range = 48

4 Factors/Subscales:

I. *Critical Existential Thinking* (CET): Sum items 1, 3, 5, 9, 13, 17, and 21.

7 items in total; range: 0-28; mid-range = 14

CET reflects that: I think about the purpose of my life and the meaning of things I've experienced, the meaning of what has happened to me, and the reason(s) for living. I also think about a greater power.

II. *Personal Meaning Production* (PMP): Sum items 7, 11, 15, 19, and 23.

5 items in total; range: 0-20; mid-range = 10

PMP reflects that: Even when I fail, I find meaning in the loss—I learn. I do have purpose and meaning in my life. I make my decisions based on what is meaningful for me; what supports my purpose.

III. *Transcendental Awareness (TA):* Sum items 2, 6*, 10, 14, 18, 20, and 22.

7 items in total; range: 0-28; mid-range = 14

Prior to summing scores, reverse score on #6-0 = 4, 1 = 3, 2 = 2, 3 = 1 and 4 = 0

TA reflects that: I think about things that go beyond the material or physical. I think about myself in ways that are not about how I look, my physical strengths or attributes. I recognize qualities in others that go beyond how they look, beyond their personality.

IV. *Conscious State Expansion (CSE):* Sum items 4, 8, 12, 16, and 24.

5 items in total; range: 0-20; mid-range = 10

CSE reflects that: I meditate, reflect, I practice mindfulness. I have an awareness beyond myself.

How I use: We obviously want to score mid-range and above, preferably closer to the maximum score in each subscale. The higher our score across all four subscales the greater our resilience (see above statements regarding coping and mental health benefits of spiritual intelligence). *These also reflect mindsets about life that enhance our resilience. Use the lower scored items to reflect on how you can change your mindset, the way you think about life, yourself, your purpose, time to enhance awareness, etc.*

Use of the SISRI is unrestricted so long as it is for academic, educational, or research purposes. Unlimited duplication of this scale is allowed with full author acknowledgement only. Alterations and/or modifications of any kind are strictly prohibited without author permission. For additional information, please visit www.dbking.net/spiritualintelligence/ or email David King at davidking2311@gmail.com.

Emmons, R. A. (2000). Is spirituality an intelligence? Motivation, cognition and the psychology of ultimate concern. *International Journal for the Psychology of Religion*, *10*, 3-26.

King, D. B. (2008). *Rethinking claims of spiritual intelligence: A definition, model, and measure*. Unpublished master thesis. Ontorio, Canada: Trent University.

King, D. B., & DeCicco, T. L. (2009). A viable model and self-report measure of spiritual intelligence. *International Journal of Transpersonal Studies*, *28*(1), 68-85.

Wigglesworth, C. (2006). Why spiritual intelligence is essential to mature leadership. *Integral Leadership Review*, *6*, 206-208.

A10 Resilience Characteristics Survey

© 2019 Dr. William Steele

Charney (2004) provides one of the most comprehensive lists of protective factors related to resilience reflected by several items in this checklist: optimism, altruism, having a moral compass, social supports, humor, role models, taking risk, mission/purpose and spirituality. This survey also reflects characteristics reported by others (King & DeCicco, 2009; Bonano, 2010; Stebbins, 2010; Seligman, 2011; Diehl, 2017).

For each item indicate 1 = Sometimes, 2 = Often, 3 = Almost always, 4 = Always

1. ___ I'm generally optimistic even when facing the hardest of challenges.
2. ___ I see problems, "failure" as opportunities to learn and grow.
3. ___ I give back to my community, to others.
4. ___ I believe in a higher power.
5. ___ I don't stop until I find what works best for challenges I face.
6. ___ I have a good sense of humor and usually see the lighter side of things.
7. ___ I have several role models I draw strength from as needed.
8. ___ Even when I am most vulnerable, I persist until the situation changes for the positive.
9. ___ I have supportive, non-judgmental others I can go to about difficult situations.
10. ___ I am not afraid to take risk, to leave my comfort zone for new experiences.
11. ___ I have a clear purpose in life.
12. ___ I surround myself with others I trust and enjoy learning from.
13. ___ I'm generally very curious and will seek out new information and resources to improve on what I am doing.
14. ___ I can advocate for myself.
15. ___ I am willing to try new approaches when what I am doing is not working.
16. ___ I generally see my future in positive ways.
17. ___ I engage in daily self-care/wellness practices.
18. ___ I trust myself, my abilities.
19. ___ In the past, I've generally found ways to overcome challenges.
20. ___ I treat my body with respect.
21. ___ I spend time weekly at "serious leisure" (hobby, sport).
22. ___ I enjoy "down time" during the week (reading, relaxing, listening to music, etc.).
23. ___ I am fairly good at noticing opportunities or pending challenges.
24. ___ During emotionally difficult times I am able to manage my feelings.
25. ___ I spend time weekly to reflect.

Scoring:

75-100 Very resilient
50-74 Somewhat resilient—room for fine tuning
Below 49 Minimally resilient—much room for improvement

Appendix A10

Consider your scores by category. Ideally you want an optimal score or be at least at the 75% level. The categories, optimal scores, 75% level scores and the questions for each category are listed below.

Optimism: #s 1, 2, 6, 16 . . . Optimal Score (OS) = 16; 75% = 12

Adaptability: #s 10, 14, 18, 19 . . . OS = 16; 75% =12

**Spiritual Intelligence: #s 3, 4, 11, 23, 24, 25 . . . OS = 24; 75% = 18

Effective Effort: #s 5, 8, 13, 15 . . . OS = 16; 75% = 12

Social Strength: #s 7, 9, 12 . . . OS = 12; 75% = 9

Self-Care/Wellness: #s 17, 20, 21, 22 . . . OS = 16; 75% = 12

**Spiritual Intelligence includes critical existential thinking: You think about your purpose in life, its meaning and about a higher power. Personal meaning production: Even when you fail, you learn, you find meaning in that loss. Conscious state expansion: You reflect, you have an awareness beyond yourself.

Bonano, G. (2010). *The other side of sadness: What the new science of bereavement tells us about life after loss.* New York: Basic Books.

Charney, D. S. (2004). Psychobiological mechanisms of resilience and vulnerability: Implications for successful adaptation to extreme stress. *American Journal of Psychiatry, 161*(2), 195–216.

Diehl, E. (2017). Growth mindsets for learning: Effective effort. In W. Steele (Ed.), *Optimizing learning outcomes: Proven brain-centric, trauma sensitive practices* (p. 122). New York: Routledge.

King, D. B., & DeCicco, T. L. (2009). A viable model and self-report measure of spiritual intelligence. *International Journal of Transpersonal Studies, 28*(1), 68–85.

Seligman, M. (2011). *Flourish: A visionary new understanding of happiness and well-being.* New York: Free Press.

Stebbins, R. (2010). *Serious leisure: A perspective for our time.* Brunswick, NJ: Transaction Publishers.

B. Symptom Checklists

CF/STS/BO and Individual/Organizational Disengagement

CF

(CF can and often does include STS yet STS can also exist without CF so STS symptoms are listed separately.)

- Overwhelmed by others suffering
- Blaming others for their suffering
- Physical and mental fatigue
- Difficulty concentrating
- Distancing self from others
- Feeling disconnected from others
- Distancing from some clients while becoming overinvolved with others
- Finding it difficult to be empathetic or sympathetic
- Increased irritability
- No longer enjoying the work
- Little satisfaction
- Feel like you are working harder but accomplishing less
- Making poor decisions re: self and clients
- Becoming cynical
- Your view of the world and yourself changes
- Easily frustrated
- Increased use of substances
- Others complaining about you and your work
- Denial of symptoms observed by others

Secondary Traumatic Stress

Avoiding any reminders of traumatic material or experience. This includes:

- Clients
- Client material that trigger unwanted memories
- Intrusive recollections of trauma experience/content
- Feeling as if you are reexperiencing what client experienced
- Easily startled
- Hypervigilant
- Constantly ready for the next bad thing to happen
- Trouble sleeping, concentrating
- Withdrawing from others and activities you once enjoyed
- Feeling numb/detached
- Experiencing negative thoughts about yourself

- Blaming yourself or others for what happened
- Unable to remember certain aspects of what you were exposed to

BO

(Some BO and CF symptoms are very similar. Keep in mind that BO is related to the work environment, its policies, conditions and practices whereas CF is related to the interactions with the people you are assisting.)

- Physically drained
- Exhausted
- Feeling overloaded, overworked
- Skipping lunches and skipping out on friends and social activities
- Experiencing physical symptoms
- Sleep problems
- Waking up tired
- Dreaming about work
- Little or no motivation to go to work
- Loss of enthusiasm and pleasure
- Concentration suffers
- Quality of work inconsistent and declining
- Missing deadlines
- Disengaged
- Negative attitude towards the work environment and its policies and practices
- Think frequently about quitting

Disengagement

Staff disengagement:

- Consistently complaining
- Trouble getting work done
- Talk about/plan on working elsewhere
- Makes excuses rather than owning mistakes
- Creates conflict/crises
- Avoids supervision
- Contributes little in meetings
- Attendance issues
- Poor work quality

Organizational disengagement:
  Leaders/managers:

- Either micro manage or ignore employees
- Do not engage/support wellness/well-being practices, polices, on site programs
- Remain remote, uninterested

Employees are:

- Frustrated by their lack of support, involvement and input
- Think they are not visible, have erratic expectations or show favoritism
- Feel open communication is not valued
- Feel feedback is ignored and emotional safety and optimism are largely absent

C. Worksheets

C1   Self-Care Checklist Worksheet

Assessment Outcomes

Record the outcomes of your assessments on this form. This information will be used to develop your self-care plan. In the final session, each of the five categories will be discussed and questions presented to help determine your primary focus in each category.

Review Post-session Questions

Before recording the outcomes of the assessment tools, please review your response to Question #4 in each of the Post-session Questions, Sessions One through Five. The question is, "How has this changed what you feel you need to do about the unavoidable stress of what you do?" Take a minute to reflect on your responses. After reflecting, list here what you consider to be "must do" related to your self-care.

_____

_____

_____

Overall Stress Outcomes

Record your answer to the Session Six question located under the heading "Overall Stress Assessment Series." The question was: *Given the accumulation of knowledge you now have about the various sources/symptoms/causes of stress, how do you now rate your stress level?*

Current Perceived Stress Level ____%

Perceived Stress Scale (PSS) Score (be sure you reversed scoring for #s 4, 5, 7 and 8 before adding the total)

_____mild _____moderate _____high

*mild = my perceptions (responses) help maintain low stress levels; *moderate* = my perceptions/reactions create stress needing my attention; *high* = my perceptions/reactions are causing high stress levels.

What specific questions did you rate *fairly often* and indicate whether these reflected problems with control, coping and/or emotional reactions (see *I also suggest the following use* under PSS scoring)?

_____, _____, _____,

_____, _____, _____.

What specific questions did you rate *very often* and indicate whether these reflected problems with control, coping and/or emotional reactions?

_____, _____, _____,

_____, _____, _____.

As you review your answers, check that area(s) that need your attention.

Controlling/managing life challenges_____, Coping (developing new coping skills) _____,

Emotional (Need for more effective emotional regulation) ____.

Stress 360 Outcomes

My total score _____rating/interpretation

Record statements checked "very often" and the category they were under (lifestyle, occupation, attitude or diet). If no statements were checked "very often," list those checked "often."

Lifestyle _____
_____
_____

Occupation_____
_____
_____

Attitude_____
_____
_____

Diet_____
_____
_____

Of these five areas, which area(s) appears to need your attention the most?

_____, _____, _____, _____.

The Stress and Well-being Survey

Record your score for each category and the comment made related to that category.

Total well-being score _____

Comment:
_____
_____

Stress management score _____

Comment:
_____
_____

Adaptability score _____

Comment:
_____
_____

Resilience score _____

Comment:

_____

_____

Emotional vitality score _____

Comment:

_____

_____

Which area(s) need my attention the most?

_____

_____

How does your PSS score compare with your answer to the Session Six question asking you to rate your current stress level? Was your self-evaluation of your stress lower or higher than the outcomes of this series of assessments, and what does this reflect about our ability to determine our stress level without completing assessments? _____

_____

_____

StressCom (Optional)

If you decided to complete this survey, check which area(s) appears to need your attention the most?

control ___, competition ___, task orientation ___, change ___, time ___, management of symptoms ___.

What suggestions were made to address the area(s) needing your attention?

_____

_____

_____

After completing these surveys, what five areas need your attention the most?

_____

_____

_____

_____

BO, STS, CF

Test-Stress.com

Record your total score and interpretation.

Emotional/physical exhaustion score _____

Interpretation

_____

_____

Depersonalization/loss of compassion score _____

Interpretation

_____

_____

Personal accomplishment score _____

Interpretation

_____

_____

What area(s) needs your attention?

_____

If you took other test from this source what was the outcome/suggestions made?

_____

_____

_____

Silencing Response Scale

Total score ___, Risk Interpretation_____

Record all statements scored "5" or above.

_____

_____

_____

_____

_____

After looking at the results what do they suggest you need - supervision, training, evaluation for STS/CF?

_____

_____

STS Checklist

Record number of items checked under each category.

Intrusion ____, Avoidance ____, Arousal ____, Cognitive/Mood Alterations ____.

After taking this survey, what stands out or surprises you the most?

_____

_____

The ProQOL

Record scores and interpretation (low, average, high) for each category.

Compassion satisfaction ____ Interpretation _____

BO ____ Interpretation ____

STS _____ Interpretation _____

After taking this survey, what stands out or surprises you the most?

_____

_____

After completing this series of surveys, what three areas need your attention the most?

_____

_____

_____

Organizational Assessment

Record the answers you provided for the three Session Four questions about organizational well-being and engagement practices. Your answers were originally recorded following the Session Four Post-session Questions.

Question One: My organizations demonstrated effort to support my well-being is Limited_____, Some focus/effort but inconsistent _____, A definite priority_____.

Question Two: Of the six domains, which domains receive the least attention or provide the fewest resources _____, _____, _____, _____.

Question Three: The level of engagement in your work setting is

Poor_____, Minimal_____, Limited_____, Somewhat good_____, Very good_____.

What concerns you the most? _____

Are your responses to these questions contributing to your BO and if so, does the ProQOL reflect a similar outcome that should be a consideration related to changing work environments? _____

Self-Engagement Survey

Record the scores in each category

Category A "yes" responses _____ (very engaged)

Category B "somewhat" responses _____ (somewhat engaged)

Category C "rarely" responses _____ (rarely engaged)

List the statements rated "rarely." These are the areas that need to be changed if possible or, if outside of your control, do you need to consider changing environments.

_____

_____

_____

_____

_____

_____

Secondary Traumatic Stress-Informed Organization Assessment (STSI-OA)

Record the organizations overall focus on STS issues and practices.

Score _____%

After taking this survey, what areas are your organization lacking that impact you directly? For example, the organization does not have defined procedures to promote resilience building among staff.

_____

_____

_____

_____

How did you answer the following question from Session Five? Hearing information about some of the factors associated with a trauma-informed organization how do rate your organization? Not informed____, Somewhat informed____, Informed with limited sensitivity____, Informed and trauma sensitive____

As you consider the outcome to this question and the previous three questions what are your conclusions about the organizational factors that may be contributing to or helping you with the stress of what you do?

_____

_____

STS Competency Survey

Record your answer to this Session Five question: Given this information how would you rate your supervisory relationship? Poor____, somewhat supportive____, trauma-informed/sensitive____, very supportive, trauma-informed and sensitive____.

(Answer the following based on your position as a supervisee or a supervisor.)

As a supervisee record your answers to the two questions that followed the *STS Competency* survey. Those questions were:

What is your immediate impression of your supervisor's STS competency?

_____

_____

Knowing what you know about supervisor STS competency, the effects of STS and the benefits of brief intervention, do you feel safe and confident that your supervisor can help? ____Yes, ____No

Do you need to seek outside help from a trauma specialist? ____Yes, ____No

As a supervisor record your scores related to the *STS Supervisor Competency Checklist.*

As a supervisor my STS competency % = _____

Practices/competencies I need to develop:

_____, _____, _____,

_____, _____, _____,

_____, _____, _____.

Self-Efficacy

The Self-Compassion Scale

(Ratings listed here reflect positive self-compassion.)

Record score for each category

Self-Kindness: Score _____ (4-5 = almost always)

**Self-Judgment: Score _____ (1-2 = almost never)

Common Humanity: Score _____ (4-5 = almost always)

**Isolation Items: Score _____ (1-2 = almost never)

Mindfulness Items: Score _____ (4-5 = almost always)

**Over-identified Items: Score _____ (1-2 = almost never)

After taking this survey, what stands out or surprises you the most?

_____

_____

Spiritual Intelligence Self-Report Inventory (SISRI-24)

Record Total Score _____ (mid-range = 48)

Record score by category

Critical Existential Thinking _____ (mid-range = 14)

Personal Meaning Production _____ (mid-range = 10)

Transcendental Awareness _____ (mid-range = 14)

Conscious State Expansion _____ (mid-range = 10)

After taking this survey, what stands out or surprises you the most?

_____

_____

Resilience Self-Assessment (Mind Tool)

Record total score _____

Brief interpretation given

_____

_____

_____

After taking this survey, what area(s) need attention?

_____

_____

_____

After completing this series of surveys what areas needing attention stand out the most for you?

_____
_____
_____
_____

Resilience Characteristics Survey

My total score _____ Interpretation_____

Category Scores

Optimism _____, Adaptability _____, Spiritual Intelligence _____, Effective Effort _____, Social Strength _____, Self-Care/Wellness _____.

After taking this survey, what areas need attention?

_____
_____
_____

Your responses on the *Self-Care Checklist* will be used to complete the *What Matters Most Worksheet*.

C2　What Matters Most Worksheet

Phase One: Reflecting on the Outcomes

To complete this worksheet, you will need the answers/outcomes recorded on your *Self-Care Checklist*.

Post-session Reflection

As you reflect on your responses to Question #4, which is, "How has this changed what you feel you need to do about the unavoidable stress of what you do?" in each of the Post-session Questions, Sessions One through Five, ask yourself what you now consider matters most to you. How would you complete the sentence, "I need to . . ."? Be as specific as possible (you may have multiple actions that are needed).

I need to . . .

_____

_____

_____

Perceived Stress Scale

As you now reflect on your *PSS* outcomes, what are the specific elements, issues, factors, thoughts associated with these outcomes that needs your attention the most? What matters most for you? How would you complete the sentence, "I need to . . ."? Be as specific as possible (you may have multiple actions that are needed).

I need to . . .

_____

_____

_____

Stress 360

As you now reflect on your *Stress 360* outcomes, what are the specific elements, issues, factors, thoughts associated with this outcome that needs your attention the most? What matters most for you? How would you complete the sentence, "I need to . . ."? Be as specific as possible (you may have multiple actions that are needed).

I need to . . .

_____

_____

_____

The Stress and Well-Being Survey

As you now reflect on your *Stress and Well-being Survey* outcomes, what are the specific elements, issues, factors, thoughts associated with these outcomes that needs my attention the most? What matters most for you? How would you complete the sentence, "I need to . . ."? Be as specific as possible (you may have multiple actions that are needed).

I need to . . .

_____

_____

_____

StressCom (Optional)

As you now reflect on your *StressCom (Optional) Survey* outcomes, what are the specific elements, issues, factors, thoughts associated with these outcomes that needs your attention the most? What matters most for you? How would you complete the sentence, "I need to . . ."? Be as specific as possible (you may have multiple actions that are needed).

I need to . . .

_____

_____

_____

Test-Stress.com

As you now reflect on your *Test-Stress.com Survey* outcomes, what are the specific elements, issues, factors, thoughts associated with these outcomes that needs your attention the most?

What matters most for you? How would you complete the sentence, "I need to . . ."? Be as specific as possible (you may have multiple actions that are needed).

I need to . . .

_____

_____

_____

Silencing Response Scale

As you now reflect on your Silencing Response Scale outcomes, what are the specific elements, issues, factors, thoughts associated with these outcomes that needs your attention the most?

What matters most for you? How would you complete the sentence, "I need to . . ."? Be as specific as possible (you may have multiple actions that are needed).

I need to . . .

_____

_____

_____

STS Outcomes

As you now reflect on your *STS* outcomes, what are the specific elements, issues, factors, thoughts associated with these outcomes that needs your attention the most? What matters most for you? How would you complete the sentence, "I need to . . ."? Be as specific as possible (you may have multiple actions that are needed).

I need to . . .

_____

_____

_____

ProQOL

As you now reflect on your ProQOL outcomes, what are the specific elements, issues, factors, thoughts associated with these outcomes that needs your attention the most? What matters most for you? How would you complete the sentence, "I need to . . ."? Be as specific as possible (you may have multiple actions that are needed).

I need to . . .

_____

_____

_____

Self-Engagement Survey

As you now reflect on your *Self-Engagement Survey* outcomes, what are the specific elements, issues, factors, thoughts associated with these outcomes that needs your attention the most? What matters most for you? How would you complete the sentence, "I need to . . ."? Be as specific as possible (you may have multiple actions that are needed).

I need to . . .

_____

_____

_____

Secondary Traumatic Stress Informed Organization Assessment (STSI-OA)

As you now reflect on your STSI-OA outcomes, what are the specific elements, issues, factors, thoughts associated with these outcomes that needs your attention the most? What matters most for you? How would you complete the sentence, "I need to . . ."? Be as specific as possible (you may have multiple actions that are needed).

I need to . . .

_____

_____

_____

STS Competency Survey

As you now reflect on your *STS Competency Survey* outcomes, what are the specific elements, issues, factors, thoughts associated with these outcomes that needs your attention the most?

What matters most for you? How would you complete the sentence, "I need to . . ."? Be as specific as possible (you may have multiple actions that are needed).

I need to . . .

_____

_____

_____

Self-Compassion Survey

As you now reflect on your *Self-Compassion Survey* outcomes, what are the specific elements, issues, factors, thoughts associated with these outcomes that needs your attention the most?

What matters most for you? How would you complete the sentence, "I need to . . ."? Be as specific as possible (you may have multiple actions that are needed).

I need to . . .

_____

_____

_____

Spiritual Intelligence Self-Report Inventory (SISRI-24)

As you now reflect on your SISRI-24 outcomes, what are the specific elements, issues, factors, thoughts associated with these outcomes that needs your attention the most? What matters most for you? How would you complete the sentence, "I need to . . ."? Be as specific as possible (you may have multiple actions that are needed).

I need to . . .

_____

_____

_____

Resilience Self-Assessment (Mind Tool)

As you now reflect on your Resilience Self-Assessment outcomes, what are the specific elements, issues, factors, thoughts associated with these outcomes that needs your attention the most? What matters most for you? How would you complete the sentence, "I need to . . ."? Be as specific as possible (you may have multiple actions that are needed).

I need to . . .

_____

_____

_____

Resilience Characteristics Survey

As you now reflect on your *Resilience Characteristics Survey* outcomes, what are the specific elements, issues, factors, thoughts associated with these outcomes that needs your attention the most? What matters most for you? How would you complete the sentence, "I need to . . ."? Be as specific as possible (you may have multiple actions that are needed).

I need to . . .

_____

_____

_____

Thoughts Following Review of Reflective Questionnaires

To complete Phase One, review the *Reflective Questionnaires* in the Appendix. Reviewing and beginning with the *IQ Matrix Questionnaire* is recommended. The other questionnaires cover various areas. Select those that apply to you and then record your responses.

After reviewing these *Reflective Questionnaires* ask yourself what stands out the most for you and then complete the sentence, "I need to . . .". Be as specific as possible (you may have multiple actions that are needed).

I need to . . .

_____

_____

_____

_____

Phase Two

List your top priorities here in the order you consider most important.

_____

_____

_____

_____

_____

Record your secondary priorities here.

_____

_____

_____

_____

_____

Phase Three: Identifying Needed Actions

The final step involves identifying those actions needed to support your priorities. To complete this step, use the *My Priorities, My Action Plans Worksheet* in the Appendix

C3 My Priorities, My Action Plan Worksheet

My Priorities, My Action Plan Worksheet

Begin with top priorities:

Priority	Actions
Priority	Actions
Priority	Actions
Priority	Actions
Priority	Actions

My Priorities, My Action Plan Worksheet

Priority	Actions
Priority	Actions
Priority	Actions
Priority	Actions
Priority	Actions

My Priorities, My Action Plan Worksheet

Priority	Actions
Priority	Actions
Priority	Actions
Priority	Actions
Priority	Actions

D. Reflective Questions

D1　Self-Reflection: How to Make the Most of Every Experience

Reprinted by permission from Adam Sicinski-IQ Matrix ©2008 https://iqmatrix.com

This series of reflective questions helps us review how we are processing our experiences, our emotions, thoughts, attitudes, decisions, beliefs, interactions, the problems we faced, the decisions made, our health, the roles we engaged, the opportunities we had and what we learned. As a balanced review it is very comprehensive and could be used as day or an end of week review, or as a focused review of one or two areas such as reflecting on your thoughts and the decisions you made. If using as a weekly reflection simply change Reflections of the Day to Reflections of the Week.

Reflections of the Day/Week

- How was my day?
- What specifically happened?
- What was great about today?
- What do I appreciate about today?
- What do I regret or wish to do over?
- Why do I feel this way?
- What valuable lessons can I learn from all this?

Reflecting Upon Decisions Made

- What specific decisions did I make today?
- What intentions did I have when making these decisions?
- Why did I make these decisions and not other decisions?
- What outcomes did all these decisions lead to?
- Where these outcomes favorable or unfavorable? Why? Why not?
- What valuable lessons can I learn from all this?

Reflecting Upon Actions and Behaviors

- What risks did I take today? Why?
- How did all these risks pan out?
- Did I give into my fears at any stage of the day? Why?
- Did I indulge in any addictions that weren't to my benefit? Why?
- What worked really well for me today? Why?
- What didn't work out so well for me today? Why?
- What valuable lessons can I learn from all this?

Reflecting Upon Thought Process

- How did I think about things today?
- Why did I think this way about these things?

- Was this an optimal way to think about these things?
- How else could I have thought about these things?
- What advantage would there have been to think about things differently than I did?
- What valuable lessons can I learn from this?

Reflecting Upon Emotions Experienced

- What emotions did I tend to experience throughout the day?
- What events, circumstances or people tended to rile up my emotions?
- How did I handle my emotional experiences?
- Did I handle them in a helpful or hurtful way?
- How could I have handled my emotional experiences in a more optimal way?
- What valuable lessons can I learn from this?

Reflecting Upon Belief Systems

- What do I believe about today?
- What do I believe about myself, other people and about the events of the day?
- Are all these beliefs valid and justified?
- Where am I possibly jumping to conclusions or making assumptions about things?
- What empowering beliefs got me through the day?
- What limiting beliefs tended to hinder me?
- What valuable insights can I gain about myself through my belief systems?

Reflecting Upon Interactions

- How did I relate with other people today?
- Did any conflicts arise? How did I handle them?
- How did I handle criticism and rejection?
- How did I express myself to others today?
- How effectively did I communicate my needs?
- How effectively did I read people's emotional needs and intentions?
- Where could I improve to upgrade how I interact with other people?

Reflecting Upon Personal Attitude

- How was my attitude today?
- Was my attitude more optimistic or more pessimistic? Why?
- What specifically tended to trigger this attitude?
- Were these triggers internal or external?
- Did I give all that I had today? How? Why not?
- Was I nurturing, generous and humble?
- What valuable lessons can I learn from all of this?

Reflecting on Problems

- How was I challenged today?
- How did I respond to these challenges?

- What was the outcome?
- What exactly did I do that helped me overcome these challenges?
- What about the challenges I didn't overcome?
- Did I make any excuses along the way? Why?
- Why specifically were these challenges so difficult to overcome today?
- What valuable lessons can I learn from dealing with these challenges?

Reflecting on Roles Played

- How was I as a parent, sister, teacher, friend, mentor, spouse, leader, teammate, manager, son, etc.?
- Where did I meet my expectations?
- Where did I fail to live up to the standards I hold for myself within each of these roles?
- Was my work-life balanced? Why? Why not?
- What can I learn from reflecting on all my roles in this way?

Reflecting on Personal Health

- Did I look after my body today?
- Did I exercise?
- Did I eat healthy?
- Did I look after my mind?
- Where did I let myself down?
- Where and how could I improve tomorrow?

Reflecting on Opportunities

- What opportunities did I get today?
- How did I take advantage of these opportunities?
- How did I fail to make full use of these opportunities? Why?
- What valuable lessons can I learn from this experience?

Reflecting on Knowledge Gained

- What valuable knowledge did I acquire today?
- How did I come about this knowledge?
- How can I make use of this knowledge to help me tomorrow?
- What knowledge am I still missing that could be of value?
- How will I go about acquiring that knowledge?
- What can I learn from today's (this weeks) experience of knowledge acquisition?

The final question above sets us up for the learning phase of this process. We have of course been learning all the way through this process, but now let's ask several questions that will help bring all the lessons learned into full view:

- What can I learn and take away from today?
- What specifically did I learn about myself today?
- What specifically did I learn about my problems and the interactions I had with others?

Appendix D1

- What specifically did I learn about other people today?
- What have other people taught me through their words, attitude, actions and behaviors? What have they taught me indirectly?
- How specifically have I grown today?
- Why is this level of growth important to me?
- Given another chance what would I have done differently?
- What would I change or do better than before?

While learning from your experiences, it's important to set your sights on the future; to plan ahead and prepare yourself for things that are still yet to come. That is after all the only way we are able to make progress. Ask yourself:

- How could I live with more purpose and intention tomorrow?
- How could I more readily express my core values?
- Given what I now know, what potential skills must I learn or upgrade?
- What knowledge do I need to acquire to help move me forward toward my desired goals and objectives?
- How will I go about acquiring this knowledge?
- Who could support me along my journey?
- How will I acquire that support from others?
- What else can I take away from today that I can use to my advantage tomorrow?

D2 Ultimate Self-Care Assessment/ Reflection

Reprinted with permission from Barbara Markway, Ph.D @ www.barbaramarkway.com

This reflective tool approaches self-care by categories: our attitudes, relationships, physical, mental, emotional and spiritual self-care. Both *Reflective Questionnaires* can help us focus on what matters most.

Self-care Attitudes

- Are you able to take time for yourself without feeling guilty?
- Do you believe you deserve self-care?
- Do you know the difference between self-care and self-indulgence?
- Do you realize self-care does not equal weakness?
- Are you okay with slowing down sometimes?
- Do you have a go-to list of self-care activities?
- Do you make leisure time a priority?
- Have you made self-care a habit?
- Do you have a basic self-care plan, preferably in writing?

Interpersonal Self-care

- Do you have a small group of people you can call on for support?
- Do you spend time with people who make you laugh?
- Do you nurture relationships with people who make you feel good about yourself?
- Are you able to set appropriate limits in your relationships?
- Are you able to seek out and accept help from others?
- Do you talk problems and concerns out with a trusted friend or relative?

Physical Self-care

- Do you exercise enough to work up a sweat several times a week?
- Do you generally nourish your body with nutritious food?
- Can you eat food you love without feeling guilty?
- Do you feel comfortable in your own body?
- Do you sleep and rest when you're tired?
- Do you unwind before bedtime so that you can sleep better?
- Do you get outside each day?
- Do you attend to your health care needs, such as getting preventative care and regular checkups?

Mental Self-care

- Do you regularly stimulate your brain learning new things?
- Do you have an outlet for creativity?
- Can you make a mistake without it being a catastrophe?
- Can you generally manage negative mental habits like worrying?
- Do you know and practice stress reduction techniques, such as deep breathing, meditation?

Emotional Self-care

- Can you identify and acknowledge your feelings?
- Do you affirm your right to experience all of your feelings?
- Do you know how to express your feelings appropriately?
- Are you aware of how you "numb out" from uncomfortable feelings?
- Do you have a plan in place for when you feel overwhelmed with feelings?
- Do you practice self-compassion?

Spiritual Self-care

- Do you pray, meditate or practice whatever feeds you spiritually?
- Do you have any serene place of your own to go when you're stressed?
- Do you make time for reflection and contemplation?
- Do you pay attention to every day beauty?
- Do you have a gratitude practice?
- Do you read inspirational materials?
- Do you have a spiritual community?
- Do you have a sense of meaning and purpose?

Dr. Steele's Additional Questions

- As you reflect on your answers, what stands out the most for you?

  _____

  _____

  _____

  _____

- How do your responses to these questions and what you consider matters the most compare with the outcomes of the assessments you may have taken?

  _____

  _____

  _____

- Consider adding any new insights to your *What Matters Most Worksheet.*

D3   Brief End-of-Day Reflection

© 2018 Dr. William Steele

The following reflective questions can be used to reflect on all aspects of your day-work, personal and professional growth, family/social, health, finances and spiritual. However, you are encouraged once a week to review the more extensive reflective questions under the *IQ Matrix Questionnaire* or the *Ultimate Self-Care Assessment/Reflection Tool*, also found in the Appendix. There are others on the Internet that address the life areas you might prefer after reviewing them. Simply Google "End-of-Day or End-of-Week Reflective Questions," and you will be introduced to a number of excellent resources.

- What was the best part of my day today and who or what made it the best part? What did this teach me?
- What am I most proud of today?
- Who or what am I most grateful for?
- What did I spend too much time doing today? Who or what caused this to happen and what can I do tomorrow to use my time more effectively?
- What did I not spend enough time doing? Who or what prevented me from taking the time I needed and what can I do to tomorrow to change this?
- If a crisis threw off my schedule, how do I need to readjust my priorities for tomorrow?
- Did I remain focused on what matters most to me and if not, what can I do tomorrow to reset my focus?
- What is it I wished I would have done differently today and how might I make this happen tomorrow or in the near future?
- Was there a person or situation that triggered an unwanted emotional reaction today? What did I learn from this and what do I need to do or change in order to better regulate my reaction should this happen again?
- What do I wish I would have said or not said today?
- What one thought helped or hurt me today?
- Did I remain optimistic in my thoughts and actions and if not, what can I do to remain more optimistically focused?
- Even though my time may have been limited, did I pursue doing what matters most to me in my personal life (mental health, stress management, my spiritual life, social, physical health and financial), with family and/or friends, and what matters most to me at work, in my professional life?
- What are my three top priorities for tomorrow?

D4 Reflecting About Client Situations, Interactions, Responses

© 2018 Dr. William Steele

Note: These reflective questions can address your interactions with one client or several clients. They can also be used to reflect on your response to a critical, potentially trauma inducing situation; simply substitute "situation" for "client." If you are in a setting that is providing comprehensive reflective supervision, these may not be necessary as they should be included in that reflective process.

- *What client interactions (situations) went well today?* Is there a theme as to which of your interactions proved productive/helpful? What was it about these clients that made it fairly easy for you to assist them? What did you learn from these interactions?
- *What client (victim) behaviors or interactions did not seem to make sense to you?* From a trauma-informed perspective what do you think the client might be trying to communicate–their hurt, fear, worry, the need for control, help with regulating their reactions, the need to feel safe and protected? How might you respond differently if this happens again?
- *What client interactions (response to trauma situation) were a challenge?* What made them a challenge–the topic, the client's response, your response to the client? What specific client response presented the most anxiety or discomfort for you? Describe what that anxiety/discomfort was like. What did that client's response make you want to do? In what way did your body respond - tighten up, started breathing shallow, began sweating, increased heart rate? What was the worst part of the reactions you had? As you think about this now is there anything familiar about this client, their experience or reaction that reminds you of a similar experience in the past? Who or what helped you the most back then? What might this experience be teaching you? What new information or skills might help you with this in the future? How can you best prepare yourself and regulate your response should this happen again?
- Of all the client reactions you experienced today what one thought stands out the most for you?
- What did you learn today about yourself and about others?
- What is that you wish you could have done or done differently today?

D5　Reflective Questions About Issues With Your Supervisor/Manager

© 2018 Dr. William Steele

- Do you feel that your S/M treats you fairly?
- Have you found that they have been as helpful as you would like?
- In what way have they not been helpful?
- Have you felt comfortable talking about areas of weakness with your S/M?
- When you tell them of your concerns, a difficulty you are having, has their response been helpful or one that tells you he/she is not going to be helpful with your difficulties such as, "This is the nature of what we do; either get used to it or think about changing careers?
- Does your S/M remind you of similar experiences you've had in the past with people like your S/M?
- Do you feel emotionally safe with your S/M, that what you say or express is safe?
- What has your supervisor/manager said to you or done in the past that causes you to be uneasy with this relationship?
- What have others said about your S/M that might cause you to be uncomfortable with them?
- If you were supervising yourself what might you say about your performance and reports?
- If you could, would you look for another supervisor/manager?
- Do you need to think about getting the support you are looking for from outside supervision or from peers?
- If you believe your S/M is not likely to change, what can you now do to continue to improve while avoiding conflict with your S/M?
- What resources would be helpful in this endeavor?
- What would you consider to be an acceptable outcome?
- In what time frame do you believe this can be accomplished?

D6 Reflective Questions About Difficulty Completing Client Records

© 2018 Dr. William Steele

- What is your primary issue with reports – on time completion/submission, accuracy or comprehensiveness, what they might reflect about your knowledge or skill?
- Knowing that licensing agents, managers and supervisors use records to determine ongoing licensing and accreditation of your organization, to determine neglect or responsibility when things go bad with clients or when clients file complaints, what do you think gets in the way of your not making completing reports a priority?
- What thought(s) is/are associated with actually writing/typing down information for records?
- What is your biggest worry about your reports being reviewed?
- We all feel the burden of paperwork, however, since completing reports is not only a primary and ongoing demand and one that reflects your compliance and the quality of your work, what is that makes it difficult for you meet this demand; is it a time issue or a fear of what your reports reflect about you?
- Do you have a problem setting limits and working within timeframes (see comment in the next section)?
- What have you tried to do to correct this problem? Since what you have tried is not helping, what else might you do (in the next section)?

When Putting It In Writing Creates Anxiety

You are not alone if recording your interactions with clients in writing creates anxiety for you to the point that you almost freeze when it comes time to complete your report. Often people who have trouble writing down necessary information are still able to verbalize it; it's just the writing that creates the anxiety. Dragon Dictate is an easy-to-use software that records your verbal answers in writing in a word document. Once your answers are in writing you can cut and paste, if using electronic records, or copy your answers into a hard copy record. Others have difficulty completing records because they are unsure of the appropriate terminology to use. There is also the issue of how much to say about the client and interactions as records can be subpoenaed by the courts, which can be very intimidating. Your supervisor ought to be able to help you with this. Frankly, organizations ought to have a series of training on record keeping that reviews the language and terms to use and specific content needed about high-risk situations.

Time management is a real issue for some, who generally do not prioritize their time, set aside quiet time for record completion, who are often distracted by other's requests, have difficulty saying "no" and setting limits. Time management training can be very helpful in this regard; however, there may be other issues that need to be addressed in supervision such as the difficulty saying "no" to other's requests. If this is a challenge for you, correcting it must be a priority as it is not only extremely stressful but a problem that can place your clients and your organization at risk and lead to your termination. Do get help if this is a problem. It is nothing to be ashamed about unless you fail to act.

E. Additional Self-care/Well-being Strategies

To save time searching various titles, Google the titles below to access numerous self-care practices in many of the areas evaluated in the assessments you completed.

- 17 Ways to Take Care of Yourself
- The Self-Compassion Project
- 20 Expert Tactics for Dealing With Difficult People
- 10 Reasons to Stop Judging People
- Stop Fighting Your Negative Thoughts
- How to Talk to Yourself
- Speak to Yourself Using Words That Soothe and Heal
- 8 Easy Meditation Tips for Beginners
- 7 Things Not to Do When Practicing Mindfulness/Meditation
- Meditation Practices
- Mindfulness Practices at Work
- 6 Reasons Why You Should Use a Daily Planner
- Overcoming BO in the Workplace
- Changing Our Perceptions
- Resilience Practices
- Self-efficacy Practices
- Self-compassion Strategies
- Finding Purpose Strategies
- Journaling to Relieve Stress
- Expressive Arts to Manage Stress
- Well-being Practices in Non-profit Settings
- Music and Stress

Additional Strategies

Nature Soothes and Heals

Spending time outdoors is definitely beneficial especially when we surround ourselves with nature. Many communities now have small parks filled with trees and paths, no cars. Nature makes us feel better; it soothes and creates a positive mood. An interesting study was done that showed that compared to those who spend 90 minutes walking in an urban setting, those who spend 90 minutes in nature see a much more significant decrease in depression and anxiety. In fact, city dwellers have a 20% higher risk of anxiety and a 40% higher risk of depression compared to those in rural areas.

Write

Sian Bielock, author of *Choke: What the Secrets of the Brain Revealed About Getting It Right When You Have To*, reported that anxiety in students uses parts of their working memory, and decreases the cognitive resources needed to do well on tests. To counter test anxiety, students in one research project were asked, before their test, to write down in detail their worries. Test scores improved significantly as a result of this one writing exercise. In another study, students, experiencing higher levels of test anxiety than other students, were asked to describe in writing something they value and why it mattered to them. This study showed that this one writing process shrank the performance gap between this group and those with low test anxiety by 40% (Paul, A. M., "Relax, It's Only A Test," *Time Magazine*, Feb. 2013, 41–45). Stated differently, the most anxious became less anxious and saw their performance on tests increase significantly.

It works and, as the research shows, it's a great way to lessen anxiety and stress. I really suggest you search the Internet on the benefits of journaling; you'll be surprised by the research, as well as find a variety of journal formats to use.

When There Are No Words, Create a Collage

Creating a collage of pictures taken from magazines that reflect our hopes, our dreams or what we are experiencing in the present is another way to bring others into our world without words. Using a camera to create photos that reflect your world, your views, what is important, what you want others to know about you is another way to communicate when you do not have the words.

After you create a collage related to your hopes and dreams (I highly recommend this), take 5 minutes in the morning to sit and look at the images and headings you put on that page or pages. These iconic images will be stronger than trying to talk to yourself into what you want. They will be embedded in your mid-brain, the emotional/sensing part of our brain or what some call your subconscious. They will help drive your behavior and keep you focused on what is important to you. Neuroscience now proves that images fire up the brain more often than words. As the saying goes,

"If you can visualize it, you can achieve it."

Paint/Create

We all have a need to express ourselves; to be heard; to share what we think, what we feel, what we know, what we experience. There are times when talk alone simply cannot make that happen. When talking is too difficult or is not helping or when words just can't be found to reflect what we are experiencing; we need to find another way. Painting, using clay and making other kinds of art allow us to express ourselves and alleviate stress. I recommended googling "creative arts to manage stress" for numerous resources.

Draw

Drawing helps our silent world speak loudly.

Drawing is a way to move what is inside outside of ourselves in a concrete tangible form. That form allows us to re-examine what we feel and think. Drawing can heal.

Drawing is like taking a virtual tour of our lives, what it was, what it is and what it can yet become.

In therapy, drawing is a structured process that asks for drawings related to what we are experiencing or did experience. It is the starting point for us to tell our story about abuse, for example, and what that experience was like. In the process it allows you to better understand what happened to you and how it is impacting you in the present and then presents the opportunity to change how you think. It helps you to respond differently to that part of your life now. If not in therapy, when times are difficult, take out some plain paper and a pencil. Start by drawing a line, straight or wavy doesn't matter; just let the pencil do whatever it wants. The simple movement of your hand transferring what you are feeling onto paper helps to reduce the intensity of what is being felt. Use additional paper if needed; you will be surprised by the relief you experience, as well as how your scribbles change with different emotions and thoughts.

Music

Music can be a wonderful way to express yourself. Create a collection of the music, songs that best reflects what life is like for you. When you play these for others, it becomes easier to find the words to describe what that music reflects about you. New research also continues to highlight the significant impact music has on emotional and physical well-being. Music has been used successfully in treatment programs to reduce stress or lower blood pressure, alleviate pain, overcome various learning disabilities, improve movement and balance, and promote endurance and strength.

You might find it interesting that biofeedback studies show that drumming along with our own heartbeat alters brain wave pattern. Using a drum to beat out what we are experiencing can bring amazingly relief. It can soothe, calms and allows us to express ourselves without words. It can also restore our energy level, focus and concentration. Since we're talking about music, dance is another form of self-expression. Put simply, explore until you find what forms of self-expression works best for you. You'll feel better, alleviate stress and become less reactive over time.

Additional Wellness/Well-being Strategies

Adapted from multiple sources.

- snooze friendly policies giving employees the opportunity to take power naps knowing that they can improve focus and energy,
- presentations/training on social emotional learning/emotional intelligence,
- conducting Improv Training sessions to improve collaboration, risk taking, confidence and conflict resolution,
- using artificial Intelligence (AI) to support employee well-being goals,
- showing pertinent TED Talks at meetings or as part of supervision,
- holding *Sensi Sessions*, such as How to Hack Your Brain to Stay Focused,
- allowing remote days of work at home to renew focus, remove distractions to get more done (paper work, for example),
- providing stress management resources, including books, music and online resources,
- holding yoga classes and meditation sessions,
- social activity, team building and fun,
- pets at the office,
- the option to download stretch break reminders to staff computers. These reminders appear throughout the day and provide employees with a different stretch each time, reminding them of the importance of stepping away from their desks throughout the day,
- scheduling 15-minute walking breaks during long meetings to help reduce stress that might have built up. Employees typically come back refreshed and ready to work, and
- coaching around positive thinking, which has been shown to increase life span, lower rates of depression, improve coping skills during hardships.

F. Suggested Websites and YouTube Segments

Websites

These websites introduce you to leaders in the field of trauma and CF, the various articles, blogs and video segments created by these individuals. Google "Secondary Traumatic Stress Programs" and a listing of multiple resources are also available.

Alvarado Consulting and Treatment Group

www.alvaradoconsultinggroup.com

Child Welfare League of America (CWLA)

www.cwla.org/addressing-secondary-traumatic-stress/

Counseling Today https://ct.counseling.org

Compassion Fatigue Awareness project @ www.compassionfatigue.org/pages/reading.html

(Kathleen Figley) Green Cross Academy of Traumatology @ www.greencross.org/

The National Child Traumatic Stress Network (NCTSN) www.nctsn.org

The National Center for Trauma Informed Care (NCTIC) www.samshsa.gov/nctic.org

The Resilience Alliance

www.nctsn.org/ . . . /resilience-alliance-promoting-resilience-and-reducing-second . . .

(Patricia Fisher) The Tend Academy @ www.tendacademy.ca/what-is-compassion-fatigue/

(Anna Baranowski) Traumatology Institute @t https://psychink.com/

(Laura van Dernoot Lipsky) The Trauma Stewardship Institute traumastewardship.com/event-host-resources/about-laura/

(Charles Figley) Tulane University Traumatology Institute @ https://tulanetraumatologyinstitute.com/

Suggested Video/YouTube Segments

These segments will introduce you to other related segments:

How to fix the exhausted brain | Brady Wilson | TEDxMississauga 18 minutes www.youtube.com/watch?v=XOU2ubWkoPw

Neuroscience of Mindfulness: What Happens to Your Brain When you Meditate *Observer*. Retrieved from: http://observer.com/2017/06/neuroscience-mindfulness-brain-when-you-meditate-development/

Long term effects of stress on your body www.youtube.com/watch?v=1BOPGFnYnv4

CF, a 3-minute segment about the hazards of helping at www.youtube.com/watch?v=a9orwFLS68I featuring Dr. Charles Figley, the Director of the Tulane University Traumatology Institute.

Appendix F

CF: The Value of saying "No" is a 10 minute segment that introduces you to Dr. Baranowsky, Director of the Traumatology Institute at www.youtube.com/watch?v=QD-HGGsCLyU

Françoise Mathieu is the founder of Compassion Fatigue Solutions. Listen to her 17-minute talk on TEDxTalk, The Edge of Compassion | Françoise Mathieu | TEDxQueensU at www.youtube.com/watch?v=IcaUA6A37q8

As indicated above, linking with any of these resources will automatically introduce you to many others.

G. Hot Walk Talk Protocol

©2012 Patricia Fisher, Ph.D., R.Psych.

Excerpted from the workbook *Building Resilient Teams: Facilitating Workplace Wellness & Organizational Health in Trauma-Exposed Environments*

Available at www.tendacademy.ca

Reprinted with permission from Patricia Fisher, Ph.D., R.Psych

This protocol applies when there has been no physical injury and the person is stable enough in the aftermath to proceed. In the event that the individual has been physically injured or is in shock you would need to follow emergency procedures and get the appropriate immediate medical resources.

This protocol is designed to provide helpful first aid immediately after a team member experiences a particularly distressing or disturbing incident and is undergoing a completely normal stress reaction. This is something either supervisors or peers can offer each other, and you will consider what would work best for you in your particular circumstances.

Remember that when we are experiencing a high stress response our body is in the flight, fight or freeze state and we are flooding with stress hormones and all the physical, emotional and cognitive responses that go with that. So, our first response introduces safety and containment for the person.

The following steps in the process are typically helpful:

1. Go to the individual, ensure that they are physically out of danger, and invite them to come walk with you.
2. Walk away from the area where the incident occurred and toward a neutral or safe area (if you can get outside that can be even more grounding).
3. Walk beside them and set a pace that is brisk enough to engage the individual and help them discharge some of the distress . . . as the walk proceeds you may find that they naturally slow the pace–let them progressively have more control over the pace as the debriefing proceeds.
4. Bring a bottle of water and have them drink the water as you walk.
5. Let them know that they are safe now and you are here to support them as they move through this absolutely normal response to high stress.
6. Ask them to tell you what happened in their own words, if they seem stuck in the incident, prompt them to move on with the narrative by asking "and then what happened." You want to help them move through the whole narrative from beginning to the end - until they get to the present where they are walking with you in safety and are no longer at risk.
7. After you have gone through this initial debrief you may work in an environment where you are required to complete an incident report. If this is the case, go with the individual and ask them how you can help in completing the report. They may want you to type in the information as they dictate it, or they may simply appreciate your presence while they complete the report.
8. Remember to remind them to focus on their breathing and open posture to help them deescalate from the stress response - especially after you have stopped walking and may be standing or sitting.
9. After the initial debrief and report (if required), ask the person what they would find helpful now? Do they want to phone a family member, get a sandwich, take a break, go back to work? They need to have control over their choices while attending to their needs.

10. Let the individual know that you will remain available to them and encourage them to access addition supports that may be available if they would find them helpful (e.g., Employee Assistance Programs, counseling, other community resources).

Following, and sometimes parallel to, this immediate first aid response, there may be additional steps needed from an institutional perspective. These may include:

- The debriefer stays with the affected person, and asks a colleague to notify the supervisor about the incident. The debriefer can provide updates to the supervisor as needed.
- The supervisor speaks with the affected person(s) and assesses whether the person should remain at work following the incident. The debriefer or supervisor assists with making travel arrangements if the affected person is not in a condition to drive home. If the affected person goes home early, the supervisor phones the affected person to ensure that they arrived home safely.
- The debriefer emails a summary of the incident to the supervisor, based on the information gathered from the affected person. The supervisor may also be responsible for submitting paperwork.
- The supervisor updates other staff in the office about the incident, as needed.
- The supervisor works with the affected person(s) to discuss any case management or other relevant decisions in relation to the incident.
- The supervisor will check in periodically with the affected person and continue to offer support in the weeks that follow.

Index

Note: Page numbers **bold** indicate a table on the corresponding page.

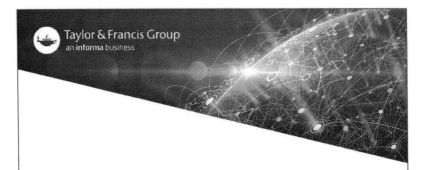

Made in the USA
Middletown, DE
11 August 2023